READINGS FROM KARL MARX

READINGS FROM
KARL MARX

EDITED BY DEREK SAYER

ROUTLEDGE
London and New York

To Miranda

First published 1989 by Routledge
11 New Fetter Lane, London EC4P 4EE

Simultaneously published in the USA and Canada
by Routledge
a division of Routledge, Chapman and Hall, Inc.
29 West 35th Street, New York, NY 10001

© 1989 Derek Sayer

Typeset by LaserScript Ltd., Mitcham, Surrey
Printed and bound in Great Britain by
The Guernsey Press Co. Ltd., Guernsey, Channel Islands.

British Library Cataloguing in Publications Data

Readings from Karl Marx.
1. Society. Theories of Marx, Karl, 1818–
1883
I. Sayer, Derek
301.′092′4

ISBN 0-415-01810-2

Library of Congress Cataloging in Publication Data

Marx, Karl, 1818–1883.
Readings from Karl Marx.
(Key texts)
Bibliography: p.
Includes index.
1. Sociology. 2. Marx, Karl, 1818–1883——Contributions in
Sociology. I. Sayer, Derek. II. Title. III. Series.
HX39.5.A224   1989   335.4   88-26465

ISBN 0-415-01810-2

Contents

Acknowledgements

The editor and publishers would like to thank the following for their permission to reprint material in this volume: Lawrence and Wishart Ltd for selections from Karl Marx and Friedrich Engels, *Collected Works*, vols 1, 3, 4, 5, 6, 8, 9, 11, 12, 19, 20, 22, 28, 40, and 41, *Selected Correspondence* and *Ireland and the Irish question*, and Karl Marx, *Capital*, vols 2 and 3, *Theories of Surplus Value*, and *A Contribution to the Critique of Political Economy*; Penguin Books Ltd and Random House Inc. for selections from Karl Marx *Grundrisse*, translated by M. Nicolaus, 1973, and *Capital*, vol. 1, translated by B. Fowkes and R. Livingstone, 1976; Associated Book Publishers for selections from T. Shanin (ed.) *Late Marx and the Russian Road*; and Basil Blackwell Ltd for selections from T. Carver (ed.) *Karl Marx: Texts on Method*.

Preface

This is the kind of anthology that indefatigable Marx scholar Hal Draper calls a 'bits and pieces collection' – passages drawn from across Marx's writings, arranged by theme. The dangers of this sort of collection are many and obvious. Marx's thought can be easily misrepresented by quotation out of context; by selection of generalizing, summary or aphoristic material at the expense of the dense and the complex; by imposition, through the choice of themes and ordering of the material, of priorities that were not his own. I have done my utmost to avoid these pitfalls. In particular, I have restricted any temptation to force Marx's thought into the categorial frameworks of later sociology. Readers will not find *separate* chapters on 'class' or 'alienation'; such themes are treated as they occur in Marx, as integral parts of his *overall* analysis of bourgeois society. On the other hand, a 'bits and pieces' collection has advantages other formats often lack. It can give wider currency to passages buried in works that none but specialists would normally read, and thereby shake up simplistic ideas of Marx gleaned from textbooks or a cursory reading of the *Communist Manifesto*. It permits comparison of Marx's ideas on particular topics across a range of texts. Most importantly of all, it allows the many who do not have the time to plough through *Capital*, or even a hefty standard anthology like McLellan's *Selected Writings*, the opportunity nonetheless to get a flavour of Marx himself. In an introductory selection, I think the advantages outweigh the risks.

I have minimized commentary in order to increase room for Marx's own writings. I do, however, provide a brief introduction, which endeavours to say something about the nature of Marx's literary legacy, and the interpretive problems it poses. This seemed to me essential in a book of this kind. I have also prefaced each chapter with a short account of its contents, and given a thumbnail chronology of Marx's life. The notes explain people and events referred to by Marx, and in some cases provide brief elaboration on difficult points in the text, particularly of economic theory. There is a detailed index of names and subjects.

This book can, I hope, be read simply as a self-contained introduction to Marx. But for readers who want to go further, I have provided a fairly full scholarly apparatus. The notes give a good deal of information on Marx's texts: their provenance, publication dates, dates of translations. They also give some guidance to the secondary literature. The bibliography lists editions and anthologies of Marx's writings, reference works and biographies, and commentaries. It is comprehensive, without claiming to be exhaustive.

Philip Corrigan, P. A. Saram, and Teodor Shanin gave advice which was gratefully taken, and I am indebted to Scott McLean for help in preparing the bibliography. I owe a particular debt to Ashraf Ghani, both for a memorable weekend in Baltimore in the course of which my ideas for how to do this book took shape, and for his detailed comments on its first draft. Thanks are due also to Chris Rojek, my editor at Routledge, and Eve Daintith for her painstaking copy-editing. But since I am presuming to present a selection of somebody else's writings (and in the case of Marx such an enterprise has often enough struck me as simply ludicrous, given their magnitude), it is more than conventionally necessary to stress that the responsibility for whatever defects this book might have is mine alone.

University of Alberta
February 1988

Abbreviations

Individual texts of Marx are identified by date codes. These are listed in full, and sources given, in the bibliography, section 2. I have abbreviated titles of various source volumes: full details are given in section 1 of the bibliography.

AME	*Arkiv K. Marksa i F. Engelsa*
Carver	*Texts on Method*, T. Carver (ed.)
CEW	*Early Writings*, L. Colletti (ed.)
CW	*Collected Works*
DFI	*Documents of the First International*
GC	General Council
Ireland	*Ireland and the Irish Question*
IWMA	International Working Men's Association
MEGA 1	*Gesamtausgabe*, 1927–36
MEGA 2	*Gesamtausgabe*, 1975 onwards
MEW	*Werke*
Nicolaus	*Grundrisse*, tr. M. Nicolaus
PW	Political Writings (3 vols, D. Fernbach (ed.))
SC	*Selected Correspondence*, 1975 edition
SC 1934	*Selected Correspondence*, 1934 edition
Shanin	*Late Marx and the Russian Road*, T. Shanin (ed.)
Value	*Value: Studies by Karl Marx*

Chronology

This is a mere skeletal outline of major events in Marx's life. See note 32 for biographies. A fuller listing of Marx's texts by date of composition is given in the bibliography, section 1B.

1818   Marx born in Trier, Rhineland, on 5 May
1830   Enters high school
1835   Attends University of Bonn
1836   Engaged to Jenny von Westphalen
          Enters University of Berlin
1841   Awarded PhD from Jena; moves to Bonn; begins journalistic career
1842   Contributor to, then editor of, *Rheinische Zeitung*
1843   *Rheinische Zeitung* suppressed (March)
          Marries Jenny (June)
          Critique of Hegel's Rechtsphilosophie (summer)
          Moves to Paris (October)
1844   *Deutsch-Französische Jahrbücher* articles
          Birth of daughter Jenny (May)
          Economic and philosophic manuscripts
          Meets Engels (September); beginning of their lifelong collaboration
          Holy Family
1845   Expelled from France, moves to Brussels (February)

	Theses on Feuerbach
	First visit to England (July)
	Birth of daughter Laura (September)
1846	*The German Ideology* (1845–6)
	Birth of son Edgar (December)
1847	Joined Communist League (January)
	Poverty of Philosophy
	Wage Labour and Capital
1848	*Communist Manifesto*
	Expelled from Belgium, returned to Paris (March)
	Moved to Cologne (June), as editor of *Neue Rheinische Zeitung*
1849	*Neue Rheinische Zeitung* suppressed; returned to Paris (May)
	Moved to London (August), thereafter to be his permanent home
	Birth of son Guido (November)
1850	Edits *Neue Rheinische Zeitung Revue*
	Class Struggles in France
	Death of Guido (September)
1851	Birth of daughter Franziska (March)
1852	Death of Franziska (April)
	18th Brumaire
	Dissolved Communist League
	Begins writing articles for *New York Daily Tribune* (1852/62); throughout this period, other journalism
1855	Birth of daughter Eleanor (January)
	Death of Edgar (April)
1857–8	*Grundrisse*
1859	*Critique of Political Economy*
1861–3	*Theories of Surplus Value*
1864	IWMA founded; Marx active in it until 1872
1864/5	*Capital* 3 drafted
1865/78	*Capital* 2 drafted
1867	*Capital* 1 published
1868	Laura marries Paul Lafargue
1870	Engels moves to London
1871	*Civil War in France*
1872	Jenny marries Charles Longuet
1881	Death of Marx's wife Jenny (December)
1883	Death of daughter Jenny (January)
	Death of Marx (14 March)

And the materialist conception of history also has a lot of friends nowadays to whom it serves as an excuse for *not* studying history. Just as Marx used to say about the French 'Marxists' of the late 'seventies: "All I know is that I am not a Marxist".

Friedrich Engels (letter to Conrad Schmidt, 5 August 1890) [Engels 1890a]

With the master what is new and significant develops vigorously amid the 'manure' of contradictions out of the contradictory phenomena. The underlying contradictions themselves testify to the richness of the living foundation from which the theory itself developed. It is different with the disciple. His raw material is no longer reality, but the new theoretical form in which the master has sublimated it. It is in part *theoretical disagreement of opponents of the new theory* and in part the *often paradoxical relationship of this theory to reality* which drive him to seek *to refute* his opponents and *explain away* reality. In doing so, he entangles himself in contradictions and with his attempt to solve these he demonstrates the beginning *disintegration of the theory* which he dogmatically espouses.

Karl Marx, *Theories of Surplus Value* [1863c: 85]

Introduction: Marx's writings

Marx wrote an enormous amount (the Marx/Engels *Gesamtausgabe*[1] will amount on completion to more than one hundred fat volumes), over a period of some forty years. This textual legacy is as varied as it is vast. Marx's writings do not form a unified corpus of doctrine, in which each and every utterance can be treated as canonically equivalent. Books like the first volume of *Capital*, finalized for the press and revised through several editions, form the smaller part of Marx's output.[2] Even these pose interpretive problems: there are major differences, for instance, between successive editions of *Capital* 1.[3] Marx also prepared for press, over a lifetime, hundreds of newspaper and journal articles. Twice he did this as editor of his own paper (the *Rheinische Zeitung*, 1842–3; and the *Neue Rheinische Zeitung*, 1848–9), though in the first case under conditions of censorship, and he also wrote occasionally for the socialist press. But much of this journalism was done on a paid basis, mainly for the *New York Daily Tribune* (1852–62). These newspaper articles were often written in haste, and sometimes on subjects that Marx had by no means researched in the same depth as he did, say, *Capital*. His own view of his 'newspaper muck' was that 'in the final analysis [it] is nothing [...] Purely scientific works are something completely different'.[4]

Many of what would now be accepted as amongst Marx's major writings, however, were *not* polished for publication, but were drafts left in various stages of completion. Amongst these are the bulk of his so-called 'early works', including the Critique of Hegel's *Rechtsphilosophie* (1843b), the Economic and Philosophical Manuscripts of 1844 (1844c), and *The German Ideology* (with Engels, 1845–6)(1846a). The publication of these writings, half a century after Marx's death, was a bombshell, playing havoc with received ideas of what he stood for. Their status in his legacy has been acrimoniously debated ever since.[5] Some see the early writings as mere juvenilia, others hail them as providing the 'humanist' key to Marx's entire *oeuvre*. *The German Ideology* (1846a), which is generally acknowledged as (at least) a major 'transitional' work in Marx's intellectual development, provides the fullest account anywhere in his writings of the overall 'premises' of his viewpoint. It also nicely illustrates the difficulties of assessing drafts. For it was abandoned by its authors to 'the gnawing criticism of the mice', whilst Friedrich Engels, unearthing the manuscript forty years later, commented that it showed 'only how incomplete our knowledge of economic history was at that time'.[6]

Such difficulties extend to the very heart of Marx's work. Of his immense 'economics' – the several 'pamphlets' he proposed in the Preface to the 1844 Manuscripts, which grew to become his 'dramatically incomplete' life-work[7] – only the 1859 *Critique* and *Capital* 1 were prepared for the press. The 'first draft' of *Capital*, the mighty *Grundrisse* (1857–8), was not. It was only effectively published in 1953, while as late as 1968 Martin Nicolaus, its eventual English translator (1973), could write an article on this text with the thoroughly accurate title 'The unknown Marx'.[8] Even volumes 2 and 3 of *Capital* were issued by Engels after Marx's death (1885, 1894b). He wove together volume 2 from eight separate manuscripts, written between 1865 and 1878, and edited volume 3 mainly from Marx's incomplete and often very scrappy first draft of 1864–5 – a text compiled before volume 1 was revised for press.[9] The three volumes of *Theories of Surplus Value*, which Marx had also intended as an integral part of his 'economics', were left in draft form too in 1861–3. *Theories* was first published in full a century after it was written.[10] There are other smaller manuscripts that are also associated with the 'economics', of various dates: of particular note is one known as 'Results of the immediate process of production', dating from some time between 1863 and 1866.[11] Other drafts of Marx's, which are today seen as important because they are fuller and more revealing than final texts, include those of *The Civil War in France* (1871) and the letter to Vera Zasulich of March 1881.[12]

Much of this material was unknown both to the generations that gave Marxism its shape and form, and to Marx's 'classical' critics. Yet these provide the interpretive grid through which he is so often still read today. The 'young Marx' was unknown to Kautsky, Plekhanov, Labriola, and Lenin,[13] the *Grundrisse* to Gramsci, Lukács, and Korsch. Max Weber, too, might have been pleasantly surprised had he been aware of some asides in the *Grundrisse* concerning the affinity between Protestant asceticism and early capitalism.[14] Even today, received ideas of Marx are being challenged (and orthodoxy, of course, aggressively reasserted) on the basis of 'new' texts hailing from his last decade, which, it seems, has been too hastily written off by successive biographers as a period of 'slow death'.[15] In many ways, arguably, Marx *still* remains 'unknown'. The problem now is less the availability of texts, than the blinkers imposed by past interpretations: the tradition of all the dead generations weighs like a nightmare on the minds of the living.[16]

Other categories of Marx's writing pose different problems. He penned a lot in the context of his political activity, notably as a founding member of the General Council of the International Working Men's Association (1864–72).[17] Much of this sort of material is of little interest save to Marx specialists (or to idolators): for instance his scurrilous portraits of political opponents in 'Great Men of the Exile' (with Engels, 1852), or his tedious polemic (on which he wasted eighteen months) against Karl Vogt (*Herr Vogt*, 1860).[18] But even the more enduring writings of this kind pose difficult questions of context and interpretation. Marx was sometimes constrained, for instance, by the pressures of organizational politics. His 'toning-down' of *The Civil War in France* from drafts to final text *may* be explained by this factor, although this is mere conjecture.[19]

The circumstances of Marx's more directly 'political' texts need always to be borne in mind when their content is at issue, whether it is a matter of the grand rolling simplicities of the *Manifesto* – it was after all precisely that, a call to arms in the heady revolutionary year of 1848, not a reasoned discourse on social theory – or the noncommital reply Marx eventually sent in 1881 to Vera Zasulich, a member of a Russian revolutionary sect he had very little time for, on the vexatious question of the destiny of the Russian peasant commune. The issue of whether or not the commune could be a possible basis for a distinctive kind of socialism bitterly divided the Russian revolutionary movement, then and later. Concern as to the uses to which his words might be put, rather than a change of mind on Marx's part, is the most plausible reason for his excision from the final text of the very detailed (and eminently 'unorthodox') analysis present in his initial three drafts.[20] The point about context also holds more generally. In seeking to interpret the famous Preface to the 1859 *Critique*, for instance, a text that has been repeatedly used to legitimate scientistic, deterministic readings of Marx, we should perhaps remember that Marx wrote this with a wary eye on the Prussian state censor.[21] He was concerned to portray the *Critique* as a work of empirical science rather than of political agitation – and to get it published.

Throughout his life, Marx had the habit of taking copious notes and excerpts from other writers, that he would annotate with his own comments. Indeed, the degree to which Marx developed his analysis of capitalism through a critique of its theorists, the political economists, rather than through empirical investigation, is worth underlining. Engels, by contrast, had first-hand acquaintance with factory production, and in his *Condition of the Working Class in England in 1844* produced a pioneering classic of empirical sociology. Some of Marx's notes and excerpts (like the 1844 notes on James Mill, the 1874 comments on Bakunin's *Statism and Anarchy*, and the 1880 marginal notes on Adolph Wagner) are now relatively well known; but amongst the most interesting are the so-called Ethnological Notebooks of 1879–80, on Lewis Henry Morgan and others, published in Holland in 1972 and still awaiting English translation.[22] Much has still to be published, at least in the West. In the early 1880s, for example, Marx compiled a massive chronology of world history from the first century BC to the 17th century, which runs to some 1500 pages in print. Apparently it focuses, amongst other things, on the rise of the modern nation state, the early development of capitalism, and the importance for both of the Reformation – topics on which Marx's views have been extensively debated. So far the only published text is in Russian.[23] Generally, Marx's notebooks are valuable for the light they shed on his sources, his working methods, and areas of his thought not developed in published writings. This is true in particular of his last decade, in which he read prodigiously and published little. The notebooks also illustrate the breadth of Marx's interests. Like many another Victorian, he was an amateur of the natural sciences, attending lectures on chemistry for 'a Sunday amusement'.[24] Amongst his notebooks are ones that deal at length with geology (complete with drawings of fossils), the uses of electricity, and even with calculus.[25]

Similar things can be said of Marx's correspondence, which was copious.[26] Not only is this of evident biographical interest. Letters, like drafts and notebooks, illuminate the development of his thought – we can watch him wrestling with problems – and its many byways. And at times, they provide brilliantly succinct summaries. The letter to Annenkov of December 1846 is as good a précis as any of Marx's general outlook at the time.[27] One of the clearest formulations of his theory of value (and, to my mind at least, the most compelling argument Marx offers for it, one not explicitly developed in the relevant part of *Capital* 1) is to be found in a letter of 1868 to his friend Ludwig Kugelmann.[28] The letters Marx wrote to Engels whilst finalizing *Capital* provide a commentary of his own on what *he* thought most important and novel in the book.[29] A letter of the late 1870s to the editorial board of the Russian periodical *Otechestvenniye Zapiski* puts it in black and white that *Capital* does not legitimate extrapolation of the trajectory of capitalist development in Western Europe into a 'universal path' all peoples are fated to tread.[30] And so on.

I have not yet mentioned Marx's youthful literary ventures, or the three volumes of poetry he dedicated, as a student, to his future wife Jenny von Westphalen.[31] These may perhaps be passed over, without too much contention, as amongst his least enduring creations. But they do, at least, have the virtue of revealing the man behind the myths. This anthology begins in this vein, with Marx's so-called 'Confessions', his answers to questions put to him as part of a parlour game by his daughters Jenny and Laura, sometime in the 1860s. Here we learn, among other things, that Marx's 'favourite heroes' were Spartacus and Kepler, his 'favourite poets' Shakespeare, Goethe, and Aeschylus (whom he read in the original), and his 'idea of misery' submission. It is salutory to find that his 'favourite motto' was '*De omnibus dubitandum*' (doubt everything). His 'favourite virtue in man' was strength. In women, however, it was 'weakness'; and his 'favourite heroine' was not a Boadicea or a Joan of Arc, but Goethe's fictional Gretchen. Marx may, of course, simply have been teasing his female children; but he was, amongst many other things, a very Victorian, if Bohemian, paterfamilias.[32] Such ephemera serve to remind us that this was not the only respect in which Marx was a man of his time and place.

Like most other Victorians, Marx thought both 'race' and family natural categories (even if subject to some 'historical modification'), and had little trouble in distinguishing between 'civilisation' (which for him was white, western, and modern) and 'barbarism'. His views on the beneficial results of European colonialism would embarrass many twentieth-century Marxists, notwithstanding his denunciations of the violence of its means, and the sharp intimations of what has since come to be called the 'development of underdevelopment' that are occasionally to be found in his work. Marx was, at best, ambivalent on claims to national self-determination, particularly where Slavic peoples were concerned; and his assessment of peasantry was not (in general) one that anticipated the peasant wars of the twentieth century, often led by 'Marxist' parties.[33] Peasant revolutions have been an enduring feature of the modern global landscape: they are a striking illustration of the way the course of history has declined to conform to Marx's expectations. There are others. What he might have made of 'Marxist–feminism' is anyone's guess; but his notes on the split in the American section of the International (1872) dismiss the American feminist Victoria C. Woodhull as 'a banker's woman, free-lover, and general humbug', and he had her section summarily expelled from the organization.[34] His ideas on education, as expressed in August 1869, might appear somewhat naive to Marxists schooled in today's ideas of the 'hidden curriculum':

> Nothing could be introduced either in primary or higher schools that admitted of party or class interpretation. Only subjects such as the physical sciences, grammar, etc., were fit matter for schools. The rules of grammar, for instance, could not differ, whether explained by a religious Tory or a free thinker. Subjects that admitted of different conclusions must be excluded and left for the adults.[35]

I could continue.

None of this is intended to diminish Marx. To criticize him for failing to transcend *all* the prejudices and preconceptions of his era (or to fault him for not foreseeing the preoccupations of ours), makes just about as much sense as berating Aristotle for omitting to invent the steam-engine – or defending slavery. But it is as well to be aware, in a world that has seen Marx's work transformed into exactly the kind of theological master-key to history he himself so emphatically spurned, that his writings *are* products of a time and place, which are steadily receding into the past. *Capital* might have been a very different book had it been written a hundred years later; Marx was not in the habit of deducing the world from his own writings.

Marx's legacy would be difficult enough to interpret, even if it had not been caught up in the tribulations of the bloodiest century in human history, and hopelessly mythologized by his foes and friends alike.[36] What weight, for example, should be given to 'early' works as against later, the 'humanist' Marx of the 1844 Manuscripts as against the 'scientific' Marx of *Capital* (or Teodor Shanin's intriguing 'late Marx', a creature of second thoughts and uncanny insight)? How are we to balance the always difficult, sometimes confused, but often brilliant *Grundrisse* against the polished masterpiece of world literature that is volume 1 of *Capital*? What are we to make of Marx's most widely read text, the Communist Manifesto, knowing both that he painted a very much more complex picture of 'the history of all hitherto existing society'[37] elsewhere, and that he later on explicitly dissociated himself from the political 'programme' of this work – still regularly reproduced in undergraduate texts – in the light of the experience of the Paris Commune of 1871?[38] What status, in reconstructing Marx's views, should we give to his journalism? To marginalia? To correspondence? Where, in short, amid that vast and varied outpouring, is the 'authentic' Marx to be found?

The short answer is: in all of it – inclusive of the many uncertainties, ambiguities, hesitations, changes of mind, and, on occasion, downright inconsistencies – and in none of it, if what is expected is a single, authoritative, talismanic statement of doctrine. 'The authentic Marx' is as chimerical a figure as the definitive production of *Hamlet*. It is often possible to show that he did *not* hold views often ascribed to him; and it is also clear what he was against – injustice, oppression, exploitation. That said, his textual legacy is still capable of legitimately sustaining a variety of interpretations, all of which can find some backing in his writings, and none of which are beyond 'refutation' by selective quotation – that favourite Marxological device – from some other part of the canon.[39] This is not to say that Marx was in any way an incoherent thinker, but – simply – that he was human. 'Marxism' did not spring fully armed from his brain, one fine day in 1845 (or whenever), like Athene from the head of Zeus; nor is it the offspring of some mysterious entelechy, smoothly unfolding itself from the Paris Manuscripts of 1844 to *Capital*. There were false starts, dead ends, chance encounters – like with the rebellious young son of a pious Barmen industrialist, who, at that stage of the game, knew far more of the modern world than he.[40] It is the posthumous translation of Marx's writings into scriptures, texts deserving of reverential exegesis rather than critical confrontation, that makes authenticity an issue in the first place. Behind its self-appointed arbiters stands the gulag.

I do not, then, intend to tell readers how Marx should be read, beyond suggesting the merits of an awareness of historical contexts – both the contexts in which Marx himself wrote, and those in which he has been variously appropriated. But one could do worse, perhaps, than bear in mind his own favourite motto.

This anthology focuses on what would nowadays be called Marx's *sociology*: it does not pretend to illustrate all his concerns equally. Neither Marx's political activities, nor the more technical reaches of his economics, are much addressed in these pages.[41] Within this rubric, I have ranged pretty widely across the various categories of his output discussed previously (there are no love poems), in the belief that a decent selection should reflect Marx's writing in its diversity. Readers will, of course, find many well-known passages. They include themselves. But if there is a bias in this collection, it is towards the less familiar, particularly towards those texts made available in English only in relatively recent years.[42] Non-specialists should find something new (and perhaps, something unexpected) in the Marx on offer in this volume.

All selections use existing translations, wherever possible from the English language *Collected Works*. This facilitates the following-up of the inevitably truncated extracts given here. But in general it is always worth comparing translations, and I give alternatives in the bibliography. I have preferred the old 1887 Moore–Aveling version of *Capital* 1 to the recent Penguin one out of respect for Friedrich Engels, who oversaw it, and a fondness for the Victorian English. To me, Marx reads better thus. This may be idiosyncratic. Each passage is numbered for ease of cross-reference. Round brackets in the text are Marx's own; square brackets insertions by editors of the sources that I employ; curly brackets mine. All emphases are Marx's. The notes are numbered sequentially throughout the book. The bibliography gives full publication details of all material cited, as well as providing guidance to English editions and collections of Marx.

It remains to say only that this anthology, like any other, is a personal selection. Others would doubtless have chosen very differently, and produced equally good (or bad) collections. But that, in a way, is itself a testimony to the continuing fecundity of Marx's thought. To transform his texts into sacred tablets is to make a mockery of the critical spirit that animates everything he wrote. Nonetheless, when all is said and done, Marx remains, for all his Victorian prejudices, our contemporary. The study of modern society still begins with his work, even if it cannot and should not end there.

1

A self-portrait

This text is discussed on p. xix. Martin Tupper was a popular Victorian writer of moralistic verse; his *Proverbial Philosophy* sold over a million copies. Gretchen is the heroine of Goethe's *Faust*.

1.1

Your favourite virtue – Simplicity.
Your favourite virtue in man – Strength.
Your favourite virtue in woman – Weakness.
Your chief characteristic – Singleness of purpose.
Your idea of happiness – To fight.
Your idea of misery – Submission.
The vice you excuse most – Gullibility.
The vice you detest most – Servility.
Your pet aversion – Martin Tupper.
Favourite occupation – Bookworming.
Poet – Shakespeare, Aeschylus, Goethe.
Prose writer – Diderot.
Hero – Spartacus, Kepler.
Heroine – Gretchen.
Flower – Daphne.
Colour – Red.

Name – Laura, Jenny.
Dish – Fish.
Favourite maxim – *Nihil humanum a me alienum puto* {I regard nothing human as alien to me}.
Favourite motto – *De omnibus dubitandum* {doubt everything}.

[Confessions, 1860s; Riazanov, *Karl Marx*, p. 269]

2

Settling accounts

This chapter draws mainly on Marx's writings of the 1840s, and illustrates major themes in his critique of the philosophical historiographies current in Germany at the time. In retrospect this can be seen as a ground-clearing exercise, a 'settling of accounts', as Marx put it later, with his 'former philosophical conscience' (see 9.2). He charges Hegelian and post-Hegelian idealist philosophy with the creation of imaginary historical subjects, through the abstraction of ideas from the material conditions and social relations that they, in his view, express. But Marx is as critical of classical materialism. It too, he argues, remains 'abstract'; it does not set out from 'real, active men', but philosophical 'phrases' like 'matter', 'substance', or 'the world of things'. It is, as Marx makes explicit in a comment on Proudhon, the *dualism* of material and ideal, 'life and ideas', that he rejects. Marx's alternative is made clearest in his criticisms of Feuerbach: his materialism starts out from 'human activity itself as *objective* activity'. Such a materialism, focused on 'the changing of circumstances and of human activity or self-change', is necessarily *historical*.

2.1 Dear Father,
There are moments in one's life which are like frontier posts

marking the completion of a period but at the same time clearly indicating a new direction [...]

In accordance with my state of mind at the time, lyrical poetry was bound to be my first subject [...] But owing to my attitude and whole previous development it was purely idealistic [...] All the poems of the first three volumes I sent to Jenny {von Westphalen, then Marx's fiancée} are marked by attacks on our times, diffuse and inchoate expressions of feeling, nothing natural, everything built out of moon-shine, complete opposition between what is and what ought to be [...]

Poetry, however, could be and had to be only an accompaniment; I had to study law and above all felt the urge to wrestle with philosophy [...]

Here {in a 300-page MS on law, which has not survived}, above all, the same opposition between what is and what ought to be, which is characteristic of idealism, stood out as a serious defect and was the source of the hopelessly incorrect division of the subject-matter. First of all came what I was pleased to call the metaphysics of law, i.e. basic principles, reflections, definitions of concepts, divorced from all actual law and every actual form of law, as occurs in Fichte, only in my case it was more modern and shallower. From the outset an obstacle to grasping the truth here was the unscientific form of mathematical dogmatism, in which the author argues hither and thither, going round and round the subject dealt with, without the latter taking shape as something living and developing in a many-sided way. A triangle gives the mathematician scope for construction and proof, it remains a mere abstract conception in space and does not develop into anything further. It has to be put alongside something else, then it assumes other positions, and this diversity added to it gives it different relationships and truths. On the other hand, in the concrete expression of a living world of ideas, as exemplified by law, the state, nature, and philosophy as a whole, the object itself must be studied in its development; arbitrary divisions must not be introduced, the rational character of the object itself must develop as something imbued with contradictions in itself and find its unity in itself [...]

From the idealism which, by the way, I had compared and nourished with the idealism of Kant and Fichte, I arrived at the point of seeking the idea in reality itself. If previously the gods had dwelt above the earth, now they became its centre.

I had read fragments of Hegel's philosophy, the grotesque craggy melody of which did not appeal to me. Once more I wanted to dive into the sea, but with the definite intention of establishing that the nature of the mind is just as necessary, concrete and firmly based as

the nature of the body. My aim was no longer to practice tricks of swordsmanship, but to bring genuine pearls into the light of day.
[Letter to his father, Nov 1837; 1837: 10–12, 18][43]

2.2 Philosophers do not spring up like mushrooms out of the ground; they are products of their time, of their nation, whose most subtle, valuable and invisible juices flow in the ideas of philosophy. The same spirit that constructs railways with the hands of workers, constructs philosophical systems in the brains of philosophers. Philosophy does not exist outside the world, any more than the brain exists outside man because it is not situated in the stomach [...] Every true philosophy is the intellectual quintessence of its time.
[The leading article in no. 179 of the *Kölnische Zeitung*, 1842; 1842: 195]

2.3 Consciousness can never be anything else than conscious being, and the being of men is their actual life-process. If in all ideology men and their relations appear upside-down as in a *camera obscura*, this phenomenon arises just as much from their historical life-process as the inversion of objects on the retina does from their physical life-process.

In direct contrast to German philosophy which descends from heaven to earth, here it is a matter of ascending from earth to heaven. That is to say, not of setting out from what men say, imagine, conceive, nor from men as narrated, thought of, imagined, conceived, in order to arrive at men in the flesh; but setting out from real, active men, and on the basis of their real life-process demonstrating the development of the ideological reflexes and echoes of this life-process. The phantoms formed in the brains of men are also, necessarily, sublimates of their material life-process, which is empirically verifiable and bound to material premises. Morality, religion, metaphysics, and all the rest of ideology as well as the forms of consciousness corresponding to these, thus no longer retain the semblance of independence. They have no history, no development; but men, developing their material production and their material intercourse, alter, along with this their actual world, also their thinking and the products of their thinking. It is not consciousness that determines life, but life that determines consciousness. For the first manner of approach the starting point is consciousness taken as the living individual; for the second manner of approach, which conforms to real life, it is the real living individuals themselves, and consciousness is considered solely as *their* consciousness.

This manner of approach is not devoid of premises. It starts out from the real premises and does not abandon them for a moment. Its premises are men, not in any fantastic isolation and fixity, but in their actual, empirically perceptible process of development under definite conditions. As soon as this active life-process is described, history ceases to be a collection of dead facts, as it is with the empiricists (themselves still abstract), or an imagined activity of imagined subjects, as with the idealists.

Where speculation ends, where real life starts, there consequently begins real, positive science, the expounding of the practical activity, of the practical process of development of men. Empty phrases about consciousness end, and real knowledge has to take its place. When the reality is depicted, a self-sufficient philosophy loses its medium of existence. At the best its place can only be taken by a summing-up of the most general results, abstractions which are derived from the observation of the historical development of men. These abstractions in themselves, divorced from real history, have no value whatsoever. They can only serve to facilitate the arrangement of historical material, to indicate the sequence of its separate strata. But they by no means afford a recipe or schema, as does philosophy, for neatly trimming the epochs of history. On the contrary, the difficulties begin only when one sets about the examination and arrangement of the material – whether of a past epoch or of the present – and its actual presentation. [*The German Ideology*, 1845 – 6; 1846a: 36–7][44]

2.4 The ideas of the ruling class are in every epoch the ruling ideas: i.e., the class which is the ruling *material* force of society is at the same time its ruling *intellectual* force. The class which has the means of material production at its disposal, consequently also controls the means of mental production, so that the ideas of those who lack the means of mental production are on the whole subject to it. The ruling ideas are nothing more than the ideal expression of the dominant material relations, the dominant material relations grasped as ideas; hence of the relations which make the one class the ruling one, therefore, the ideas of its dominance [...]

If now in considering the course of history we detach the ideas of the ruling class from the ruling class itself and attribute to them an independent existence, if we confine ourselves to saying that these or those ideas were dominant at a given time, without bothering ourselves about the conditions of production and the producers of these ideas, if we thus ignore the individuals and world conditions which are the source of the ideas, then we can say, for instance, that during the time the aristocracy was dominant, the concepts honour, loyalty, etc., were dominant, during the dominance of the bourgeoisie the concepts freedom, equality, etc. The ruling class itself on the whole imagines this to be so [...]

Once the ruling ideas have been separated from the ruling individuals and, above all, from the relations which result from a given stage of the mode of production, and in this way the conclusion has been reached that history is always under the sway of ideas, it is very easy to abstract from these various ideas 'the Idea', the thought, etc., as the dominant force in history, and thus to consider all these separate ideas and concepts as 'forms of self-determination' of the Concept developing in history. It follows then naturally, too, that all the relations of men can be derived from the concept of man, man as conceived, the essence of man, Man. This has been done by speculative philosophy [...]

The whole trick of proving the hegemony of the spirit in history [...] is thus confined to the following three attempts.

No. 1. One must separate the ideas of those ruling for empirical reasons, under empirical conditions and as corporeal individuals, from these rulers, and thus recognise the rule of ideas or illusions in history.

No. 2. One must bring an order into this rule of ideas, prove a mystical connection among the successive ruling ideas, which is managed by regarding them as 'forms of self-determination of the concept' (this is possible because by virtue of their empirical basis these ideas really are connected with one another and because, conceived as *mere* ideas, they become self-distinctions, distinctions made by thought).

No. 3. To remove the mystical appearance of this 'self-determining concept' it is changed into a person – 'self-consciousness' – or, to appear thoroughly materialistic, into a series of persons, who represent the 'concept' in history, into the 'thinkers', the 'philosophers', the ideologists, who again are understood as the manufacturers of history [...] Thus the whole body of materialistic elements has been eliminated from history and now full rein can be given to the speculative steed.

[Ibid: 59–62][45]

2.5   1

The chief defect of all previous materialism – that of Feuerbach included – is that things, reality, sensuousness are conceived only in the form of the *object, or of contemplation*, but not as *human sensuous activity, practice*, not subjectively. Hence, in contradistinction to materialism, the *active* side was set forth abstractly by idealism – which, of course, does not know real, sensuous activity as such. Feuerbach wants sensuous objects, really distinct from conceptual objects, but he does not conceive human activity itself as *objective* activity. In *Das Wesen des Christenthums* {*The Essence of Christianity*}, he therefore regards the theoretical attitude as the only genuinely human attitude, while practice is conceived and defined only in its dirty-Jewish form of appearance. Hence he does not grasp the significance of 'revolutionary', of 'practical–critical', activity.

2

The question whether objective truth can be attributed to human thinking is not a question of theory but is a *practical* question. Man must prove the truth, i.e., the reality and power, the this-worldliness of his thinking in practice. The dispute over the reality or non-reality of thinking which is isolated from practice is a purely *scholastic* question.

3

The materialist doctrine concerning the changing of circumstances and upbringing forgets that circumstances are changed by men and that the educator must himself be educated. This doctrine must, therefore, divide society into two parts, one of which is superior to society.

The coincidence of the changing of circumstances and of human activity or self-change can be conceived and rationally understood only as *revolutionary* practice.

4

Feuerbach starts out from the fact of religious self- estrangement, of the duplication of the world into a religious world and a secular one. His work consists in resolving the religious world into its secular basis. But that the secular basis lifts off from itself and establishes itself as an independent realm in the clouds can only be explained by the inner strife and intrinsic contradictoriness of this secular basis. The latter must, therefore, itself be both understood in its contradiction and revolutionised in practice. Thus, for instance, once the earthly family is discovered to be the secret of the holy family, the former must then itself be destroyed in theory and in practice.

5

Feuerbach, not satisfied with *abstract thinking*, wants [*sensuous*] *contemplation*; but he does not conceive sensuousness as *practical*, human-sensuous activity.

6

Feuerbach resolves the essence of religion into the essence of *man*. But the essence of man is no abstraction inherent in each single individual. In its reality it is the ensemble of the social relations.

Feuerbach, who does not enter upon a criticism of this real essence, is hence obliged:

1. To abstract from the historical process and to define the religious sentiment by itself, and to presuppose an abstract – *isolated* – human individual.

2. Essence, therefore, can be regarded only as 'species', as an inner, mute, general character which unites the many individuals *in a natural way*.

7

Feuerbach, consequently, does not see that the 'religious sentiment' is itself a social product, and that the abstract individual which he analyses belongs to a particular form of society.

8

All social life is essentially *practical*. All mysteries which lead theory to mysticism find their rational solution in human practice and in the comprehension of this practice.

9

The highest point reached by contemplative materialism, that is, materialism which does not comprehend sensuousness as practical activity, is the contemplation of single individuals and of civil society.

10

The standpoint of the old materialism is civil society; the standpoint of the new is human society, or social humanity.

11

The philosophers have only *interpreted* the world in various ways; the point is to *change* it.

[Theses on Feuerbach, 1845; 1845b: 3–5][46]

2.6 Feuerbach's 'conception' of the sensuous world is confined on the one hand to mere contemplation of it, and on the other to mere feeling; he posits 'Man' instead of 'real historical man'. 'Man' is really 'the German'. In the first case, the *contemplation* of the sensuous world, he necessarily lights on things which contradict his consciousness and feeling, which disturb the harmony he presupposes, the harmony of all parts of the sensuous world and especially of man and nature. To remove this disturbance, he must take refuge in a double perception, a profane one which perceives 'only the flatly obvious', and a higher, philosophical, one which perceives the 'true essence' of things. He does not see that the sensuous world around him is not a thing given direct from all eternity, remaining ever the same, but the product of industry and of the state of society; and, indeed [a product] in the sense that it is an historical product, the result of the activity of a whole succession of generations, each standing on the shoulders of the preceding one, developing its industry and its intercourse, and modifying its social system according to the changed needs. Even the objects of the simplest 'sensuous certainty' are only given him through social development, industry and commercial intercourse. The cherry-tree, like almost all fruit trees, was, as is well known, only a few centuries ago transplanted by *commerce* into our zone, and therefore only *by* this action of a definite society in a definite age has it become 'sensuous certainty' for Feuerbach.

Incidentally, when things are seen in this way, as they really are and happened, every profound philosophical problem is resolved [...] quite simply into an empirical fact. For instance, the important question of the relation of man to nature (Bruno {Bauer} goes so far as to speak of 'the antitheses in nature and history', as though these were two separate 'things' and man did not always have before him an historical nature and a natural history), which gave rise to all the 'unfathomably lofty works' on 'substance' and 'self-consciousness', crumbles of itself when we understand that the celebrated 'unity of man with nature' has always existed in industry and has existed in various forms in each epoch according to the lesser or greater development of industry, and so has the 'struggle' of man with nature, right up to the development of his productive forces on a corresponding basis [...]

Certainly Feuerbach has a great advantage over the 'pure'

materialists since he realises that man too is an 'object of the senses'. But apart from the fact that he only conceives him as an 'object of the senses', not as 'sensuous activity', because he still remains in the realm of theory and conceives of men not in their given social connection, not under their existing conditions of life, which have made them *what* they are, he never arrives at the actually existing, active men, but stops at the abstraction 'man', and gets no further than recognising 'the actual, individual, corporeal man' emotionally, i.e. he knows no other 'human relations' 'of man to man' than love and friendship, and even these idealised. He gives no criticism of the present conditions of life. Thus he never manages to conceive the sensuous world as the total living sensuous *activity* of the individuals composing it [...]

As far as Feuerbach is a materialist he does not deal with history, and as far as he considers history he is not a materialist. With him materialism and history diverge completely.
[*The German Ideology*, 1845–6; 1846a: 39–41]

2.7 Mr Proudhon, chiefly because he doesn't know history, fails to see that, in developing his productive faculties, i.e. in living, man develops certain inter-relations, and that the nature of these relations necessarily changes with the modification and the growth of the said productive faculties. He fails to see that *economic categories* are but *abstractions* of those real relations, that they are truths only in so far as those relations continue to exist. Thus he falls into the error of bourgeois economists who regard those economic categories as eternal laws and not as historical laws which are laws only for a given historical development, a specific development of the productive forces. Thus, instead of regarding politico–economic categories as abstractions of actual social relations that are transitory and historical, Mr Proudhon, by a mystical inversion, sees in the real relations only the embodiment of those abstractions. [...]

Mr Proudhon understands perfectly well that men manufacture worsted, linens and silks [...] What Mr Proudhon does not understand is that, according to their faculties, men also produce the *social relations* in which they produce worsteds and linens. Still less does Mr Proudhon understand that those who produce social relations in conformity with their material productivity also produce the *ideas*, *categories*, i.e. the ideal abstract expressions of those same social relations. Indeed, the categories are no more eternal than the relations they express. They are historical and transitory products. To Mr Proudhon, on the contrary, the prime cause consists in abstractions and categories. According to him it is these and not men which make history. *The abstraction, the category regarded as such*, i.e. as distinct from man and his material activity, is, of course, immortal, immutable, impassive. [...]

Because Mr Proudhon posits on the one hand eternal ideas, the categories of pure reason, and, on the other, man and his practical life which, according to him, is the practical application of these categories, you will find in him from the very outset a *dualism* between life and ideas, between soul and body - a dualism which recurs in many forms. So you now see that the said antagonism is nothing other than Mr Proudhon's inability to understand either the origin or the profane history of the categories he has deified.

[Letter to Annenkov, December 28, 1846; 1846b: 100, 102, 104][47]

2.8 {Stirner} has nothing real and mundane to say about real mundane history, except that under the name of 'nature', the 'world of things', etc., he always opposes it to consciousness, as an object of speculation of the latter, as a world which, in spite of its continual annihilation, continues to exist in a mystical darkness, in order to reappear on every convenient occasion [...] Concerning such historical and non-historical constructions, good old *Hegel* wrote with regard to Schelling – the model for all constructors – that one can say the following in this context:

> It is no more difficult to handle the instruments of this monotonous formalism than a painter's palette which has only two colours, say black [...] and yellow [...], in order to use the former to paint a surface when something historical (the 'world of things') is required, and the latter when a landscape ('heaven', spirit, holiness, etc.) is needed.

[*The German Ideology*, 1845–6; 1846a: 134]

2.9 A philosophical *phrase* about a real question is for {Bauer} the real question itself. Consequently, on the one hand, instead of real people and their real consciousness of their social relations, which apparently confront them as something independent, he has the mere abstract expression: *self-consciousness*, just as, instead of real production, he has *the activity of this self-consciousness, which has become independent*. On the other hand, instead of real nature and the actually existing social relations, he has the philosophical summing-up of all the philosophical categories or names of these relations in the expression: *substance*; for Bruno, along with all philosophers and ideologists, erroneously regards thoughts and ideas – the independent intellectual expression of the existing world – as the basis of this existing world. It is obvious that with these two abstractions, which have become senseless and empty, he can perform all kinds of tricks without knowing anything at all about real people and their relations. [Ibid: 99]

2.10 The last attempt to exploit further the criticism of religion as an independent sphere (a criticism which has been flogged to the point of exhaustion), to remain within the premises of German theory and yet to appear to be going beyond them [...] consisted in attacking material relations, not in their actual form, and not even in the form of the mundane illusions of those who are practically involved in the present-day world, but in the heavenly extract of their mundane form as predicates, as emanations from God, as angels [...] Thus, the struggle against religious illusions, against God, was again substituted for the real struggle [...] These predicates of God are again nothing but deified names for the ideas of people about their definite, empirical relations, ideas which subsequently they hypocritically retain because of practical considerations. With the theoretical equipment inherited from Hegel it is, of course, not possible even to understand the empirical, material attitude of these people. Owing to the fact that Feuerbach showed the religious world as an illusion of the earthly world – a world which in his writing appears merely as a *phrase* – German theory too was confronted with the question which he left unanswered: how did it come about that people 'got' these illusions 'into their heads'? Even for the German theoreticians this question paved the way to the materialistic view of the world, a view which is *not without premises*, but which empirically observes the actual material premises as such and for that reason is, for the first time, *actually* a critical view of the world. This path was already indicated in the *Deutsch-Französische Jahrbücher* – in the *Einleitung zur Kritik der Hegelschen Rechtsphilosophie* and *Zur Judenfrage*. But since at that time this was done in philosophical phraseology, the traditionally occurring philosophical expressions such as 'human essence', 'species', etc., gave the German theoreticians the desired reason for misunderstanding the real trend of thought and believing that here again it was a question merely of giving a new turn to their worn-out theoretical garment [...] One has to 'leave philosophy aside' [...] one has to leap out of it and devote oneself like an ordinary man to the study of actuality, for which there exists also an enormous amount of literary material, unknown, of course, to the philosophers [...] Philosophy and the study

of the actual world have the same relation to one another as onanism and sexual love.
[Ibid: 235–6][48]

3

Real, living individuals

This chapter attempts to outline some of the most general
'premises' of Marx's sociology. These include his rejection of both
a reified conception of 'society as subject', and the 'abstract
individual', as valid starting-points for sociological or historical
analysis, these being explained as illusions of modernity; his own
conception of society as a set of relations, spanning both space and
time, between social individuals; his insistence that 'human nature',
and with it, the nature of individual human subjectivity, varies
historically; his stress on 'material life', humanity's relation with the
natural world, as the basis of any social life; and the broadness
of his conception of what 'material life' entails. Though *The
German Ideology* is the work most quoted here, these passages
range across Marx's writings, from the 1844 Paris Manuscripts to
the Notes on Wagner of 1880.

3.1 *Just as* society itself produces *man as man*, so is society *produced*
by him. Activity and enjoyment, both in their content and in their *mode
of existence*, are *social*; *social* activity and *social* enjoyment. The
human aspect of nature exists only for *social* man; for only then does
nature exist for him as a *bond* with *man* – as his existence for the
other and the other's existence for him – and as the life-element of

human reality. Only then does nature exist as the *foundation* of his own *human* existence. Only here has what is to him his *natural* existence become his *human* existence, and nature become man for him. Thus *society* is the complete unity of man with nature – the true resurrection of nature – the accomplished naturalism of man and the accomplished humanism of nature.

Social activity and social enjoyment exist by no means *only* in the form of some *directly* communal activity and directly *communal* enjoyment [...] But also when I am active *scientifically*, etc. – an activity which I can seldom perform in direct community with others – then my activity is *social*, because I perform it as a *man*. Not only is the material of my activity given to me as a social product (as is even the language in which the speaker is active): my *own* existence *is* social activity, and therefore that which I make of myself, I make of myself for society and with the consciousness of myself as a social being [...]

Above all we must avoid postulating 'society' again as an abstraction *vis-à-vis* the individual. The individual *is the social being*. His manifestations of life – even if they may not appear in the direct form of *communal* manifestations of life carried out in association with others – *are* therefore an expression and confirmation of *social life*. Man's individual and species life are not *different* [...]

[Economic and philosophic manuscripts of 1844; 1844c: 298–9][49]

3.2 [...] let us look at this in its subjective aspect. Just as only music awakens in man the sense of music, and just as the most beautiful music has *no* sense for the unmusical ear – is [no] object for it, because my object can only be the confirmation of one of my essential powers – it can therefore only exist for me insofar as my essential power exists for itself as a subjective capacity; because the meaning of an object for me goes only so far as *my* sense goes (has only a meaning for a sense corresponding to that object) – for these reasons the *senses* of the social man *differ* from those of the non-social man. Only through the objectively unfolded richness of man's essential being is the richness of subjective *human* sensibility (a musical ear, an eye for beauty of form – in short, *senses* capable of human gratification, senses affirming themselves to be essential powers of *man*) either cultivated or brought into being. For not only the five senses but also the so-called mental senses, the practical senses (will, love, etc.), in a word, *human* sense, the human nature of the senses, comes to be by virtue of *its* object, by virtue of *humanised* nature. The *forming* of the five senses is a labour of the entire history of the world down to the present.

[Ibid: 301–2]

Marx goes on to argue that 'the nature which develops in human history – the genesis of human society – is man's *real* nature' (p. 303), and 'the *entire so-called history of the world* is nothing but the creation of man through human labour' (p. 305). Three years later he summarizes his point by saying that 'all history is nothing but a continuous transformation of human nature' [1847a: 192]

3.3 We should be only too pleased to believe that 'all the social virtues' of our true socialist {Rudolph Mattäi} are based 'upon the feeling of natural human affinity and unity', even though feudal bondage, slavery and all the social inequalities of every age have also been based upon this 'natural affinity'. Incidentally, 'natural human affinity' is an historical product which is daily changed at the hands of men; it has always been perfectly natural, however inhuman and contrary to nature it may seem, not only in the judgement of 'Man', but also of a later evolutionary generation.

We learn further, quite by chance, that present-day society is based upon 'external compulsion'. By 'external compulsion' the true socialists do not understand the restrictive material conditions of life of given individuals. They see it only as the compulsion exercised by the *state*, in the form of bayonets, police and cannons, which far from being the foundation of society, are only a consequence of its structure [...]

The socialist opposes to present-day society, which is 'based upon external compulsion', the ideal of true society, which is based upon the 'consciousness of man's *inward* nature, i.e., upon reason'. It is based, that is, upon the consciousness of consciousness, upon the thought of thought. The true socialist does not differ from the philosophers even in his choice of terms. He forgets that the 'inward nature' of men, as well as their 'consciousness' of it, 'i.e.', their 'reason', has at all times been an historical product and that even when, as he believes, the society of men was based 'upon external compulsion', their 'inward nature' corresponded to this 'external compulsion'.

[*The German Ideology*, 1845–6; 1846a: 479–80]

3.4 The difference between the individual as a person and whatever is extraneous to him is not a conceptual difference but a historical fact. This distinction has a different significance at different times – e.g., the estate as something extraneous to the individual in the eighteenth century, and so too, more or less, the family. It is not a distinction that we have to make for each age, but one which each age itself makes from among the different elements which it finds in existence, and indeed not according to any idea, but compelled by material collisions in life.

What appears accidental to a later age as opposed to an earlier – and this applies also to the elements handed down by an earlier age – is a form of intercourse which corresponded to a definite stage of development of the productive forces. The relation of the productive forces to the form of intercourse is the relation of the form of intercourse to the occupation or activity of the individuals [...] The conditions under which individuals have intercourse with each other, so long as this contradiction {between new productive forces and old forms of intercourse} is absent, are conditions appertaining to their individuality, in no way external to them; conditions under which alone these definite individuals, living under definite relations, can produce their material life and what is connected with it, are thus the conditions of their self-activity and are produced by this self-activity. The definite condition under which they produce thus corresponds, as long as the contradiction has not yet appeared, to the reality of their conditioned nature, their one-sided existence, the one-sidedness of which only becomes evident when the contradiction enters on the scene and thus exists solely for those who live later. Then this condition appears as an accidental fetter, and the consciousness that it is a fetter is imputed to the earlier age as well.

These various conditions, which appear at first as conditions of self-activity, later as fetters upon it, form in the whole development of history a coherent series of forms of intercourse, the coherence of which consists in this: an earlier form of intercourse, which has become a fetter, is replaced by a new one corresponding to the more developed productive forces and, hence, to the advanced mode of the self-activity of individuals – a form which in its turn becomes a fetter and is then replaced by another. Since these conditions correspond at every stage to the simultaneous development of the productive forces, their history is at the same time the history of the evolving productive forces taken over by each new generation, and is therefore the history of the development of the forces of the individuals themselves.
[Ibid: 81–2]

3.5 In these writings you have provided – I don't know whether

intentionally – a philosophical basis for socialism and the Communists have immediately understood them in this way. The unity of man with man, which is based on the real differences between men, the concept of the human species brought down from the heaven of abstraction to the real earth, what is this but the concept of *society*!
[Letter to Feuerbach, 11 August 1844; 1844d: 354][30]

3.6   In history up to the present it is certainly [...] an empirical fact that separate individuals have, with the broadening of their activity into world-historical activity, become more and more enslaved under a power alien to them (a pressure which they have conceived of as a dirty trick on the part of the so-called world-spirit, etc.), a power which has become more and more enormous and, in the last instance, turns out to be the *world-market* [...] *All-round* dependence, this primary natural form of the *world-historical* co-operation of individuals, will be transformed by this communist revolution into the control and conscious mastery of these powers, which, born of the action of men on one another, have till now overawed and ruled men as powers completely alien to them. Now this view can be expressed again in a speculative–idealistic, i.e., fantastic, way as 'self-generation of the species' ('society as the subject'), and thereby the consecutive series of interrelated individuals can be regarded as a single individual, which accomplishes the mystery of generating itself. In this context it is evident that individuals undoubtedly make *one another*, physically and mentally, but do not make themselves, either in the nonsense of Saint Bruno {Bauer}, or in {Stirner's} sense of the 'unique', the 'made man'.
[*The German Ideology*, 1845–6; 1846a: 51–2]

Marx's hostility to the reification or personification of society remained a consistent theme in his work: Stirner is criticized in *The German Ideology* for his abstraction of 'society as a person, as a subject' [1846a: 206]; similarly Proudhon in *The Poverty of Philosophy* [1847a: 152–3]; while in the 'General Introduction' of 1857, Marx reiterates that 'to consider society as a single subject is wrong: a speculative approach' [1857: 31].

3.7   '*Man*'? If the category 'man' is meant here, then he has, in general, 'no' needs; if it is man who confronts nature as an individual, then he is to be understood as a non-herd animal; if it is man situated in any form of society – and Herr Wagner implies this, since, for him, 'man', even if he does not have a university education, has language at any

rate –, then the determinate character of this social man is to be brought forward as the starting point, i.e. the determinate character of the existing community in which he lives, since production here, hence his *process of securing life*, already has some kind of social character.
[Notes on Adolph Wagner, 1879–80; 1880b: 189][51]

3.8 Individuals producing in a society – hence the socially determined production by individuals is of course the point of departure. The individual and isolated hunter and fisherman, who serves Adam Smith and Ricardo as a starting point, is one of the unimaginative fantasies of the 18th century Robinsonades which, contrary to the fancies of the historians of civilisation, by no means signify simply a reaction against over-refinement and a reversion to a misconceived natural life. No more is Rousseau's *contrat social*, which by means of a contract establishes a relationship and connection between subjects that are by nature independent, based on this kind of naturalism. This is an illusion and nothing but the aesthetic illusion of the small and big Robinsonades. It is, rather, the anticipation of 'bourgeois society' [*bürgerliche Gesellschaft*], which began to evolve in the 16th century and was making giant strides towards maturity in the 18th. In this society of free competition the individual seems to be rid of the natural, etc., ties which in earlier historical epochs made him an appurtenance of a particular, limited aggregation of human beings. The prophets of the 18th century, on whose shoulders Smith and Ricardo were still standing completely, envisaged this 18th-century individual – a product of the dissolution of the feudal forms of society on the one hand, and of the new productive forces evolved since the 16th century on the other – as an ideal whose existence belonged to the past. They saw this individual not as a historical result, but as the starting point of history; not as something evolving in the course of history, but posited by nature, because for them this individual was the natural individual, according to their idea of human nature. This delusion has been characteristic of every new epoch hitherto. Steuart, who in many respects was in opposition to the 18th century and as an aristocrat tended rather to regard things from an historical standpoint, avoided this naive view.

The further back we go in history, the more does the individual, and accordingly also the producing individual, appear to be dependent and belonging to a larger whole. At first, he is still in a quite natural manner part of the family, and of the family expanded into the tribe; later he is part of a community, of one of the different forms of community which arise from the conflict and the merging of tribes. It is not until

the 18th century, in 'bourgeois society' [*bürgerliche Gesellschaft*], that the various forms of the social nexus confront the individual as merely a means towards his private ends, as external necessity. But the epoch which produces this standpoint, that of the isolated individual, is precisely the epoch of the hitherto most highly developed social (according to this standpoint, general) relations. Man is a *zoon politikon* {political being} in the most literal sense: he is not only a social animal, but an animal that can isolate itself only within society. Production by an isolated individual outside society – something rare, which might occur when a civilised person already dynamically in possession of the social forces is accidentally cast into the wilderness – is just as preposterous as the development of language without individuals who live *together* and speak to one another.
[General Introduction, 1857; 1857: 17–18][52]

3.9 Man is, if not as Aristotle contends, a political, at all events a social animal. Strictly, Aristotle's definition is that man is by nature a town-citizen. This is quite as characteristic of ancient classical society as Franklin's definition of man, as a tool-making animal, is characteristic of Yankeedom.
[*Capital* I, 1867; 1867a: 326 (text and note)]

3.10 Nothing is more erroneous than the way in which both the economists and the socialists consider *society* in relation to economic conditions. Proudhon, for example, replies to Bastiat by saying [...]:

> '*For society*, the distinction between capital and product does not exist. This distinction is a purely *subjective* one, existing only for individuals.'

Thus it is precisely the social aspect which he calls social and the subjective abstraction which he calls society. The distinction between product and capital is precisely that, as capital, the product expresses a specific relation belonging to an historical form of society. This so-called consideration from the point of view of society means nothing more than to overlook precisely the *differences* which express the *social relation* (relation of civil society). Society does not consist of individuals, but expresses the sum of the relationships and conditions in which these individuals stand to one another. As if someone were to say: for society, slaves and citizens do not exist: both are men. They *are* both men, if we consider them outside society. To be a slave and to be a citizen are social determinations, relations between human

beings A and B. Human being A as such is not a slave; he is a slave in and through society. Mr Proudhon's remarks about capital and product mean that in his view there is no distinction between capitalists and workers from the point of view of society. But actually this distinction exists only from the point of view of society.
[*Grundrisse*, 1857–8; 1858a: 195–6]

3.11 The premises from which we begin are not arbitrary ones, not dogmas, but real premises from which abstraction can be made only in the imagination. They are the real individuals, their activity and the material conditions of their life, both those which they find already existing and those produced by their activity. These premises can thus be verified in a purely empirical way.

The first premise of all human history is, of course, the existence of living human individuals. Thus the first fact to be established is the physical organisation of these individuals and their consequent relation to the rest of nature. Of course, we cannot go here either into the actual physical nature of man, or into the natural conditions in which man finds himself – geological, oro-hydrographical, climactic and so on. All historical writing must set out from these natural bases and their modification in the course of history through the action of men.

Men can be distinguished from animals by consciousness, by religion or anything else you like. They themselves begin to distinguish themselves from animals as soon as they begin to *produce* their means of subsistence, a step which is conditioned by their physical organisation. By producing their means of subsistence men are indirectly producing their material life.

The way in which men produce their means of subsistence depends first of all on the nature of the means of subsistence they actually find in existence and have to reproduce.

This mode of production must not be considered simply as being the reproduction of the physical existence of the individuals. Rather it is a definite form of activity of these individuals, a definite form of expressing their life, a definite *mode of life* on their part. As individuals express their life, so they are. What they are, therefore, coincides with their production, both with *what* they produce and with *how* they produce. Hence what individuals are depends on the material conditions of their production.

This production only makes its appearance with the *increase of population*. In its turn this presupposes the *intercourse* [*Verkehr*] of individuals with one another. The form of this intercourse is again determined by production.

[*The German Ideology*, 1845–6; 1846a: 31–2]

3.12 Since we are dealing with the Germans, who are devoid of premises, we must begin by stating the first premise of all human existence, and, therefore, of all history, the premise, namely, that men must be in a position to live in order to be able to 'make history'. But life involves before everything else eating and drinking, housing, clothing, and various other things. The first historical act is thus the production of the means to satisfy these needs, the production of material life itself. And indeed this is an historical act, a fundamental condition of all history, which today, as thousands of years ago, must daily and hourly be fulfilled merely in order to sustain human life [...] Therefore in any conception of history one has first of all to observe this fundamental fact in all its significance and all its implications and to accord it its due importance [...]

The second point is that the satisfaction of the first need, the action of satisfying and the instrument of satisfaction which has been acquired, leads to new needs; and this creation of new needs is the first historical act [...]

The third circumstance which, from the very outset, enters into historical development, is that men, who daily re-create their own life, begin to make other men, to propagate their kind: the relation between man and woman, parents and children, the *family*. The family, which to begin with is the only social relation, becomes later, when increased needs create new social relations and the increased population new needs, a subordinate one (except in Germany), and must then be treated and analysed according to the existing empirical evidence, not according to 'the concept of the family', as is the custom in Germany.

These three aspects of social activity are not of course to be taken as three different stages, but just as three aspects or, to make it clear to the Germans, three 'moments', which have existed simultaneously since the dawn of history and the first men, and which still assert themselves in history today.

The production of life, both of one's own in labour and of fresh life in procreation, now appears as a twofold relation: on the one hand as a natural, on the other as a social relation – social in the sense that it denotes the co-operation of several individuals, no matter under what conditions, in what manner and to what end. It follows from this that a certain mode of production, or industrial stage, is always combined with a certain mode of co-operation, or social stage, and this mode of co-operation is itself a 'productive force'. Further, that the aggregate of productive forces accessible to men determines the condition of society, hence, the 'history of humanity' must always be studied and treated in relation to the history of industry and exchange [...] Thus it is quite obvious from the start that there exists a materialist connection of men with one another, which is determined by their needs and their mode of production, and which is as old as men themselves. This connection is ever taking on new forms, and thus presents a 'history' irrespective of the existence of any political or religious nonsense which would especially hold men together.

Only now, after having considered four moments, four aspects of primary historical relations, do we find that man also possesses 'consciousness'.
[Ibid: 41–3]

3.13 In production, men enter into relation not only with nature. They produce only by co-operating in a certain way and mutually exchanging their activities. In order to produce, they enter into definite connections and relations with one another, and only within these social connections and relations does their relation with nature, does production, take place.
[Wage Labour and Capital, 1847; 1847b: 211][53]

3.14 Man himself is the basis of his material production, as of any other production that he carries on. All circumstances, therefore, which affect man, the *subject* of production, more or less modify all his functions and activities, and therefore too his functions and activities as the creator of material wealth, of commodities. In this respect it can in fact be shown that *all* human relations and functions, however and in whatever form they may appear, influence material production and have a more or less decisive influence upon it.
[*Theories of Surplus Value*, 1861–3; 1863a: 288][54]

3.15 The form of intercourse [*Verkehrsform*] determined by the existing productive forces at all previous historical stages, and in its turn determining these, is *civil society*. The latter [...] has as its premise and basis the simple family and the multiple, called the tribe [...] Already here we see that this civil society is the true focus and theatre of all history, and how absurd is the conception of history held hitherto, which neglects the real relations and confines itself to spectacular historical events.

In the main we have so far considered only one aspect of human activity, the *reshaping of nature* by men. The other aspect, the *reshaping of men by men* ... [{Marginal note by Marx}: intercourse and productive power.]
[*The German Ideology*, 1845–6; 1846a: 50]

3.16 Civil society embraces the whole material intercourse of individuals within a definite stage of the development of productive forces. It embraces the whole commercial and industrial life of a given stage, and, insofar, transcends the state and the nation, though, on the other hand again, it must assert itself in its external relations as nationality and internally must organise itself as state. The term 'civil society' [*bürgerliche Gesellschaft*] emerged in the eighteenth century, when property relations had already extricated themselves from the ancient and medieval community. Civil society as such only develops with the bourgeoisie; the social organisation evolving directly out of production and intercourse, which in all ages forms the basis of the state and the rest of the idealistic superstructure, has, however, always been designated by the same name.
[Ibid: 89]

Marx identifies this dual reference – historically specific (*bourgeois* society) and transhistorical (civil society) – of the concept *bürgerliche Gesellschaft*, as a more general feature of such 'simple abstractions': see 4.8.

3.17 What Mr. Proudhon calls the *extra-economic* origin of property – by which he means precisely landed property – is the *pre-bourgeois* relation of the individual to the objective conditions of labour, and initially to the *natural*, objective, conditions of labour. For, just as the working subject is a natural individual, a natural being, so the first objective condition of his labour appears as nature, earth, as his inorganic body. He himself is not only the organic body, but also this inorganic nature as a subject. This condition is not something he has produced, but something he finds to hand; as the natural world outside himself and presupposed to him.

Before proceeding in our analysis, one further point: the worthy Proudhon would not only be able to, he would have to, accuse *capital* and *wage labour* – as forms of property – of having an *extra-economic* origin. For the worker's encounter of the objective conditions of his labour as something separate from him, as *capital*, and the capitalist's encounter of the propertyless *worker*, as an abstract worker – the exchange as it takes place between value and living labour – presupposes an *historical process*, however much capital and labour themselves reproduce this relation and elaborate it in its objective scope, as well as in depth. And this historical process [...] is the history of the emergence of both capital and wage labour.

In other words, the *extra-economic origin* of property means nothing but the *historical origin* of the bourgeois economy, of the forms of production to which the categories of political economy give theoretical or conceptual expression. The statement that pre-bourgeois history, and each phase of it, has its own *economy* and an *economic basis* of its movement, is *au fond* {at base} merely the tautology that human life has from the beginning rested on production, and, *d'une manière ou d'une autre* {in one way or another}, on *social* production, whose relations are precisely what we call economic relations.
[*Grundrisse*, 1857–8; 1858a: 412–13]

3.18 The division of labour in which all these contradictions are implicit, and which in its turn is based on the natural division of labour in the family and the separation of society into individual families opposed to one another, simultaneously implies the *distribution*, and indeed the *unequal* distribution, both quantitative and qualitative, of labour and its products, hence property, the nucleus, the first form of which lies in the family, where wives and children are the slaves of the husband. This latent slavery in the family, though still very crude, is the first form of property, but even at this stage it corresponds perfectly to the definition of modern economists, who call it the power of disposing of the labour-power of others. Division of labour and property are, after all, identical expressions: in the one the same thing is affirmed with reference to activity as is affirmed in the other with reference to the product of the activity.
[*The German Ideology*, 1845–6; 1846a: 46]

3.19 The most important division of material and mental labour is the separation of town and country. The contradiction between town and country begins with the transition from barbarism to civilisation, from tribe to state, from locality to nation, and runs through the whole history of civilisation to the present day (the Anti-Corn Law League).

The advent of the town implies, at the same time, the necessity of administration, police, taxes, etc., in short, of the municipality, and thus of politics in general. Here first became manifest the division of the population into two great classes, which is directly based on the division

of labour and of the instruments of production. The town is in actual fact already the concentration of the population, of the instruments of production, of capital, of pleasures, of needs, while the country demonstrates just the opposite fact, isolation and separation. The contradiction between town and country can exist only within the framework of private property. It is the most crass expression of the subjection of the individual under the division of labour, under a definite activity forced upon him – a subjection which makes one man into a restricted town-animal, another into a restricted country-animal, and daily creates anew the strife between their interests. Labour is here again the chief thing, power *over* individuals, and as long as this power exists, private property must exist. [...] The separation of town and country can also be understood as the separation of capital and landed property, as the beginning of the existence and development of capital independent of landed property – the beginning of property having its basis only in labour and exchange.
[Ibid: 64]

3.20 Whatever the social form of production, labourers and means of production always remain factors of it. But in a state of separation from each other either of these factors can be such only potentially. For production to go on at all they must unite. The specific manner in which this union is accomplished distinguishes the different economic epochs of the structure of society from one another.
[*Capital* 2, MS VI, between October 1877 and July 1878; 1878: 36–37]

3.21 The essential difference between the various economic forms of society, between, for instance, a society based on slave-labour, and one based on wage-labour, lies only in the mode in which [...] surplus-labour is in each case extracted from the actual producer, the labourer.
[*Capital* 1, 1867; 1867a: 217]

3.22 The specific economic form, in which unpaid surplus-labour is pumped out of direct producers, determines the relationship of rulers and ruled, as it grows directly out of production itself and, in turn, reacts upon it as a determining element. Upon this, however, is founded the entire formation of the economic community which grows up out of the production relations themselves, thereby simultaneously its specific political form. It is always the direct relationship of the owners

of the conditions of production to the direct producers – a relation always naturally corresponding to a definite stage in the development of the methods of labour and thereby its social productivity – which reveals the innermost secret, the hidden basis of the entire social structure, and with it the political form of the relation of sovereignty and dependence, in short, the corresponding specific form of the state. This does not prevent the same economic basis – the same from the standpoint of its main conditions – due to innumerable different empirical circumstances, natural environment, racial relations, external historical influences, etc., from showing infinite variations and gradations in appearance, which can be ascertained only by analysis of the empirically given circumstances.
[*Capital* 3, 1863–5; 1865a: 791–2][55]

3.23 This conception of history thus relies on expounding the real process of production – starting from the material production of life itself – and comprehending the form of intercourse connected with and created by this mode of production, i.e., civil society in its various stages, as the basis of all history; describing it in its action as the state, and also explaining how all the different theoretical products and forms of consciousness, religion, philosophy, morality, etc., etc., arise from it, and tracing the process of their formation from that basis; thus the whole thing can, of course, be depicted in its totality (and therefore, too, the reciprocal action of these various sides on one another). It has not, like the idealist view of history, to look for a category in every period, but constantly remains on the real *ground* of history; it does not explain practice from the idea but explains the formation of ideas from material practice [...] It shows that history does not end by being resolved into 'self-consciousness' as 'spirit of the spirit', but that each stage contains a material result, a sum of productive forces, a historically created relation to nature and of individuals to one another, which is handed down to each generation from its predecessor; a mass of productive forces, capital funds and circumstances, which on the one hand is indeed modified by the new generation, but on the other also prescribes for it its conditions of life and gives it a definite development, a special character. It shows that circumstances make men just as much as men make circumstances.
[*The German Ideology*, 1845–6; 1846a: 53–4]

3.24 Men make their own history, but they do not make it just as they please; they do not make it under circumstances chosen by

themselves, but under circumstances directly encountered, given and transmitted from the past. The tradition of all the dead generations weighs like a nightmare on the brain of the living. And just when they seem engaged in revolutionising themselves and things, in creating something that has never yet existed, precisely in such periods of revolutionary crisis they anxiously conjure up the spirits of the past to their service and borrow from them names, battle-cries and costumes in order to present the new scene of world history in this time-honoured disguise and borrowed language. Thus Luther donned the mask of the Apostle Paul, the revolution of 1789 to 1814 draped itself alternately as the Roman Republic and the Roman Empire, and the revolution of 1848 knew nothing better to do than to parody, now 1789, now the revolutionary tradition of 1793 to 1795.
[*Eighteenth Brumaire*, 1852; 1852a: 103–4][56]

3.25 What is society, irrespective of its form? The product of man's interaction upon man. Is man free to choose this or that form of society? By no means. If you assume a given state of development of man's productive faculties, you will have a corresponding form of commerce and consumption. If you assume given stages of development in production, commerce or consumption, you will have a corresponding form of social constitution, a corresponding organisation, whether of the family, of the estates or of the classes – in a word, a corresponding civil society. If you assume this or that civil society, you will have this or that political system, which is but the official expression of civil society. This is something Mr Proudhon will never understand, for he imagines he's doing something great when he appeals from the state to civil society, i.e. to official society from the official epitome of society.

Needless to say, man is not free to choose *his productive forces* – upon which his whole history is based – for every productive force is an acquired force, the product of previous activity. Thus the productive forces are the result of man's practical energy, but that energy is in turn circumscribed by the conditions in which man is placed by the productive forces already acquired, by the form of society which exists before him, which he does not create, which is the product of the preceding generation. The simple fact that every succeeding generation finds productive forces acquired by the preceding generation and which serve it as the raw material of further production, engenders a relatedness in the history of mankind, which is all the more a history of mankind as man's productive forces, and hence his social relations, have expanded. From this it can only be concluded that the social

history of man is never anything else than the history of his individual development, whether he be conscious of this or not. His material relations form the basis of all his relations. These material relations are but the necessary forms in which his material and individual activity is realised.
[Letter to Annenkov, 28 December 1846; 1846b: 96]

3.26 Mr Proudhon the economist understands very well that men make cloth, linen or silk materials in definite relations of production. But what he has not understood is that these definite social relations are just as much produced by men as linen, flax, etc. Social relations are closely bound up with productive forces. In acquiring new productive forces men change their mode of production; and in changing their mode of production, in changing the way of earning their living, they change all their social relations. The hand-mill gives you society with the feudal lord; the steam-mill, society with the industrial capitalist.

The same men who establish their social relations in conformity with their material productivity, produce also principles, ideas and categories, in conformity with their social relations.

Thus these ideas, these categories, are as little eternal as the relations they express. They are *historical and transitory products*.

There is a continual movement of growth in productive forces, of destruction in social relations, of formation in ideas; the only immutable thing is the abstraction of movement – *mors immortalis* {immortal death}.
[*The Poverty of Philosophy*, 1847; 1847a: 165–6][57]

3.27 When we consider bourgeois society in the long view and as a whole, then the final result of the process of social production always appears as the society itself, i.e. the human being itself in its social relations. Everything that has a fixed form, such as the product etc., appears merely as a moment, a vanishing moment, in this movement. The direct production process itself here appears only as a moment. The conditions and objectifications of the process are themselves equally moments of it, and its only subjects are individuals, but individuals in mutual relationships, which they equally reproduce and produce anew. The constant process of their own movement, in which they renew themselves even as they renew the world of wealth which they create.
[*Grundrisse*, 1857–8; Nicolaus: 712]

4

Reproducing the concrete by way of thought

I have argued elsewhere that Marx's most enduring contribution to the understanding of human social life is to be found less in his substantive conclusions than in his method of analysis: a critique of apparently 'natural' social forms of life, which in turn makes possible their recovery as historical products of 'real, living individuals'.[58] This chapter tries to illustrate key tenets of Marx's methodology. This is not easy to do, since Marx did not write anything comparable to Durkheim's *Rules*.[59] His most telling methodological observations are frequently found in his critical asides on other writers, particularly political economists, and my selection here reflects this. Whilst often difficult, the extracts given in this chapter are (in my view) basic to an understanding of Marx's sociology, and repay careful study. Some may make better sense *after* reading chapters 5 and 6, which set out the fundamentals of Marx's own analysis of capitalism. At the very least, this chapter should deter readers from abstracting out of Marx a disembodied general 'theory' of society or history, which can be mechanically 'applied'.

4.1 The truly philosophical criticism of the present state constitution not only shows up contradictions as existing; it *explains* them, it comprehends their genesis, their necessity. It considers them in their *specific* significance. But *comprehending* does not consist, as Hegel imagines, in recognising the features of the logical concept everywhere, but in grasping the specific logic of the specific subject.
[Critique of Hegel's *Rechtsphilosophie*, 1843; 1843b: 91][60]

4.2 The fact is, therefore, that definite individuals who are productively active in a definite way enter into these definite social and political relations. Empirical observation must in each separate instance bring out empirically, and without any mystification and speculation, the connection of the social and political structure with production.
[*The German Ideology*, 1845–6; 1846a: 35]

4.3   Dear Sir,
The author of the article 'Karl Marx on trial before Mr. Zhukovski' {N. Mikhailovskii} is obviously a clever man, and if, in my account of primitive accumulation {in *Capital* 1, Part 8}, he had found a single passage to support his conclusions, he would have quoted it. For want of such a passage, he is forced to seize upon an incidental text – a kind of polemic against a Russian 'man of letters' {A. Herzen} appended to the first German edition of *Capital*. My reproach against this writer had been that he discovered the Russian commune not in Russia but in the book by Haxthausen, a Prussian government councillor; and that, in his hands, the Russian commune merely served as an argument to show that old, rotten Europe must be regenerated through the victory of pan-Slavism. My assessment of this writer may be right and it may be wrong, but it cannot in any event supply the key to my views on the efforts by the Russian people to find for their motherland a road of development different from the one along which Western Europe has proceeded and still proceeds [...]

In the afterword to the second German edition of *Capital* [...] I speak of a 'great Russian scholar and critic' {N. Chernyshevskii} with the high regard he deserves. In an outstanding series of articles, he discussed whether Russia, as its liberal economists would have it, must begin by destroying the rural commune in order to pass on to the capitalist regime, or whether, on the contrary, it may develop on its own historical foundations and thus, without experiencing all the tortures of this regime, nevertheless appropriate all its fruits. He, himself, pronounces for the second solution. And my respected critic

would have at least as much reason to infer from my regard for this
'great Russian scholar and critic' that I shared his views on this matter,
as to conclude from my polemic against the pan-Slavist 'man of letters'
that I rejected them.

Finally, as I do not like to leave 'anything to guesswork', I shall
be direct and to the point. In order to reach an informed judgement on
Russia's economic development, I learned Russian and then for many
years studied official and other publications relating to the question. I
have come to the conclusion that if Russia continues along the path it
has followed since 1861, it will lose the finest chance ever offered by
history to a people and undergo all the fateful vicissitudes of the
capitalist regime.

II

The chapter on primitive accumulation {*Capital* 1, Part 8} claims no
more than to trace the path by which, in Western Europe, the capitalist
economic order emerged from the womb of the feudal economic order.
It therefore presents the historical movement which, by divorcing the
producers from their means of production, converted the former into
wage-labourers (proletarians in the modern sense of the word) and the
owners of the latter into capitalists. In this history 'all revolutions are
epoch-making that serve as a lever for the advance of the emergent
capitalist class, above all those which, by stripping great masses of
people of their traditional means of production and existence,
suddenly hurl them on to the labour-market. But the basis of the whole
development is the expropriation of the agricultural producers. Only
in England has it so far been accomplished in a radical manner ... but
all the countries of Western Europe are following the same course' etc.
(*Capital*, French edition, p. 315). At the end of the chapter, the
historical tendency of production is said to consist in the fact that it
'begets its own negation with the inexorability presiding over the
metamorphoses of nature'; that it has itself created the elements of a
new economic order, giving the greatest impetus both to the
productive forces of social labour and to the all-round development of
each individual producer; that capitalist property, effectively already
resting upon a collective mode of production, cannot but be
transformed into social property. I furnish no proof at this point, for
the good reason that this statement merely summarises in brief the
long expositions given previously in the chapters on capitalist
production.

Now, what application to Russia could my critic make of this
historical sketch? Only this: if Russia is tending to become a capitalist
nation like the nations of Western Europe – and in the last few years

she has been at great pains to achieve this – she will not succeed without first transforming a large part of her peasants into proletarians; subsequently, once brought into the fold of the capitalist regime, she will pass under its pitiless laws like other profane peoples. That is all. But it is too little for my critic. He absolutely insists on transforming my historical sketch of the genesis of capitalism in Western Europe into a historico–philosophical theory of the general course fatally imposed on all peoples, whatever the historical circumstances in which they find themselves placed, in order to arrive ultimately at this economic formation which assures the greatest expansion of the productive forces of social labour, as well as the most complete development of man. But I beg his pardon. That is to do me both too much honour and too much discredit. Let us take an example.

At various points in *Capital* I allude to the fate that befell the plebeians of ancient Rome. They were originally free peasants, each tilling his own plot on his own behalf. In the course of Roman history they were expropriated. The same movement that divorced them from their means of production and subsistence involved the formation not only of large landed property but also of big money capitals. Thus one fine morning there were, on the one side, free men stripped of everything but their labour-power, and, on the other, ready to exploit their labour, owners of all the acquired wealth. What happened? The Roman proletarians became, not wage-labourers, but an idle mob more abject than those who used to be called 'poor whites' in the southern United States; and what opened up alongside them was not a capitalist but a slave mode of production. Thus events of striking similarity, taking place in different historical contexts, led to totally disparate results. By studying each of these developments separately, and then comparing them, one may easily discover the key to this phenomenon. But success will never come with the master-key of a general historico–philosophical theory, whose supreme virtue consists in being supra-historical.

[Letter to editors of *Otechestvenniye Zapiski*, November 1877 or late 1878; 1877; Shanin: 134–6][61]

Interestingly, Marx clarified the French edition of *Capital* on this very point. The Preface to the first German edition reads: 'The country that is more developed industrially only shows, to the less developed, the image of its own future' [1867a: 9]. The French modification runs: 'The country that is more developed industrially only shows, *to those which follow it on the industrial path* [*à ceux qui le suivent sur l'échelle industrielle*], the image of their own future' (1875a: 36, my italics).

4.4 History is nothing but the succession of the separate generations, each of which uses the materials, the capital funds, the productive forces handed down to it by all preceding generations and thus, on the one hand, continues the traditional activity in completely changed circumstances, and, on the other, modifies the old circumstances with a completely changed activity. This can be speculatively distorted so that later history is made the goal of earlier history, e.g., the goal ascribed to the discovery of America is to further the eruption of the French revolution. Thereby history receives its own special goals [...] What is designated with the words 'destiny', 'goal', 'germ', or 'idea' of earlier history is nothing more than an abstraction from later history, from the active influence which earlier history exercises on later history.

[*The German Ideology*, 1845–6; 1846a: 50]

4.5 Darwin's work {*On the Origin of Species by Means of Natural Selection*} is most important in that it provides a basis in natural science for the historical class struggle. One does, of course, have to put up with the clumsy English style of argument. Despite all shortcomings, it is here that, for the first time, 'teleology' in natural science is not only dealt a mortal blow but its rational meaning is empirically explained.

[Letter to Lassalle, 16 January 1861; 1861a: 246–7][62]

4.6 When we speak of production, we always have in mind production at a definite stage of social development, production by social individuals. It might therefore seem that, in order to speak of production at all, we must either trace the historical process of development in its various phases, or else declare at the very beginning that we are dealing with one particular historical epoch, for instance with modern bourgeois production, which is indeed our real subject-matter. All epochs of production, however, have certain features in common, certain common determinations. *Production in general* is an abstraction, but a reasonable abstraction in so far as it actually emphasizes and defines the common aspects and thus spares us the need of repetition. Yet this *general aspect*, or the common element which is brought to light by comparison, is itself multiply divided and diverges into different determinations. Some features are found in all epochs, others are common to a few epochs. The most modern epoch and the most ancient will have [certain] determinations in common. Without them production is inconceivable. But although the most highly developed languages have laws and categories in common with the most primitive ones, it is precisely what constitutes their development that distinguishes them from this general and common element. The determinations which apply to production in general must rather be set apart in order not to allow the unity which stems from the very fact that the subject, mankind, and the object, nature, are the same – to obscure the essential difference. On failure to perceive this difference rests, for instance, the entire wisdom of modern economists who are trying to prove the eternity and harmony of the existing social relations. For example, no production is possible without an instrument of production, even if this instrument is simply the hand. None is possible without past, accumulated labour, even if this labour is merely the skill accumulated and concentrated in the hand of the savage by repeated exercise. Capital is amongst other things also an instrument of production, also past, objectified labour. Consequently [modern economists say] capital is a universal and eternal relation given by nature – that is, provided one omits precisely those specific factors which turn the 'instrument of production' or 'accumulated labour' into capital. The whole history of the relations of production therefore appears, for instance in Carey, as a falsification maliciously brought about by the governments [...]

It is fashionable to preface economic works with a general part [...] which deals with the *general conditions* of all production.

This general part comprises or purports to comprise:

1. The conditions without which production is impossible. This means in fact only that the essential moments of all production are indicated. But actually this boils down, as we will see, to a few very simple definitions, which are expanded into trivial tautologies.

2. The conditions which promote production to a larger or smaller degree [...]

But all that is not really what the economists are concerned with in this general part. It is rather – see for example Mill – that production, as distinct from distribution, etc., is to be presented as governed by eternal natural laws independent of history, and then *bourgeois* relations are quietly substituted as irrefutable natural laws of society *in abstracto*. This is the more or less conscious purpose of the whole procedure. As regards distribution, however, men are said to have indeed indulged in all sorts of arbitrary action. Quite apart from the crude separation of production and distribution and from their real relation, it should be obvious from the outset that, however dissimilar [the mode of] distribution at the various stages of society may be, it must be possible, just as in the case of production, to [single out] common determinations, and it must be likewise possible to confuse or efface all historical differences in *general human* laws. For example, the slave, the serf, the wage worker, all receive an amount of food enabling them to exist as a slave, serf, or wage worker. The conqueror who lives by tribute, or the official who lives by taxes, or the landowner who lives by rent, or the monk who lives by alms, or the Levite who lives by tithes, all receive a portion of the social product which is determined by laws different from those that determine the portion of the slave, etc. The two principal items which all economists include in this section are: (1) property and (2) safeguarding of property by the judiciary, police, etc.

To this, only a brief reply is needed:

Regarding (1): All production is appropriation of nature by the individual within and by means of a definite form of society. In this sense it is a tautology to say that property (appropriation) is a condition of production. But it is ridiculous to make a leap from this to a definite form of property, e.g. private property (this is moreover an antithetical form, which presupposes *non-property* as a condition, too). History shows, on the contrary, that common property (e.g., among the Indians, Slavs, ancient Celts, etc.) is the earlier form, a form which in the shape of communal property continues to play a significant role for a long time. The question whether wealth develops better under this or under that form of property is not yet under discussion here. But it is tautological to say that where no form of property exists there can be no production and hence no society either. Appropriation which appropriates nothing is a *contradictio in subjecto* {contradiction in terms}.

Regarding (2): Safeguarding what has been acquired, etc. If these trivialities are reduced to their real content, they say more than their preachers realise, namely, that each form of production produces its own legal relations, forms of government, etc. The crudity and lack of comprehension lies precisely in that organically coherent factors are brought into haphazard relation with one another, i.e., into a merely speculative connection. The bourgeois economists only have in view that production proceeds more smoothly with modern police than, e.g., under club-law. They forget, however, that club-law is law, and that the law of the stronger survives, in a different form, even in their 'constitutional state' [...]

To recapitulate: there are determinations which are common to all

stages of production and are fixed by reasoning as general; the so-called *general conditions* of all production, however, are nothing but these abstract moments, which do not define any of the actual historical stages of production.
[General Introduction, 1857: 1857: 23–26][63]

4.7 In each historical epoch, property has developed entirely differently and under a set of entirely different social relations. Thus to define bourgeois property is nothing else than to give an exposition of all the social relations of bourgeois production. To try and give a definition of property as of an independent relation, a category apart, an abstract and eternal idea, can be nothing but an illusion of metaphysics or jurisprudence.
[*The Poverty of Philosophy*, 1847; 1847a: 197]

4.8 Labour seems to be a very simple category. The notion of labour in this universal form, as labour in general, is also as old as the hills. Nevertheless, considered economically in this simplicity, 'labour' is just as modern a category as the relations which give rise to this simple abstraction [...]

The fact that the specific kind of labour is irrelevant {in the way in which modern economists conceive 'labour'} presupposes a highly developed totality of actually existing kinds of labour, none of which is any more the dominating one. Thus the most general abstractions arise on the whole only with the most profuse concrete development, when one [phenomenon] is seen to be common to many, common to all. Then it is no longer perceived simply in a particular form. On the other hand, this abstraction of labour in general is not simply the conceptual result of a concrete totality of labours. The fact that the particular kind of labour is irrelevant corresponds to a form of society in which individuals easily pass from one kind of labour to another, the particular kind of labour being accidental to them and therefore indifferent. Labour, not only as a category but in reality, has become here a means to create wealth in general, and has ceased as a determination to be tied with the individuals in any particularity. This state of affairs is most pronounced in the most modern form of bourgeois society, the United States. It is only there that the abstract category 'labour', 'labour as such', labour *sans phrase* {pure and simple}, the point of departure of modern [political] economy, is first seen to be true in practice.

The simplest abstraction which plays the key role in modern

[political] economy, and which expresses an ancient relation existing in all forms of society, appears to be true in practice in this abstract form only as a category of the most modern society [...]

This example of labour strikingly demonstrates that even the most abstract categories, despite their being valid – precisely because they are abstractions – for all epochs, are, in the determinateness of their abstraction, just as much a product of historical conditions and retain their full validity only for and within these conditions.

Bourgeois society is the most developed and many-faceted historical organisation of production. The categories which express its relations, an understanding of its structure, therefore, provide, at the same time, an insight into the structure and the relations of production of all previous forms of society the ruins and components of which were used in the creation of bourgeois society. Some of these remains are still dragged along within bourgeois society unassimilated, while elements which previously were barely indicated have developed and attained their full significance, etc. The anatomy of man is a key to the anatomy of the ape. On the other hand, indications of higher forms in the lower species of animals can only be understood when the higher forms themselves are already known. Bourgeois economy thus provides a key to that of antiquity, etc. But by no means in the manner of those economists who obliterate all historical differences and see in all forms of society the bourgeois forms. One can understand tribute, tithe, etc., if one knows rent. But they must not be treated as identical.

Since bourgeois society is, moreover, only a contradictory form of development, it contains relations of earlier forms of society often only in very stunted shape or as mere travesties, e.g. communal property. Thus, if it is true that the categories of bourgeois economy are valid for all other forms of society, this has to be taken *cum grano salis* {with a grain of salt}, for they may contain them in a developed, stunted, caricatured, etc., form, always with substantial differences. [General Introduction, 1857; 1857: 40–42]

In a letter to Engels of April 2, 1858 Marx observes, more tersely: 'On closer examination, the most abstract definitions invariably point to a broader, definite, concrete, historical basis. (Of course, since to the extent that they are definite they have been abstracted therefrom.)' [1858d: 302]

4.9 Now behold [...] the vapid arguments of the degenerate political economy of the most recent times, claiming to *prove* that economic relationships always express the *same* simple determinations and hence

always express the equality and freedom of the simply determined exchange of exchange values, which amounts to nothing but infantile abstraction. For example: the relationship of capital and interest is reduced to the exchange of exchange values. No sooner is it admitted on the basis of experience that exchange value not only exists in this simple determinateness but also in the essentially different one as capital, than capital is reduced once more to the simple concept of exchange value; and, what is more, interest, which expresses a definite relationship of capital as such, is likewise divested of its specific form and equated to exchange value. The entire relationship in its specific form is turned into an abstraction and reduced to the undeveloped relationship of commodity for commodity. If I abstract from that which distinguishes something concrete from its abstract form it [the result] is naturally the abstract and [turns out to be] in no way different from it. *According to this procedure, all economic categories are only various names given to one and the same relationship, and this crude inability to grasp the real differences between them is then supposed to represent pure common sense as such. Hence the 'economic harmonies' of Mr Bastiat amount au fond to asserting that only a single economic relationship exists which adopts different names, or that difference can occur only in nomenclature.* His reductionism is not even formally scientific in the sense that everything is reduced to one real economic relationship inherent in development.
[*Grundrisse*, 1857–8; 1857: 180–1]

4.10 That the '*forms of exchange*' seem to Rossi to be a matter of complete indifference is just as if a physiologist said that the different forms of life are a matter of complete indifference, that they are all only forms of organic matter. It is precisely these forms that are alone of importance when the question is the specific character of a mode of social production. A coat is a coat. But have it made in the first form of exchange, and you have capitalist production and modern bourgeois society; in the second, and you have a form of handicraft which is compatible even with Asiatic relations or those of the Middle Ages, etc. And these *forms* are decisive for material wealth itself.
[*Theories of Surplus Value*, 1861–3; 1863a: 295–6]

4.11 The first category in which bourgeois wealth presents itself is that of the *commodity*. The commodity itself appears as unity of two aspects. It is *use value*, i.e. object of the satisfaction of any system whatsoever of human needs. This is its material side, which the most

disparate epochs of production may have in common, and whose examination therefore lies beyond political economy. Use value falls within the realm of political economy as soon as it becomes modified by the modern relations of production, or as it, in turn, intervenes to modify them. What it is customary to say about it in general terms, for the sake of good form, is confined to commonplaces which had a historic value in the first beginnings of the science, when the social forms of bourgeois production had still laboriously to be peeled out of the material, and, at great effort, to be established as independent objects of study. In fact, however, the use value of the commodity is a given presupposition – the material basis in which a specific economic relation presents itself. It is only this specific relation which stamps the use value as a commodity.
[*Grundrisse*, 1857–8; Nicolaus: 881][64]

4.12 Well (it is difficult for me today to write), let us now come to the *corpus delicti* {heart of the matter}.

I. *Capital. First section*: *Capital in general* [...]

1. *Value.* Simply reduced to the quantity of labour; time as a measure of labour. Use-value – whether regarded subjectively as the usefulness of labour, or objectively as the utility of the product – is shown here simply as the material prerequisite of value, and one which for the present is entirely irrelevant to the formal economic definition. Value as such has no 'substance' other than actual labour. This definition of value, first outlined by Petty and neatly elaborated by Ricardo, is simply bourgeois wealth in its most abstract form. As such, it already presupposes 1. the transcending of indigenous communism (India, etc.), 2. of all undeveloped, pre-bourgeois modes of production which are not in every respect governed by exchange. Although an abstraction, it is an historical abstraction and hence feasible only when grounded on a specific economic development of society.

[Letter to Engels, 2 April 1858; 1858d: 298][65]

4.13 Herr Wagner forgets that neither 'value' nor 'exchange-value' are my subjects, but *the commodity* [...]

In the first place [*De prime abord*] I do not start out {in *Capital*} from 'concepts', hence I do not start out from 'the concept of value', and do not have 'to divide' these in any way. What I start out from is the simplest social form in which the labour-product is presented in contemporary society, and this is the *'commodity'*. I analyse it, and right from the beginning, in *the form in which it appears*. Here I find that it is, on the one hand, in its natural form, a *useful thing*, alias a *use-value*; on the other hand it is a *bearer of exchange-value*, and from this viewpoint, it is itself 'exchange-value'. Further analysis of the latter shows me that exchange-value is only a *'form* of appearance', the autonomous mode of presentation of the *value* contained in the commodity, and I then move on to the analysis of the latter [...] Hence I do not divide *value* into use-value and exchange-value as antitheses into which the abstraction 'value' splits, rather [I divide] the *concrete social form* of the labour-product; *'commodity'* is, on the one hand, use-value, and on the other hand, 'value', not exchange-value, since the mere form of appearance is not its proper *content*.

[Notes on Adolph Wagner, 1879–80; 1880b: 183, 198]

4.14 Political Economy has indeed analysed, however incompletely, value and its magnitude, and has discovered what lies beneath these forms. But it has never once asked the question why labour is represented by the value of its product and labour-time by the magnitude of that value. * It is one of the chief failings of classical economy that it has never succeeded, by means of its analysis of commodities, and, in particular, of their value, in discovering that form under which value becomes exchange-value. Even Adam Smith and Ricardo, the best representatives of the school, treat the form of value as a thing of no importance, as having no connection with the inherent nature of commodities. The reason for this is not solely that their attention is entirely absorbed in the analysis of the magnitude of value. It lies deeper. The value-form of the product of labour is not only the most abstract, but is also the most universal form, taken by the product in bourgeois production, and stamps that production as a particular species of social production, and thereby gives it its special historical character. If then we treat this mode of production as one eternally fixed by Nature for every state of society, we necessarily overlook that which is the differentia specifica of the value-form, and consequently of the commodity-form, and of its further developments, money-form, capital-form, &c. [...]* These formulae, which bear it stamped upon them in unmistakeable letters that they belong to a state of society, in which the process of production has the mastery over man, instead of being controlled by him, such formulae appear to the bourgeois intellect to be as much a self-evident necessity imposed by nature as productive labour itself. Hence forms of production that preceded the bourgeois form, are treated by the bourgeoisie in much the same way as the

Fathers of the Church treated pre-Christian religions.
[*Capital* 1, 1867, as substantially modified, in the case of this
passage, in 1871–3; 1867a: 80–81 (footnote incorporated into text
between asterisks)]

4.15 The best points in my book {*Capital*} are: 1) the *two-fold
character of labour* {useful and abstract}, according to whether it is
expressed in use value or exchange value. (*All* understanding of the
facts depends upon this.) It is emphasised immediately, in the *first*
chapter; 2) the treatment of *surplus value independently of its particular*
forms as profit, interest, rent, etc. This will be seen especially in the
second volume. The treatment of the particular forms by political
economy, which always mixes them up with the general form, is a
regular hash.
[Letter to Engels, 24 August 1867; 1867b: 180][66]

Writing again to Engels on January 8, 1868, Marx reiterated these
as two of 'the three fundamentally new elements of the book', and
described recognition of the two-fold character of labour as 'in fact,
the whole secret of the critical conception'. His third 'new element'
was: 'That for the first time wages are presented as an irrational
manifestation of a relation concealed behind them, and that this is
scrupulously formulated with regard to the two forms of wages –
time rates and piece rates' [1868a: 186–7].

4.16 The labour-process, resolved as above into its simple elementary
factors {'1, the personal activity of man, i.e., work itself, 2, the subject
of that work, and 3, its instruments'} is human action with a view to
the production of use-values, appropriation of natural substances to
human requirements; it is the necessary condition for effecting
exchange of matter between man and Nature; it is the everlasting
Nature-imposed condition of human existence, and therefore is
independent of every social phase of that existence, or rather, is
common to every such phase. It was, therefore, not necessary to
represent our labourer in connection with other labourers; man and his
labour on the one side, Nature and its materials on the other, sufficed.
As the taste of the porridge does not tell you who grew the oats, no
more does this simple process tell you of itself what are the social
conditions under which it is taking place, whether under the
slave-owner's brutal lash, or the anxious eye of the capitalist, whether
Cincinnatus carries it on in tilling his modest farm or a savage in killing
wild animals with stones.

[*Capital* 1, 1867; 1867a: 183–4, parenthesis from p. 178]
In *Grundrisse* Marx likewise speaks of the labour process as a
process which 'because of its abstractness, its pure materiality, is
equally common to all forms of production' [1858a: 230].

4.17 Labour is organized, is divided differently according to the
instruments it has at its disposal. The hand-mill presupposes a different
division of labour from the steam-mill. Thus it is slapping history in
the face to want to begin with the division of labour in general, in
order to arrive subsequently at a specific instrument of production,
machinery.

Machinery is no more an economic category than the bullock that
drags the plough. Machinery is merely a productive force. The modern
workshop, which is based on the application of machinery, is a social
production relation, an economic category.
[*The Poverty of Philosophy*, 1847; 1847a: 183][67]

4.18 When considering a given country from the standpoint of political
economy, we begin with its population, the division of the population
into classes, town and country, sea, the different branches of production,
export and import, annual production and consumption, commodity
prices, etc.

It would seem right to start with the real and concrete, with the
actual presupposition, e.g. in political economy to start with the
population, which forms the basis and the subject of the whole social
act of production. Closer consideration shows, however, that this is
wrong. Population is an abstraction if, for instance, one disregards the
classes of which it is composed. These classes in turn remain an empty
phrase if one does not know the elements on which they are based,
e.g. wage labour, capital, etc. These presuppose exchange, division of
labour, prices, etc. For example, capital is nothing without wage labour,
without value, money, price, etc. If one were to start with population,
it would be a chaotic conception of the whole, and through closer
definition one would arrive analytically at increasingly simple concepts;
from the imagined concrete, one would move to more and more tenuous
abstractions until one arrived at the simplest determinations. From there
it would be necessary to make a return journey until one finally arrived
once more at population, which this time would be not a chaotic
conception of a whole, but a rich totality of many determinations and
relations.

The first course is the one taken by political economy historically at its inception. The 17th-century economists, for example, always started with the living whole, the population, the nation, the State, several States, etc., but analysis always led them in the end to the discovery of a few determining abstract, general relations, such as division of labour, money, value, etc. As soon as these individual moments were more or less clearly deduced and abstracted, economic systems were evolved which from the simple [concepts], such as labour, division of labour, need, exchange value, advanced to the State, international exchange and world market.

The latter is obviously the correct scientific method. The concrete is concrete because it is a synthesis of many determinations, thus a unity of the diverse. In thinking, it therefore appears as a process of summing-up, as a result, not as the starting point, although it is the real starting point, and thus also the starting point of perception and conception. The first procedure attenuates the comprehensive visualisation to abstract determination, the second leads from abstract determinations by way of thought to the reproduction of the concrete. [General Introduction, 1857; 1857: 37–38]

4.19 In Book I {of *Capital*} we analysed the phenomena which constitute the *process of capitalist production as such*, as the immediate productive process, with no regard for any of the secondary effects of outside influences. But this immediate process of production does not exhaust the life-span of capital. It is supplemented in the actual world by the *process of circulation*, which was the object of study in Book II. In the latter, namely in Part III, which treated the process of circulation as a medium for the process of social reproduction, it developed that the capitalist process of production taken as a whole represents a synthesis of the processes of production and circulation. Considering what this third book treats, it cannot confine itself to general reflection relative to this synthesis. On the contrary, it must locate and describe the concrete forms which grow out of the *movements of capital as a whole*. In their actual movement capitals confront each other in such concrete shape, for which the form of capital in the immediate process of production, just as its form in the process of circulation, appear only as special instances. The various forms of capital, as evolved in this book, thus approach step by step the form which they assume on the surface of society, in the action of different capitals upon one another, in competition, and in the ordinary consciousness of the agents of production themselves.
[*Capital* 3, 863–5; 1865a: 25][68]

4.20 At last {at the end of *Capital 3*} we have arrived at the *phenomena* which serve as the *starting-point* for the vulgar economist: rent originating from the land, profit (interest) from capital, wages from labour. But from our point of view the thing now looks differently. The apparent movement is explained. Moreover, Adam Smith's nonsense, which has become the *main pillar* of all hitherto existing economics, i.e. that the price of a commodity consists of those three revenues, that is only of variable capital (wages) and surplus value (rent, profit, interest), is overthrown. Finally since these three (wages, rent, profit (interest)) constitute the respective sources of income of the three classes of landowners, capitalists and wage labourers, we have, in conclusion, the *class struggle* into which the movement and the analysis of the whole business resolves itself.
[Letter to Engels, 30 April 1868; 1868b: 195][69]

4.21 Of course the method of presentation must differ in form from that of inquiry. The latter has to appropriate the material in detail, to analyse its different forms of development, to trace out their inner connection. Only after this work is done, can the actual movement be adequately described. If this is done successfully, if the life of the subject-matter is adequately reflected as in a mirror, it may appear as if we had before us a mere a priori construction.
[Afterword to second German edition of *Capital*, 1873; 1867a: 19]

This entire text (especially pp. 17–20) – too long to quote in full here – bears on Marx's method in *Capital*, and incidentally contains a famous discussion of Hegel's dialectic.

4.22 It is plain to me [...] that, in his second grand opus, the fellow {Lassalle} intends to expound political economy in the manner of Hegel. He will discover to his cost that it is one thing for a critique to take a science to the point at which it admits of a dialectical presentation, and quite another to apply an abstract, ready-made system of logic to vague presentiments of just such a system.
[Letter to Engels, 1 February 1858; 1858b: 261]

4.23 Classical political economy seeks to reduce the various fixed and mutually alien forms of wealth to their inner unity by means of analysis and to strip away the form in which they exist independently alongside one another. It seeks to grasp the inner connection in contrast to the multiplicity of outward forms. It therefore reduces rent to surplus profit, so that it ceases to be a specific, *separate* form and is divorced from

its apparent source, the land. It likewise divests interest of its independent form and shows that it is a part of profit. In this way it reduces all types of revenue and all independent forms and titles under cover of which the non-workers receive a portion of the value of commodities, to the single form of profit. Profit, however, is reduced to surplus-value since the value of the whole commodity is reduced to labour; the amount of paid labour embodied in the commodity constitutes wages, consequently the surplus over and above it constitutes unpaid labour, surplus labour called forth by capital and appropriated gratis under various titles. Classical political economy occasionally contradicts itself in this analysis. It often attempts directly, leaving out the intermediate links, to carry through the reduction and to prove that the various forms are derived from one and the same source. This is however a necessary consequence of its analytical method, with which criticism and understanding must begin. Classical economy is not interested in elaborating how the various forms come into being, but seeks to reduce them to their unity by means of analysis, because it starts from them as given premises. But analysis is the necessary prerequisite of genetical presentation, and of the understanding of the real, formative process in its different phases. Finally a failure, a deficiency of classical political economy is the fact that it does not conceive the *basic form of capital*, i.e., production designed to appropriate other people's labour, as a *historical* form but as a *natural form* of social production; the analysis carried out by the classical economists themselves nevertheless paves the way for the refutation of this conception.
[*Theories of Surplus Value*, 1861–3; 1863c: 500–1][70]

4.24 The bourgeois economists, who consider capital to be an eternal and *natural* (not historical) form of production, nevertheless try to justify it by declaring the conditions of its becoming as the conditions of its present realisation, i.e., they present the moments in which the capitalist still appropriates as non-capitalist – because he is only in the process of becoming – as the very conditions in which he appropriates *as capitalist*. These attempts at apologetics demonstrate a bad conscience and the inability to bring the mode of appropriation of capital as capital into harmony with the *general laws of property* proclaimed by capitalist society itself.

On the other hand – and this is much more important for us – our method indicates the points at which historical analysis must be introduced, or at which bourgeois economy as a mere historical form of the production process points beyond itself towards earlier historical

modes of production. To present the laws of the bourgeois economy, it is not necessary therefore to write the *real history of the production relations*. But the correct analysis and deduction of these relations as relations which have themselves arisen historically, always leads to primary equations – like e.g. empirical numbers in natural science – which point to a past lying behind this system. These indications, together with the correct grasp of the present, then also offer the key to the understanding of the past – a work in its own right, which we hope to be able to undertake as well. This correct approach, moreover, leads to points which indicate the transcendence of the present form of production relations, the movement coming into being, thus foreshadowing the future. If, on the one hand, the pre-bourgeois phases appear as *merely historical*, i.e. transcended premises, so [on the other hand] the present conditions of production appear as conditions which *transcend themselves* and thus posit themselves as *historical premisses* for a new state of society.
[*Grundrisse*, 1857–8: 1858a: 388–9]

4.25 Let us admit with M. Proudhon that real history, history according to the order in time, is the historical sequence in which ideas, categories and principles have manifested themselves.

Each principle has had its own century in which to manifest itself. The principle of authority, for example, had the eleventh century, just as the principle of individualism had the eighteenth century. In logical sequence, it was the century that belonged to the principle, and not the principle that belonged to the century. In other words it was the principle that made the history, and not the history that made the principle. When, consequently, in order to save principles as much as to save history, we ask ourselves why a particular principle was manifested in the eleventh or in the eighteenth century rather than in any other, we are necessarily forced to examine minutely what men were like in the eleventh century, what they were like in the eighteenth, what were their respective needs, their productive forces, their mode of production, the raw materials of their production – in short, what were the relations between man and man which resulted from all these conditions of existence. To get to the bottom of all these questions – what is this but to draw up the real, profane history of men in every century and to present these men as both the authors and the actors of their own drama?
[*The Poverty of Philosophy*, 1847; 1847a: 169–70]

5

The laws of bourgeois economy

In this chapter we come to Marx's analysis of capitalist society. Everything here is from *Capital* and associated works of the late 1850s and 60s. Marx is often portrayed as offering an economic theory of society and history. But it would be more accurate to describe *Capital* as a historical sociology of economic forms. Marx moves analytically from 'phenomenal forms' like commodity, money, or capital – the forms in which we experience things in everyday life – to the 'essential relations' which explain *why* things should take these forms. These are *social* relations, which are historically specific. The commodity is thus argued to rest on a particular form of division of labour, and capital on a definite class relation. Such social forms are thereby stripped of their apparent naturalness, and shown to be the products of history. The economic categories in which they are habitually apprehended are concurrently revealed as historical in their reference. I have followed the order of *Capital* in terms of the various economic forms Marx deals with: the commodity, money, capital. We have here the theoretical core of his 'economics'. But it is also the core of Marx's *sociology* of capitalism.

5.1 The work I am presently concerned with is a *Critique of Economic Categories*, or, if you like, a critical exposé of the system of bourgeois economy. It is at once an exposé and, by the same token, a critique of the system.

[Letter to Lassalle, 22 February 1858; 1858c: 270]

5.2 The wealth of those societies in which the capitalist mode of production prevails, presents itself as 'an immense accumulation of commodities', its unit being a single commodity. Our investigation must therefore begin with the analysis of a commodity.

A commodity is, in the first place, an object outside us, a thing that by its properties satisfies human wants of some sort or another. The nature of such wants, whether, for instance, they spring from the stomach or from fancy, makes no difference. Neither are we here concerned to know how the object satisfies these wants, whether directly as means of subsistence, or indirectly as means of production.

Every useful thing, as iron, paper, &c., may be looked at from the two points of view of quality and quantity. It is an assemblage of many properties, and may therefore be of use in various ways. To discover the various uses of things is the work of history. So also is the establishment of socially-recognised standards of measure for the quantities of these useful objects. The diversity of these measures has its origin partly in the diverse nature of the objects to be measured, partly in convention.

The utility of a thing makes it a use-value. But this utility is not a thing of air. Being limited by the physical properties of a commodity, it has no existence apart from that commodity. A commodity, such as iron, corn, or a diamond, is therefore, so far as it is a material thing, a use-value, something useful. This property of a commodity is independent of the amount of labour required to appropriate its useful qualities. [...] Use-values become a reality only by use or consumption: they also constitute the substance of all wealth, whatever may be the social form of that wealth. In the form of society we are about to consider, they are, in addition, the material depositories of exchange-value.

Exchange-value, at first sight, presents itself as a quantitative relation, as the proportion in which values in use of one sort are exchanged for those of another sort, a relation constantly changing with time and place. Hence exchange-value appears to be something accidental and purely relative, and consequently an intrinsic value, i.e., an exchange-value that is inseparably connected with, inherent in commodities, seems a contradiction in terms. Let us consider the matter a little more closely.

A given commodity, e.g., a quarter of wheat is exchanged for x blacking, y silk, or z gold, &c. – in short, for other commodities in the most different proportions. Instead of one exchange-value, the wheat has, therefore, a great many. But since x blacking, y silk, or z gold, &c., each represent the exchange-value of one quarter of wheat, x blacking, y silk, z gold, &c., must, as exchange-values, be replaceable by each other, or equal to each other. Therefore, first: the valid exchange-values of a given commodity express something equal; secondly, exchange-value, generally, is only the mode of expression, the phenomenal form, of something contained in it, yet distinguishable from it.

Let us take two commodities, e.g., corn and iron. The proportions in which they are exchangeable, whatever these proportions may be, can always be represented by an equation in which a given quantity of corn is equated to some quantity of iron: e.g., 1 quarter corn = x cwt. iron. What does this equation tell us? It tells us that in two different things – in 1 quarter of wheat and x cwt. iron, there exists in equal quantities something common to both. These two things must therefore be equal to a third, which is itself neither one nor the other. Each of them, so far as it is exchange-value, must therefore be reducible to this third. [...]

This common 'something' cannot be either a geometrical, a chemical, or any other natural property of commodities. Such properties claim our attention only in so far as they affect the utility of these commodities, make them use-values. But the exchange of commodities is evidently an act characterised by a total abstraction from use-value. Then one use-value is just as good as another, provided only it be present in sufficient quantity. [...] As use-values, commodities are, above all, of different qualities, but as exchange-values they are merely different quantities, and consequently do not contain an atom of use-value.

If then we leave out of consideration the use-value of commodities, they have only one common property left, that of being products of labour. But even the product of labour itself has undergone a change in our hands. If we make abstraction from its use-value, we make abstraction at the same time from the material elements and shapes that make the product a use-value; we see in it no longer a table, a house, yarn, or any other useful thing. Neither can it any longer be regarded as the product of the labour of the joiner, the mason, the spinner, or of any other definite kind of productive labour. Along with the useful qualities of the products themselves, we put out of sight both the useful character of the various kinds of labour embodied in them, and the concrete forms of that labour; there is nothing left but what is common to them all; all are reduced to one and the same sort of labour, human labour in the abstract.

Let us now consider the residue of each of these products; it consists of the same unsubstantial reality in each, a mere congelation of homogeneous human labour, of labour-power expended without regard to the mode of its expenditure. All that these things now tell us is, that human labour-power has been expended in their production, that human labour is embodied in them. When looked at as crystals of this social substance, common to them all, they are – Values.

We have seen that when commodities are exchanged, their exchange-value manifests itself as something totally independent of their use-value. But if we abstract from their use-value, there remains their Value as defined above. Therefore, the common substance that manifests itself in the exchange-value of commodities, whenever they are exchanged, is their value. The progress of our investigation will show that exchange-value is the only form in which the value of commodities can manifest itself or be expressed. For the present, however, we have to consider the nature of value independently of this, its form.

A use-value, or useful article, therefore, has value only because human labour in the abstract has been embodied or materialised in it. How, then, is the magnitude of this value to be measured? Plainly, by the quantity of the value-creating substance, the labour, contained in the article. The quantity of labour, however, is measured by its duration, and labour-time in its turn finds its standard in weeks, days, and hours. [...]

We see then that that which determines the magnitude of the value of any article is the amount of labour socially necessary, or the labour-time socially necessary, for its production. Each individual commodity, in this connection, is to be considered as an average sample of its class. Commodities, therefore, in which equal quantities of labour are embodied, or which can be produced in the same time, have the same value. The value of one commodity is to the value of any other, as the labour-time necessary for the production of the one is to that necessary for the production of the other. 'As values, all commodities are only definite masses of congealed labour-time.'
[*Capital* 1, 1867; 1867a: 35–40][12]

5.3 Every product of labour is, in all states of society, a use-value; but it is only at a definite epoch in a society's development that such a product becomes a commodity, viz., at the epoch when the labour spent on the production of a useful article becomes expressed as one of the objective qualities of that article, i.e., as its value.
[Ibid: 61]

5.4 Even if there were no chapter on 'value' in my book {*Capital*}, the analysis of the real relations which I give would contain the proof and demonstration of the real value relations. All that palaver about the necessity of proving the concept of value comes from complete ignorance both of the subject dealt with and of scientific method. Every child knows that a nation which ceased to work, I will not say for a year, but even for a few weeks, would perish. Every child knows, too, that the volume of products corresponding to the different needs require different and quantitatively determined amounts of the total labour of society. That this *necessity* of the *distribution* of social labour in definite proportions cannot possibly be done away with by a *particular form* of social production but can only change the *mode of its appearance*, is self-evident. Natural laws cannot be abolished at all. What can change in historically different circumstances is only the *form* in which these laws assert themselves. And the form in which this proportional distribution of labour asserts itself, in a social system where the interconnection of social labour manifests itself through the *private exchange* of individual products of labour, is precisely the *exchange-value* of these products [...] The essence of bourgeois society consists precisely in this, that *a priori* there is no conscious social regulation of production. The rational and naturally necessary asserts itself only as a blindly working average.
[Letter to Kugelmann, 11 July 1868; 1868c: 196–7]

5.5 Under capitalist production the proportionality of the individual branches of production springs as a continual process from disproportionality, because the cohesion of the aggregate production imposes itself as a blind law upon the agents of production, and not as a law which, being understood and hence controlled by their common mind, brings the productive process under their joint control.
[*Capital* 3, 1864-5; 1865a: 257][73]

5.6 How deeply our wiseacre {the author of *Observations on certain Verbal Disputes in Political Economy*, London, 1821} has sunk into *fetishism* and how he transforms what is relative into something positive, is demonstrated most strikingly in the following passage:

> *Value* is a *property of things*, *riches of men*. Value, in this sense, necessarily implies exchange, riches do not.

Riches here are use-values. These, as far as men are concerned, are, of course, riches, but it is through its *own properties*, its own qualities, that a thing is a use-value and therefore an element of wealth for men. Take away from grapes the qualities that make them grapes, and their use-value as grapes disappears for men and they cease to be an element of wealth for men. Riches which are identical with use-values are *properties of things* that are made use of by men and which express a relation to their wants. But 'value' is supposed to be a 'property of things'.

As values, commodities are *social* magnitudes, that is to say, something absolutely different from their 'properties' as 'things'. As values, they constitute only relations of men in their productive activity. Value indeed 'implies exchanges', but exchanges are exchanges of things between men, exchanges which in no way affect the things as such. A thing retains the same 'properties' whether it is owned by A or B. In actual fact, the concept 'value' presupposes 'exchanges' of the products. Where labour is communal, the relations of men in their social production do not manifest themselves as 'values' of 'things'. Exchange of products as commodities is a method of exchanging labour, [it demonstrates] the dependence of the labour of each upon the labour of others [and corresponds to] a certain mode of social labour or social production.

In the first part of my book {the 1859 *Critique of Political Economy*} I mentioned that it is characteristic of labour based on private exchange that the social character of labour 'manifests' itself in a perverted form – as the 'property' of things; that a social relation appears as a relation between things (between products, values in use, commodities). This *appearance* is accepted as something real by our fetish-worshipper, and he actually believes that the exchange-value of things is determined by their properties as things, and is altogether a natural property of things. No scientist to date has yet discovered what natural qualities make definite proportions of snuff tobacco and paintings 'equivalents' for one another.

Thus he, the wiseacre, transforms value into something absolute, 'a property of things', instead of seeing in it only something relative, the relation of things to social labour, social labour based on private

exchange, in which things are defined not as independent entities, but as mere expressions of social production.
[*Theories of Surplus Value*, 1863–5; 1863c: 129–30]

5.7 Whence, then, arises the enigmatical character of the product of labour, so soon as it assumes the form of commodities? Clearly from this form itself. The equality of all sorts of human labour is expressed objectively by their products all being equally values; the measure of the expenditure of labour-power by the duration of that expenditure, takes the form of the quantity of value of the products of labour; and finally, the mutual relations of the producers, within which the social character of their labour affirms itself, takes the form of a social relation between the products.

A commodity is therefore a mysterious thing, simply because in it the social character of men's labour appears to them as an objective character stamped upon the product of that labour; because the relation of the producers to the sum total of their labour is presented to them as a social relation, existing not between themselves, but between the products of their labour. This is the reason why the products of labour become commodities, social things whose qualities are at the same time perceptible and imperceptible by the senses. In the same way the light from an object is perceived by us not as the subjective excitation of the optic nerve, but as the objective form of something outside the eye itself. But, in the act of seeing, there is at all events, an actual passage of light from one thing to another, from the external object to the eye. There is a physical relation between physical things. But it is different with commodities. There, the existence of the things *qua* commodities, and the value-relation between the products of labour which stamps them as commodities, have absolutely no connection with their physical properties and with the material relations arising therefrom. There it is a definite social relation between men, that assumes, in their eyes, the fantastic form of a relation between things. In order, therefore, to find an analogy, we must have recourse to the mist-enveloped regions of the religious world. In that world the productions of the human brain appear as independent beings endowed with life, and entering into relation both with one another and the human race. So it is in the world of commodities with the products of men's hands. This I call the Fetishism which attaches itself to the products of labour, so soon as they are produced as commodities, and which is therefore inseparable from the production of commodities.

This Fetishism of commodities has its origin, as the foregoing analysis {in *Capital* 1: Chapter 1} has already shown, in the peculiar social character of the labour that produces them.

As a general rule, articles of utility become commodities, only because they are products of the labour of private individuals or groups of individuals who carry on their work independently of each other. The sum total of the labour of all these private individuals forms the aggregate labour of society. Since the producers do not come into social contact with each other until they exchange their products, the specific social character of each producer's labour does not show itself except in the act of exchange. In other words, the labour of the individual asserts itself as a part of the labour of society, only by means of the relations which the act of exchange establishes directly between the products, and indirectly, through them, between the producers. To the latter, therefore, the relations connecting the labour of one individual with that of the rest appear, not as direct social relations between individuals at work, but as what they really are, material relations between persons and social relations between things. It is only by being exchanged that the products of labour acquire, as values, one uniform social status, distinct from their varied forms of existence as objects of utility. This division of a product into a useful thing and a value becomes practically important, only when exchange has acquired such an extension that useful articles are produced for the purpose of being exchanged, and their character as values has therefore to be taken into account, beforehand, during production. From this moment the labour of the individual producer acquires socially a two-fold character. On the one hand, it must, as a definite useful kind of labour, satisfy a definite social want, and thus hold its place as part and parcel of the collective labour of all, as a branch of a social division of labour that has sprung up spontaneously. On the other hand, it can satisfy the manifold wants of the individual producer himself, only in so far as the mutual exchangeability of all kinds of useful private labour is an established social fact, and therefore the private useful labour of each producer ranks on an equality with that of all others. The equalisation of the most different kinds of labour can be the result only of an abstraction from their inequalities, or of reducing them to their common denominator, viz., expenditure of human labour-power or human labour in the abstract. The two-fold social character of the labour of the individual appears to him, when reflected in his brain, only under those forms which are impressed upon that labour in everyday practice by the exchange of products. In this way, the character that his own labour possesses of being socially useful takes the form of the condition, that the product must be not only useful, but useful for others, and the social character that his particular labour has of being the equal of all other particular kinds of labour, takes the form that all the physically different articles that are the products of labour, have one common quality, viz., that of having value.

Hence, when we bring the products of our labour into relations with each other as values, it is not because we see in these articles the material receptacles of homogeneous human labour. Quite the contrary: whenever, by an exchange, we equate as values our different products, by that very act, we also equate, as human labour, the different kinds of labour expended upon them. We are not aware of this, nevertheless we do it. Value, therefore, does not stalk about with a label describing what it is. It is value, rather, that converts every product into a social hieroglyphic. Later on, we try to decipher the hieroglyphic, to get behind the secret of our own social products; for to stamp an object of utility as a value, is just as much a social product as language. The recent scientific discovery {by Political Economy}, that the products of labour, so far as they are values, are but material expressions of the labour spent in their production, marks, indeed, an epoch in the history of the development of the human race, but, by no means, dissipates the mist through which the social character of labour appears to us to be an objective character of the products themselves. The fact, that in the particular form of production with which we are dealing, viz., the production of commodities, the specific social character of private labour carried on independently, consists in the equality of every kind of that labour, by virtue of its being human labour, which character, therefore, assumes in the product the form of value – this fact appears to the producers, notwithstanding the discovery above referred to, to be just as real and final, as the fact, that, after the discovery by science of the component gases of air, the atmosphere itself remained unaltered.

What, first of all, practically concerns producers when they make an exchange, is the question, how much of some other product they get for their own? in what proportions the products are exchangeable? When these proportions have, by custom, attained a certain stability, they appear to result from the nature of the products, so that, for instance, one ton of iron and two ounces of gold appear as naturally to be of equal value as a pound of gold and a pound of iron in spite of their different physical and chemical qualities appear to be of equal weight. The character of having value, when once impressed upon products, obtains fixity only by reason of their acting and reacting upon each other as quantities of value. These quantities vary continually, independently of the will, foresight and action of the producers. To them, their own social action takes the form of the action of objects, which rule the producers instead of being ruled by them. It requires a fully developed production of commodities before, from accumulated experience alone, the scientific conviction springs up, that all the different kinds of private labour, which are carried on independently of each other, and yet as spontaneously developed branches of the social division of labour, are continually being reduced to the quantitative proportions in which society requires them. And why? Because, in the midst of all the accidental and ever fluctuating exchange-relations between the products, the labour-time socially necessary for their production forcibly asserts itself like an over-riding law of Nature. The law of gravity thus asserts itself when a house falls about our ears. The determination of the magnitude of value by labour-time is therefore a secret, hidden under the apparent fluctuations in the relative values of commodities. Its discovery, while removing all appearance of mere accidentality from the determination of the values of products, yet in no way alters the mode in which that determination takes place.

Man's reflections on the forms of social life, and consequently, also, his scientific analysis of those forms, takes a course directly opposite to that of their actual historical development. He begins, post festum, with the results of the process of development ready to hand before him. The characters that stamp products as commodities, and whose establishment is a necessary preliminary to the circulation of commodities, have already acquired the stability of natural, self-understood forms of social life, before man seeks to decipher, not their historical character, for in his eyes they are immutable, but their meaning. Consequently it was the analysis of the prices of commodities that alone led to the determination of the magnitude of value, and it was the common expression of all commodities in money that alone led to the establishment of their characters as values. It is, however, just this ultimate money-form of the world of commodities that actually conceals, instead of disclosing, the social character of private labour, and the social relations between the individual producers. When I state that coats or boots stand in a relation to linen, because it is the universal incarnation of abstract human labour, the absurdity of the statement is self-evident. Nevertheless, when the producers of coats and boots compare those articles with linen, or, what is the same thing, with gold or silver, as the universal equivalent, they express the relation between their own labour and the collective labour of society in the same absurd form.

The categories of bourgeois economy consist of such like forms. They are forms of thought expressing with social validity the conditions and relations of a definite, historically determined mode of production, viz., the production of commodities. The whole mystery of commodities, all the magic and necromancy that surrounds the products of labour as long as they take the form of commodities, vanishes therefore, so soon as we come to other forms of production.
[*Capital* 1, 1867 (as substantially modified, in the case of this passage, in 1871–2); 1867a: 71–6]

5.8 Hodgskin says that the effects of a certain social form of labour are ascribed to objects, to the product of labour; the relationship itself is imagined to exist in *material* form. [...] Hodgskin regards this as a pure subjective illusion which conceals the deceit and the interests of the exploiting classes. He does not see that the way of looking at things arises out of the relationship itself; the latter is not an expression of the former, but vice versa.
[*Theories of Surplus Value*, 1861–3; 1863c: 295–6][74]

5.9 We have already seen, from the most elementary expression of value, x commodity A = y commodity B {Marx refers to the two poles of the expression as the *relative* and *equivalent* forms of value respectively}, that the object in which the magnitude of the value of another object is represented, appears to have the equivalent form independently of this relation, as a social property given to it by Nature. We followed up this false appearance to its final establishment, which is complete so soon as the universal equivalent form {i.e., where the relative value of *all* commodities is expressed in quantities of a *single* standard equivalent} becomes identified with the bodily form of a particular commodity, and thus crystalized into the money-form. What appears to happen is, not that gold becomes money, in consequence of all other commodities expressing their values in it, but, on the contrary, that all other commodities universally express their values in gold, because it is money. The intermediate steps of the process vanish in the result and leave no trace behind. Commodities find their own value already completely represented, without any initiative on their part, in another commodity existing in company with them. These objects, gold and silver, just as they come out of the bowels of the earth, are forthwith the direct incarnation of all human labour. Hence the magic of money. In the form of society now under consideration, the

behaviour of men in the social process of production is purely atomic. Hence their relations to each other in production assume a material character independent of their control and conscious individual action. These facts manifest themselves at first by products as a general rule taking the form of commodities. We have seen how the progressive development of a society of commodity-producers stamps one privileged commodity with the character of money. Hence the riddle presented by money is but the riddle presented by commodities; only it now strikes us in its most glaring form.
[*Capital* 1, 1867; 1867a: 92–3]

5.10 We have seen that the money-form is but the reflex, thrown upon one single commodity, of the value-relations between all the rest. That money is a commodity is therefore a new discovery only for those who, when they analyse it, start from its fully developed shape. The act of exchange gives to the commodity converted into money, not its value, but its specific value-form. By confounding these two distinct things some writers have been led to hold that the value of gold and silver is imaginary. The fact that money can, in certain functions, be replaced by mere symbols of itself, gave rise to that other mistaken notion, that it is itself a mere symbol. Nevertheless under this error lurked a presentiment that the money-form of an object is not an inseparable part of that object, but is simply the form under which certain social relations manifest themselves. In this sense every commodity is a symbol, since, in so far as it is value, it is only the material envelope of the human labour spent upon it. But if it be declared that the social characters assumed by objects, or the material forms assumed by the social qualities of labour under the regime of a definite mode of production, are mere symbols, it is in the same breath also declared that these characteristics are arbitrary fictions sanctioned by the so-called universal consent of mankind. This suited the mode of explanation in favour during the 18th century. Unable to account for the origin of the puzzling forms assumed by social relations between man and man, people sought to denude them of their strange appearance by ascribing to them a conventional origin.
[Ibid: 90–1]

In *Grundrisse* Marx argues similarly: 'money does not originate by convention, any more than the State does. It arises from exchange, grows naturally out of exchange, is a product of exchange' [1858a: 102].

5.11 The dissolution of all products and activities into exchange values presupposes both the dissolution of all established personal (historical) relations of dependence in production, and the all-round dependence of producers upon one another. The production of each individual producer is dependent upon the production of all the others, as also the transformation of his product into means of subsistence for himself has become dependent upon the consumption of all the others. Prices are old; so is exchange; but both the increasing determination of the former by production costs, and the increasing penetration of the latter into all relations of production only develop fully, and continue to develop ever more completely, in bourgeois society. What Adam Smith in the true 18th-century manner placed in pre-history, what he assumed to have preceded history, is rather its product.

This mutual dependence expressed in the constant need for exchange and in exchange value as the universal mediator. The economists express it thus: everyone pursues his private interest and only his private interest, and thereby unintentionally and unwittingly serves the private interests of all, the general interest. [...] The point is rather that private interest is itself already a socially determined interest and can be attained only within the conditions laid down by society and with the means provided by society, and is therefore tied to the reproduction of these conditions and means. It is the interest of private persons; but its content, as well as the form and means of its realisation, are given by social conditions that are independent of them all.

The absolute mutual dependence of individuals, who are indifferent to one another, constitutes their social connection. This social connection is expressed in *exchange value*, in which alone his own activity or his product becomes an activity or product for the individual himself. He must produce a general product – *exchange value*, or exchange value isolated by itself, individualised; *money*. On the other hand, the power that each individual exercises over the activity of others or over social wealth exists in him as the owner of *exchange values*, of *money*. He carries his social power, as also his connection with society, in his pocket.

The activity, whatever its individual form of manifestation, and the product of the activity, whatever its particular nature, is *exchange value*, i.e. something general in which all individuality, all particularity, is negated and extinguished. This is indeed a condition very different to that in which the individual, or the individual extended by a natural or historical process into a family and a tribe (later community), directly reproduces himself from nature, or in which his productive activity and his share in production are dependent upon a particular form of labour and of the product, and his relationship to others is determined in this particular way.

The social character of the activity, as also the social form of the product and the share of the individual in production, appear here as something alien to and existing outside the individuals; not as their relationship to each other, but as their subordination to relationships existing independently of them and arising from the collision between different individuals. The general exchange of activities and products, which has become the condition of life for every single individual, their mutual connection, appears to the individuals themselves alien, independent, as a thing. In exchange value, the social relationship of persons is transformed into a social attitude of things; personal capacity into a capacity of things. The less social power the means of exchange possesses, the more closely it is still connected with the nature of the immediate product of labour and the immediate needs of the exchangers, the greater must that power of the community still be which binds together the individuals, the patriarchal relationship, the community of antiquity, feudalism and the guild system.

Every individual possesses social power in the form of a thing. Take away this social power from the thing, and you must give it to persons [to exercise] over persons. Relationships of personal dependence (which originally arise quite spontaneously) are the first forms of society, in which human productivity develops only to a limited extent and at isolated points. Personal independence based upon dependence *mediated by things* is the second great form, and only in it is a system of general social exchange of matter, a system of universal relations, universal requirements and universal capacities, formed. Free individuality, based on the universal development of the individuals and the subordination of their communal, social productivity, which is their social possession, is the third stage. The second stage creates the conditions for the third. Patriarchal conditions and those of antiquity (likewise feudal ones) therefore decline with the development of trade, luxury, *money*, *exchange value*, in the same measure in which modern society grows with them step by step.

Exchange and division of labour condition each other. Since each person works for himself but his product is nothing by itself, he must naturally engage in exchange, not only so as to take part in the general capacity to produce, but to transform his own product into means of subsistence for himself. Of course, exchange as mediated by exchange value and money presupposes the absolute mutual dependence of the producers, but at the same time the complete isolation of their private interests and a division of social labour, whose unity and complementarity exists as it were as a natural relationship outside the individuals, independently of them. The pressure of general demand and supply upon each other provides the connection between the mutually indifferent individuals.

The very necessity to transform the product or the activity of the individuals first into the form of *exchange value*, into *money*, and the fact that they obtain and demonstrate their social *power* only in this *objective* [*sachlichen*] form, proves two things: (1) that the individuals now only produce for and within society; (2) that their production is not *directly* social, not the offspring of association distributing labour within itself. The individuals are subsumed under social production, which exists outside them as their fate; but social production is not subsumed under the individuals who manage it as their common wealth. [*Grundrisse*, 1857–8; 1858a: 93–6]

Capital adds an interesting footnote to one of the themes of this passage: 'Money itself is a commodity, an external object, capable of becoming the private property of any individual. Thus social power becomes the private power of private persons. The ancients therefore denounced money as subversive of the economic and moral order of things' [1867a: 132].

5.12 {Money's} relationship to the individual appears [...] as a purely fortuitous one; while this relationship to a thing quite unconnected with his individuality gives him at the same time, because of the thing's character, general domination over society, over the whole world of enjoyment, labour, etc. It is the same as if e.g. my discovery of a stone, quite independent of my individuality, were to procure me mastery over all fields of learning. The possession of money relates me to (social) wealth in very much the same way as that in which the philosopher's stone would relate me to all fields of learning.

Money is therefore not only *an* object of the quest for enrichment, it is *the* object of it. It is essentially *auri sacra fames* {the accursed hunger for gold (Virgil, *Aeneid*, 3, 57)}. The quest for enrichment as such, as a particular form of impulse, i.e. as distinct from the quest for particular wealth, e.g. the quest for clothes, weapons, jewellery, women, wine, etc., becomes possible only when general wealth, wealth as such, has been individualised as a particular thing {money} [...] Money is therefore not only the object but at the same time the source of the quest for enrichment. Avarice is possible without money, but the quest for enrichment is itself the product of a definite social development,

not a *natural*, in contrast to an *historical*, development.
[*Grundrisse*, 1857–8; 1858a: 154–5]

5.13 The social division of labour [...] forms the foundation of all production of commodities.
[*Capital* 1, 1867; 1867a: 351]

5.14 The owners of commodities [...] find out, that the same division of labour that turns them into independent private producers, also frees the social process of production and the relations of the individual producers to each other within that process, from all dependence on the will of those producers, and that the seeming mutual independence of the individuals is supplemented by a system of general and mutual dependence through or by means of the products.
[Ibid: 107–8]

Elsewhere in *Capital* Marx writes similarly that 'on the one hand, [...] the exchange of commodities breaks through all local and personal bounds inseparable from direct barter, and develops the circulation of the products of social labour; and on the other hand, [...] it develops a whole network of social relations spontaneous in their growth and entirely beyond the control of the actors' [Ibid: 112].

5.15 The conversion of money into capital[75] has to be explained on the basis of the laws that regulate the exchange of commodities, in such a way that the starting-point is the exchange of equivalents. Our friend, Moneybags, who is as yet only an embryo capitalist, must buy his commodities at their value, must sell them at their value, and yet at the end of the process must withdraw more value from circulation than he threw into it at starting. His development into a full-grown capitalist must take place, both within the sphere of circulation and without it. These are the conditions of the problem. Hic Rhodus, hic salta! {Here is Rhodes, jump here! – The reply to a character in one of Aesop's fables who boasted he had leaped over the colossus of Rhodes} [...]

The change of value that occurs in the case of money intended to be converted into capital, cannot take place in the money itself, since in its function as means of purchase and of payment, it does no more than realise the price of the commodity; and, as hard cash, it is value petrified, never varying. Just as little can it originate in the second act of circulation, the re-sale of the commodity, which does no more than transform the article from its bodily form back again into its money-form. The change must, therefore, take place in the commodity bought by the first act, M{oney} – C{ommodity}, but not in its value, for equivalents are exchanged, and the commodity is paid for at its full value. We are, therefore, forced to the conclusion that the change originates in the use-value, as such, of the commodity, i.e., in its consumption. In order to be able to extract value from the consumption of a commodity, our friend, Moneybags, must be so lucky as to find, within the sphere of circulation, in the market, a commodity, whose use-value possesses the peculiar property of being a source of value, whose actual consumption, therefore, is itself an embodiment of labour, and, consequently, a creation of value. The possessor of money does find on the market such a special commodity in capacity for labour or labour-power.

By labour-power or capacity for labour is to be understood the aggregate of those physical or mental capabilities existing in a human being, which he exercises whenever he produces a use-value of any description.

But in order that our owner of money may be able to find labour-power offered for sale as a commodity, various conditions must first be fulfilled.

[...]

For the conversion of his money into capital [...] the owner of money must meet in the market with the free labourer, free in the double sense, that as a free man he can dispose of his labour-power as his own commodity, and that on the other hand he has no other commodity for sale, is short of everything necessary for the realisation of his labour-power.

[...] One thing, however, is clear – Nature does not produce on the one side owners of money or commodities, and on the other men possessing nothing but their own labour-power. This relation has no natural basis, neither is its social basis one that is common to all historical periods. It is clearly the result of a past historical development, the product of many economic revolutions, of the extinction of a whole series of older forms of social production.

So, too, the economic categories, already discussed by us, bear the stamp of history. Definite historical conditions are necessary that a product may become a commodity. It must not be produced as the immediate means of subsistence of the producer himself. Had we gone further, and inquired under what circumstances all, or even the majority of products take the forms of commodities, we should have found that this can only happen with production of a very specific kind, capitalist production. Such an inquiry, however, would have been foreign to the analysis of commodities. Production and circulation of commodities can take place, although the great mass of the objects produced are intended for the immediate requirements of their producers, are not turned into commodities, and consequently social production is not yet by a long way dominated in its length and breadth by exchange-value. The appearance of products as commodities pre-supposes such a development of the social division of labour, that the separation of use-value from exchange-value, a separation which first begins with barter, must already have been completed. But such a degree of development is common to many forms of society, which in other respects present the most varying historical features. On the other hand, if we consider money, its existence implies a definite stage in the exchange of commodities. The particular functions of money which it performs, either as the mere equivalent of commodities, or as means of circulation, or means of payment, as hoard or as universal money, point, according to the extent and relative preponderance of the one function or the other, to very different stages in the process of production. Yet we know by experience that a circulation of commodities relatively primitive, suffices for the production of all these forms. Otherwise with capital. The historical conditions of its existence are by no means given with the mere circulation of money and commodities. It can spring into life, only when the owner of the means of production and subsistence meets in the market with the free labourer selling his labour-power. And this one historical condition comprises a world's history. Capital, therefore, announces from its first appearance a new epoch in the process of social production. *The capitalist epoch is therefore characterised by this, that labour-power takes in the eyes of the labourer himself the form of a commodity which is his property; his labour consequently becomes wage-labour. On the other hand, it is only from this moment that the produce of labour universally becomes a commodity.*

We must now examine more closely this peculiar commodity, labour-power. Like all others it has a value. How is that value determined?

The value of labour-power is determined, as in the case of every other commodity, by the labour-time necessary for the production, and consequently also the reproduction, of this special article. So far as it has value, it represents no more than a definite quantity of the average labour of society incorporated in it. Labour-power exists only as a capacity, or power of the living individual. Its production consequently presupposes his existence. Given the individual, the production of labour-power consists in his reproduction of himself or his maintenance. For his maintenance he requires a given quantity of the means of subsistence. Therefore the labour-time requisite for the production of labour-power reduces itself to that necessary for the production of those means of subsistence; in other words, the value of labour-power is the value of the means of subsistence necessary for the maintenance of the labourer [...] His means of subsistence must therefore be sufficient to maintain him in his normal state as a labouring individual. His natural wants, such as food, clothing, fuel, and housing, vary according to the climactic and other physical conditions of his country. On the other hand, the number and extent of his so-called necessary wants, as also the means of satisfying them, are themselves the product of historical development, and depend therefore to a great extent on the degree of civilisation of a country, more particularly on the conditions under which, and consequently on the habits and degree of comfort in which, the class of free labourers has been formed. In contradistinction therefore to the case of other commodities, there enters into the determination of the value of labour-power a historical and moral element. Nevertheless, in a given country, at a given period, the average quantity of the means of subsistence necessary for the labourer is practically known.

The owner of labour-power is mortal. If then his appearance in the market is to be continuous, and the continuous conversion of money into capital assumes this, the seller of labour-power must perpetuate himself, 'in the way that every living individual perpetuates himself, by procreation'. The labour-power withdrawn from the market by wear and tear and death, must be continually replaced by, at the very least, an equal amount of fresh labour-power. Hence the sum of the means of subsistence necessary for the production of labour-power must include the means necessary for the labourer's substitutes, i.e., his children, in order that this race of peculiar commodity owners may perpetuate its appearance in the market.

In order to modify the human organism, so that it may acquire skill and handiness in a given branch of industry, and become labour-power of a special kind, a special education or training is requisite, and this, on its part, costs an equivalent in commodities of a greater or lesser amount. This amount varies according to the more or less complicated character of the labour-power. The expenses of this education (excessively small in the case of ordinary labour-power), enter pro tanto into the total value spent in its production.

The value of labour-power resolves itself into the value of a definite quantity of the means of subsistence. It therefore varies with the value of these means or with the quantity of labour requisite for their production.

[...] Suppose that in this mass of commodities requisite for {the labourer's subsistence during} the average day there are embodied six hours of labour, then there is incorporated daily in labour-power half a day's average social labour {Marx is assuming here a 12-hour working day}, in other words, half a day's labour is requisite for the daily production of labour-power. This quantity of labour forms the value of a day's labour-power or the value of the labour-power daily reproduced. If half a day's average social labour is incorporated in three shillings, then three shillings is the price corresponding to the value of a day's labour-power. If its owner therefore offers it for sale at three shillings a day, its selling price is equal to its value, and according to our supposition, our friend Moneybags, who is intent on converting his three shillings into capital, pays this value.

[...]

We now know how the value paid by the purchaser to the possessor of this peculiar commodity, labour-power, is determined. The use-value which the former gets in exchange, manifests itself only in the actual usufruct, in the consumption of the labour-power. The money-owner buys everything necessary for this purpose, such as raw material, in the market, and pays for it at its full value. The consumption of labour-power is at one and the same time the production of commodities and of surplus-value. The consumption of labour-power is completed, as in the case of every other commodity, outside the limits of the market or of the sphere of circulation. Accompanied by Mr Moneybags and by the possessor of labour-power, we therefore take leave for a time of this noisy sphere, where everything takes place on the surface and in view of all men, and follow them both into the hidden abode of production, on whose threshold there stares us in the face 'No admittance except on business'. Here we shall see, not only how capital produces, but how capital is produced. We shall at last force the secret of profit-making.

This sphere that we are deserting, within whose boundaries the sale and purchase of labour-power goes on, is in fact a very Eden of the innate rights of man. There alone rule Freedom, Equality, Property and Bentham. Freedom, because both buyer and seller of a commodity, say of labour-power, are constrained only by their own free will. They contract as free agents, and the agreement they come to, is but the form in which they give legal expression to their common will. Equality, because each enters into relation with the other, as with a simple owner of commodities, and they exchange equivalent for equivalent. Property, because each disposes only of what is his own. And Bentham, because each looks only to himself. The only force that brings them together and brings them into relation with each other, is the selfishness, the gain and the private interests of each. Each looks to himself only, and no one troubles himself about the rest, and just because they do so, do they all, in accordance with the pre-established harmony of things, or under the auspices of an all-shrewd providence, work together to their mutual advantage, for the common weal and in the interest of all.

On leaving this sphere of simple circulation or of exchange of commodities, which furnishes the 'Free-trader Vulgaris' with his views and ideas, and with the standard by which he judges a society based on capital and wages, we think we can perceive a change in our dramatis personae. He, who before was the money-owner, now strides in front as capitalist; the possessor of labour-power follows as his labourer. The one with an air of importance, smirking, intent on business; the other, timid and holding back; like one who is bringing his own hide to market and has nothing to expect but – a hiding. [*Capital* 1, 1867; 1867a: 166–176; footnote incorporated into text between asterisks]

The next chapter (VII) of *Capital* 1 develops Marx's explanation of the 'secret of profit-making', his theory of surplus value, in detail. It is too long to give in full here, and difficult to extract from because Marx's exposition proceeds via numerical examples. He summarizes the argument elsewhere:[76]

5.16 Now suppose that the average amount of the daily necessaries of a labouring man require *six hours of average labour* for their production. Suppose, moreover, six hours of average labour to be also realised in a quantity of gold equal to 3s. { 3 shillings}. Then 3s. would be the *Price*, or the monetary expression of the *Daily Value* of that man's *Labouring Power*. If he worked daily six hours he would produce a value sufficient to buy the average amount of his daily necessaries, or to maintain himself as a labouring man.

But our man is a wages labourer. He must, therefore, sell his labouring power to a capitalist. If he sells it at 3s. daily, or 18s. weekly {assuming a six-day week}, he sells it at its value. Suppose him to be a spinner. If he works six hours daily he will add to the cotton a value of 3s. daily. This value, daily added by him, would be an exact equivalent for the wages, or the price of his labouring power, received daily. But in that case no *surplus-value* or *surplus-produce* whatever would go to the capitalist. Here, then, we come to the rub.

In buying the labouring power of the workman, and paying his value, the capitalist, like every other purchaser, has acquired the right to consume or use the commodity bought. You consume or use the labouring power of a man by making him work as you consume or use a machine by making it run. By paying the daily or weekly value of the labouring power of the workman, the capitalist has, therefore, acquired the right to use or make that labouring power work during the *whole day or week*. The working day or the working week has, of course, certain limits, but those we shall afterwards look more closely at.

For the present I want to turn your attention to one decisive point.

The *value* of the labouring power is determined by the quantity of labour necessary to maintain or reproduce it, but the *use* of that labouring power is only limited by the active energies and physical strength of the labourer. The daily or weekly *value* of the labouring power is quite distinct from the daily or weekly *exercise* of that power, the same as the food a horse wants and the time it can carry the horseman are quite distinct. The quantity of labour by which the *value* of the workman's labouring power is limited forms by no means a limit to the quantity of labour which his labouring power is apt to perform. Take the example of our spinner. We have seen that, to daily reproduce his labouring power, he must daily reproduce a value of three shillings, which he will do by working six hours daily. But this does not disable him from working ten or twelve or more hours a day. But by paying the daily or weekly *value* of the spinner's labouring power, the capitalist has acquired the right of using that labouring power during the *whole day or week*. He will, therefore, make him work daily, say, *twelve* hours. *Over and above* the six hours required to replace his wages, or the value of his labouring power, he will, therefore, have to work *six other hours*, which I shall call hours of *surplus-labour*, which surplus-labour will realise itself in a *surplus-value* and a *surplus-produce*. If our spinner, for example, by his daily labour of six hours, added three shillings' value to the cotton, a value forming an exact equivalent to his wages, he will, in twelve hours, add six shillings' worth to the cotton, and produce a *proportional surplus of yarn*. As he has sold his labouring power to the capitalist, the whole value or produce created by him belongs to the capitalist, the owner *pro tempore* of his labouring power. By advancing three shillings, the capitalist will, therefore, realise a value of six shillings, because, advancing a value in which six hours of labour are crystallized, he will receive in return a value in which twelve hours of labour are crystallized. By repeating this same process daily, the capitalist will daily advance three shillings and daily pocket six shillings, one-half of which will go to pay wages anew, and the other half of which will form *surplus-value*, for which the capitalist pays no equivalent. It is *this sort of exchange between capital and labour* upon which capitalistic production, or the wages system, is founded, and which must constantly result in reproducing the working man as a working man, and the capitalist as a capitalist.

The rate of surplus-value, all other circumstances remaining the same, will depend on the proportion between that part of the working day necessary to reproduce the value of the labouring power and the *surplus-time* or *surplus-labour* performed for the capitalist. It will, therefore, depend on the *ratio in which the working day is prolonged over and above that extent*, by working which the working man would only reproduce the value of his labouring power, or replace his wages. [Value, Price and Profit, 1865; 1865c: 130–1]

5.17 We saw that on the one side the possessor of value or money, on the other, the possessor of the value-creating substance; on the one side, the possessor of the means of production and subsistence, on the other, the possessor of nothing but labour-power, must confront one another as buyer and seller. The separation of labour from its product, of subjective labour-power from the objective conditions of labour, was therefore the real foundation in fact, and the starting-point of capitalist production.

But that which at first was but a starting-point, becomes, by the mere continuity of the process, by simple reproduction, the peculiar result, constantly renewed and perpetuated, of capitalist production. On the one hand, the process of production incessantly converts material wealth into capital, into means of creating more wealth and means of enjoyment for the capitalist. On the other hand, the labourer, on quitting the process, is what he was on entering it, a source of wealth, but devoid of all means of making that wealth his own. Since, before entering on the process, his own labour has already been alienated from himself by the sale of his labour-power, has been appropriated by the capitalist and incorporated with capital, it must, during the process, be realised in a product that does not belong to him. Since the process of production is also the process by which the capitalist consumes labour-power, the product of the labourer is constantly converted, not only into commodities, but into capital, into value that sucks up the value-creating power, into means of subsistence that buy the person of the labourer, into means of production that command the producers. The labourer therefore constantly produces material, objective wealth, but in the form of capital, of an alien power that dominates and exploits him; and the capitalist as constantly produces labour-power, but in the

form of a subjective source of wealth, separated from the objects in and by which it can alone be realised; in short he produces the labourer, but as a wage-labourer. This incessant reproduction, this perpetuation of the labourer, is the sine qua non of capitalist production.
[*Capital* 1, 1867; 1867a: 570–1]

5.18 Property in past objectified alien labour appears as the sole condition for further appropriation of present or living alien labour. In so far as a surplus capital [...] was created by means of simple exchange between objectified labour and living labour capacity – an exchange wholly based on the laws of exchange of equivalents as estimated by the quantity of labour or labour time contained in them – and *in so far as* this exchange, speaking juridically, presupposed nothing but the right of property of each person in his own products and his right freely to dispose of them [...] we see that by a peculiar logic the right of property on the side of capital is dialectically transformed into the right to an alien product or into the right to property in alien labour, the right to appropriate alien labour without equivalent; on the side of labour capacity it is transformed to the duty to relate itself towards its own labour or its own product as *alien property.* The right to property is inverted into the right on the one side to appropriate alien labour and the duty on the other side to respect the product of one's own labour and one's own labour itself as values belonging to others.

But the exchange of equivalents which appeared as the initial operation, and which juridically expressed the right to property, has been reversed in such a way that on the one side only an apparent exchange takes place, in that the part of capital exchanged for living labour capacity is, in the first place, itself *alien labour* appropriated without equivalent, and in that, secondly, it *must be replaced by labour capacity with a surplus*, i.e. it is not in fact given away but only transformed from one form into another. The relationship of exchange has therefore completely disappeared, or it has become a *mere semblance.*

Furthermore, the right to property originally appeared to be based on one's own labour. Now property appears as the right to alien labour and as the impossibility for labour to appropriate its own product. The complete separation of property, and even more of wealth, from labour now appears as a consequence of the law which arose from their identity.

Finally, the result of the process of production and valorisation {creation of value} now appears to be above all the reproduction and

new production of the *very relationship of capital and labour*, of *capitalist and worker*. In fact, this social relationship, this relationship of production, appears to be an even more important result of the process than its material results.
[*Grundrisse*, 1857–8; 1858a: 386–7]

*Marx here means that (1) once capitalist production is under way, the wages paid to the worker are paid out of *previously* created surplus-value, for which no equivalent has been given, while (2) once employed, the worker in any case *replaces* the value of the wage, as well as producing additional surplus-value.

5.19 The surplus-value is his {the capitalist's} property; it has never belonged to anyone else. If he advances it for the purposes of production, the advances made come from his own funds, exactly as on the day when he first entered the market. The fact that on this occasion the funds are derived from the unpaid labour of his workers makes absolutely no difference. If worker B is paid out of the surplus-value that worker A produced, then, in the first place, A furnished that surplus-value without having the just price of his commodity cut by a halfpenny, and, in the second place, the transaction is no concern of B's whatsoever. What B claims, and has a right to claim, is that the capitalist should pay him the value of his labour-power [...]

To be sure, the matter looks quite different if we consider capitalist production in the uninterrupted flow of its renewal, and if, in place of the individual capitalist and the individual worker, we view them in their totality, the capitalist class and the working class confronting each other. But in so doing we would be applying standards entirely foreign to commodity production.

Only buyer and seller, mutually independent, face each other in commodity production [...] If, therefore, commodity production, or one of its associated processes, is to be judged according to its own economic laws, we must consider each act of exchange by itself, apart from any connection with the act of exchange preceding it and that following it. And since sales and purchases are negotiated solely between particular individuals, it is not admissible to seek here for relations between whole social classes.

However long a series of periodical reproductions and preceding accumulations the capital functioning today may have passed through, it always preserves its original virginity. So long as the laws of exchange are observed in every single act of exchange the mode of appropriation can be completely revolutionised without in any way affecting the property rights which correspond to commodity production. These same rights remain in force both at the outset, when the product belongs to the producer, who, exchanging equivalent for equivalent, can enrich himself only by his own labour, and also in the period of capitalism, when social wealth becomes to an ever-increasing degree the property of those who are in a position to appropriate continually and ever afresh the unpaid labour of others.

This result becomes inevitable from the moment there is a free sale, by the labourer himself, of labour-power as a commodity. But it is also only from then onwards that commodity production is generalised and becomes the typical form of production; it is only from then onwards that, from the first, every product is produced for sale and all wealth produced goes through the sphere of circulation. Only when and where wage-labour is its basis does commodity production impose itself upon society as a whole; but only then and there also does it unfold all its hidden potentialities.

[*Capital* 1, 1867; 1867a: 586–7]

5.20 We see here how even economic categories appropriate to earlier modes of production acquire a new and specific historical character under the impact of capitalist production.

The transformation of money, itself only a different form of the commodity, into capital occurs only when a worker's labour-power has been converted into a commodity for him. This implies that the category of trade has been extended to embrace a sphere from which it had previously been excluded or into which it had made only sporadic inroads. In other words the working population must have ceased either to be part of the *objective* conditions of labour {like slaves}, or to enter the market-place as the independent producer of commodities; instead of selling the products of its labour it must sell that labour itself, or more accurately, its labour-power. Only then can it be said that production has become the *production of commodities* through its entire length and breadth. Only then does all produce become commodity and the objective conditions of each and every sphere of production enter into it as commodities themselves. Only on the basis of capitalist production does the commodity actually become the *universal elementary form of wealth*. For example, where capital has not yet taken over agriculture, a large proportion of agricultural produce is still used directly as means of subsistence and not as a commodity. In that event a large proportion of the working population will not have been transformed into wage-labourers and a large proportion of the conditions of labour will not yet have become capital. It is implicit in this situation that the developed division of labour which appears *by chance* within society, and the capitalist division of labour within the workshop {Marx discusses these in detail in *Capital* 1, Chapter 14, section 4}, are things that mutually condition and produce one another. For the *commodity* as the necessary form of the product, and hence the alienation of the product as the necessary means of appropriating it, entail a fully developed *division of social labour*. While, conversely, it is only on the basis of capitalist production, and hence of the *capitalist division of labour* within the workshop, that all produce necessarily assumes the form of the commodity and hence all producers are necessarily commodity producers. Therefore, it is only with the emergence of capitalist production that use-value is universally mediated by exchange-value.

These three points are crucial:

(1) Capitalist production is the first to make the commodity into the general form of all produce.
(2) The production of commodities leads inexorably to capitalist production, once the worker has ceased to be a part of the conditions of production (as in slavery, serfdom), or once primitive common ownership has ceased to be the basis of society (India). In short, from the moment when labour-power in general becomes a commodity.
(3) Capitalist production destroys the basis of commodity production in so far as the latter involves independent individual production and the exchange of commodities between owners or the exchange of equivalents. The formal exchange of capital and labour-power becomes general.

[Results of the Immediate Process of Production, between 1863 and 1866; 1866: 950-1]

5.21 Capital is not a thing, but a social relation between persons, established by the instrumentality of things. *'A negro is a negro. In certain circumstances he becomes a slave. A mule is a machine for spinning cotton. Only under certain circumstances does it become capital. Outside these circumstances, it is no more capital than gold is intrinsically money or sugar is the price of sugar [...] Capital is a social relation of production. It is a historical relation of production.'*

[*Capital* 1, 1867: 1867a; 766; footnote (a quote by Marx of his own 1847b) incorporated in text between asterisks]

5.22 Capital is not a thing, but rather a definite social production relation, belonging to a definite historical formation of society, which is manifested in a thing and lends this thing a specific social character. Capital is not the sum of material and produced means of production. Capital is rather the means of production transformed into capital, which in themselves are no more capital than gold or silver in itself is money. It is the means of production monopolised by a certain section of society, confronting living labour-power as products and working conditions rendered independent of this very labour-power, which are personified through this antithesis in capital. It is not merely the products of labourers turned into independent powers, products as rulers and buyers of their producers, but rather also the social forces of their labour and socialised form of this labour, which confronts the labourers as properties of their products. Here, then, we have a definite and, at first glance, very mystical, social form, of one of the factors in a historically produced social production process.
[*Capital* 3, 1864–5; 1865a: 814–5]

5.23 Looking at the process of production from its real side, i.e. as a process which creates new use-values by performing useful labour with existing use-values, we find it to be a *real labour process*. As such its elements, its conceptually specific components, are those of the labour process itself, of any *labour process*, irrespective of the mode of production or the stage of economic development in which they find themselves. Now this real form, the form of the objective use-values in which *capital is incorporated*, its material substratum, is necessarily the form assumed by the means of production – the means and object of labour – which are required for the creation of new products. Furthermore, these use-values are already present (on the market) in the circulation process, in the form of commodities, i.e. in the possession of the capitalist as the owner of commodities, even before they become active in the labour process in fulfilment of their specific purpose. In view of this, and since, therefore, capital – to the extent to which it manifests itself in the *objective* conditions of labour – *consists* of *means of production*, raw materials, auxiliary materials, means of labour, tools, buildings, machines etc., people tend to conclude that all means of production are capital *potentially*, and that they are so *actually* when they function as means of production. Capital then is held to be

a necessary feature of the *human labour process as such*, irrespective of the historical forms it has assumed; it is consequently something permanent, determined by the nature of human labour itself. In the same way, it is urged that because the process of production of capital in general is the labour process, the *labour process as such*, it follows that the labour process in all forms of society is necessarily capitalist in nature. Thus capital comes to be thought of as a *thing*, and as a thing it plays a certain role, a role appropriate to it as a thing in the process of production. It is the same logic that infers that because money is gold, gold is intrinsically money; that because wage-labour is labour, all labour is necessarily wage-labour. The *identity* is proved by holding fast to the features common to all processes of production, while neglecting their *specific differentiae*. We shall return to this crucial point in greater detail in the course of this chapter.
[Results of the Immediate Process of Production, between 1863 and 1866; 1866: 981–2]

5.24 Within the framework of capitalist production this ability of objectified labour to transform itself into *capital*, i.e. to transform the means of production into the means of controlling and exploiting living labour, appears as something utterly appropriate to them [...], as inseparable from them and hence as a *quality* attributable *to them as things, as use-values, as means of production.* These appear, therefore, intrinsically as capital and hence as capital which expresses a *specific relationship of production*, a specific social relationship in which the owners of the conditions of production treat living labour-power as a *thing*, just as value had appeared to be the attribute of a thing and the *economic definition* of the thing as a *commodity* appeared to be an aspect of its thinghood, just as the social form conferred on labour in the shape of money presented itself as the *characteristics of a thing*.
[Ibid: 988–9]

5.25 The folly of identifying a specific *social relationship of production* with the thing-like qualities of certain articles simply because it represents itself in terms of certain articles is what strikes us most forcibly whenever we open any textbook on economics and see on the first page how the elements of the process of production, reduced to their basic form, turn out to be land, *capital*, and labour. One might just as well say that they were *landed property*, knives, scissors, spindles, cotton, grain, in short, the *materials* and *means* of labour, and – *wage-labour*. On the one hand, we name the elements of the labour process combined with the *specific social characteristics* peculiar to them in a given *historical* phase, and on the other hand we add an element which forms an integral part of the *labour process* independently of any particular social formation, as part of an eternal commerce between man and nature. By confusing the appropriation of the labour process by capital with the labour process itself, the economists transform the *material elements* of the labour process into capital, simply because capital itself changes into the material elements of the labour process *among other things*. [...] This illusion is one that springs from the nature of capitalist production itself. But it is evident even now that this is a very convenient method by which to demonstrate the eternal validity of the capitalist mode of production and to regard *capital* as an *immutable natural element* in human production as such. Work is the eternal natural condition of human existence. The process of labour is nothing but work itself, viewed at the moment of its creative activity. Hence the universal features of the labour process are independent of every specific social development. The materials and means of labour, a proportion of which consists of the products of previous work, play their part in every labour process in every age and in all circumstances. If, therefore, I label them 'capital' in the confident knowledge that '*semper aliquid haeret*' {something always sticks}, then I have *proved* that the existence of capital is an eternal law of nature of human production and that the Kirghiz who cuts down rushes with a knife he has stolen from a Russian so as to weave them together to make a canoe is just as true a capitalist as Herr von Rothschild. I could prove with equal facility that the Greeks and Romans celebrated communion because they drank wine and ate bread, and that the Turks sprinkle themselves daily with holy water like Catholics because they wash themselves daily.

[Ibid: 998–9]

5.26 In {the vulgar economists' formula}[77] capital – profit, or better still capital – interest, land – rent, labour – wages, in this economic trinity represented as the connection between the component parts of value and wealth in general and its sources, we have the complete mystification of the capitalist mode of production, the conversion of social relations into things, the direct coalescence of the material production relations with their historical and social determination. It is an enchanted, perverted, topsy-turvy world, in which Monsieur le Capital and Madame la Terre do their ghost-walking as social characters and at the same time as mere things. It is the great merit of classical economy to have destroyed this false appearance and illusion, this

mutual independence and ossification of the various social elem
wealth, this personification of things and conversion of production
relations into entities, this religion of everyday life. It did so by
reducing interest to a portion of profit, and rent to the surplus above
average profit, so that both of them converge in surplus-value; and by
representing the process of circulation as a mere metamorphosis of
forms, and finally reducing value and surplus-value of commodities to
labour in the direct production process [...] On the other hand, it is just
as natural for the actual agents of production to feel completely at
home in these estranged and irrational forms of capital – interest, land
– rent, labour – wages, since these are precisely the forms of illusion
in which they move about and find their daily occupation. It is therefore
just as natural that vulgar economy, which is no more than a didactic,
more or less dogmatic, translation of everyday conceptions of the actual
agents of production, and which arranges them in a certain rational
order, should see precisely in this trinity, which is devoid of all inner
connection, the natural and indubitably lofty basis for its shallow
pompousness. This formula simultaneously corresponds to the interests
of the ruling classes by proclaiming the physical necessity and eternal
justification of their sources of revenue and elevating them to a dogma.
[*Capital* 3, 1864–5; 1865a: 830]

6

The real history of the relations of production

A critical analysis of the kind developed in Chapter 5 may give us the 'laws of bourgeois economy', but to write the 'real history of the relations of production' is 'a work in its own right' (see 4.23 and 4.24 above). To use the language of the 1857 Introduction (4.18), we have arrived at 'simple abstractions' which anatomize capitalism – like value, or surplus value – but we have yet to return to the 'concrete'. That return journey above all entails respecifying such abstractions in terms of the actions over time of 'real living individuals'. Thus, 'primitive accumulation' is a narrative of enclosures, clearances, and legislation against 'sturdy beggars', 'absolute surplus value' a tale of struggles over the length of the working day, 'relative surplus value' a story of changing labour processes. This chapter traces Marx's account of this 'real history of the relations of production'.

6.1 It is [...] severance of the conditions of production, on the one hand, from the producers, on the other, that forms the conception of capital. It begins with primitive accumulation ({*Capital* 1, Part 8}), appears as a permanent process in the accumulation and concentration

of capital, and expresses itself finally as centralisation of capitals in a few hands and a deprivation of many of their capital (to which appropriation is now changed).
[*Capital* 3, 1864–5; 1865a: 246]

6.2 We have seen how money is changed into capital; how through capital surplus-value is made, and from surplus-value more capital. But the accumulation of capital pre-supposes surplus-value; surplus-value presupposes capitalistic production; capitalistic production presupposes the pre-existence of considerable masses of capital and of labour-power in the hands of producers of commodities. The whole movement, therefore, seems to turn in a vicious circle, out of which we can only get by supposing a primitive accumulation (previous accumulation of Adam Smith) preceding capitalistic accumulation; an accumulation not the result of the capitalist mode of production, but its starting-point.

This primitive accumulation plays in Political Economy about the same part as original sin in theology. Adam bit the apple, and thereupon sin fell on the human race. Its origin is supposed to be explained when it is told as an anecdote of the past. In times long gone by there were two sorts of people; one, the diligent, intelligent, and, above all, frugal elite; the other, lazy rascals, spending their substance, and more, in riotous living. [...] Thus it came to pass that the former sort accumulated wealth, and the latter sort had at last nothing to sell except their own skins. And from this original sin dates the poverty of the great majority that, despite all its labour, has up to now nothing to sell but itself, and the wealth of the few that increases constantly although they have long since ceased to work. Such insipid childishness is every day preached to us in defence of property. [...] In actual history it is notorious that conquest, enslavement, robbery, murder, briefly force, play the great part. [...]

The capitalist system pre-supposes the complete separation of the labourers from all property in the means by which they can realise their labour. As soon as capitalist production is once on its own legs, it not only maintains this separation, but reproduces it on a continually extending scale. The process, therefore, that clears the way for the capitalist system, can be none other than the process which takes away from the labourer the possession of his means of production; a process that transforms, on the one hand, the social means of subsistence and of production into capital, on the other, the immediate producers into wage-labourers. The so-called primitive accumulation, therefore, is nothing else than the historical process of divorcing the producer from the means of production. It appears as primitive, because it forms the pre-historic stage of capital and of the mode of production corresponding with it.

The economic structure of capitalistic society has grown out of the economic structure of feudal society. The dissolution of the latter set free the elements of the former.

The immediate producer, the labourer, could only dispose of his own person after he had ceased to be attached to the soil and ceased to be the slave, serf, or bondman of another. To become a free seller of labour-power, who carries his commodity wherever he finds a market, he must further have escaped from the regime of the guilds, their rules for apprentices and journeymen, and the impediments of their labour regulations. Hence, the historical movement which changes the producers into wage-workers, appears, on the one hand, as their emancipation from serfdom and from the fetters of the guilds, and this side alone exists for our bourgeois historians. But, on the other hand, these new freedmen became sellers of themselves only after they had been robbed of all their own means of production, and of all the guarantees of existence afforded by the old feudal arrangements. And the history of this, their expropriation, is written in the annals of mankind in letters of blood and fire.

The industrial capitalists, these new potentates, had on their part not only to displace the guild masters of handicrafts, but also the feudal lords, the possessors of the sources of wealth. In this respect their conquest of social power appears as the fruit of a victorious struggle both against feudal lordship and its revolting prerogatives, and against the guilds and the fetters they laid on the free development of production and the free exploitation of man by man. [...]

In the history of primitive accumulation, all revolutions are epoch-making that act as levers for the capitalist class in course of formation; but, above all, those moments when great masses of men are suddenly and forcibly torn from their means of subsistence, and hurled as free and 'unattached' proletarians on the labour-market. The expropriation of the agricultural producer, of the peasant, from the soil, is the basis of the whole process.

[*Capital* 1, 1867; 1867a: 713–16]

6.3 The prelude of the revolution[78] that laid the foundation of the capitalist mode of production, was played in the last third of the 15th, and the first decade of the 16th century. A mass of free proletarians was hurled on the labour-market by the breaking-up of the bands of feudal retainers [...] In insolent conflict with king and parliament, the great feudal lords created an incomparably larger proletariat by the forcible driving of the peasantry from the land, to which the latter had the same feudal right as the lord himself, and by the usurpation of the common lands. The rapid rise of the Flemish wool manufactures, and the corresponding rise in the price of wool in England, gave the direct impulse to these evictions. The old nobility had been devoured by the great feudal wars. The new nobility was the child of its time, for which money was the power of all powers. Transformation of arable land into sheep-walks was, therefore, its great cry.

[...]

The process of forcible expropriation of the people received in the 16th century a new and frightful impulse from the Reformation, and from the consequent colossal spoliation of the church property. The Catholic church was, at the time of the Reformation, feudal proprietor of a great part of the English land. The suppression of the monasteries, &c., hurled their inmates into the proletariat. The estates of the church were to a large extent given away to rapacious royal favourites, or sold at a nominal price to speculating farmers and citizens, who drove out, *en masse*, the hereditary sub-tenants and threw their holdings into one. The legally guaranteed property of the poorer folk in a part of the church's tithes was tacitly confiscated. 'Pauper ubique jacet' {the poor man is everywhere neglected; Ovid, *Fasti*, Book 1, verse 218}, cried Queen Elizabeth, after a journey through England. In the 43rd year of her reign the nation was obliged to recognise pauperism officially by the introduction of a poor-rate.[79] [...] These immediate results of the Reformation were not its most lasting ones. The property of the church formed the religious bulwark of the traditional conditions of landed property. With its fall these were no longer tenable.

[...] About 1750, the yeomanry had disappeared, and so had, in the last decade of the 18th century, the last trace of the common land of the agricultural labourer. We leave on one side here the purely economic causes of the agricultural revolution. We deal only with the forcible means employed.

After the restoration of the Stuarts, the landed proprietors carried, by legal means, an act of usurpation,[80] effected everywhere on the Continent without any legal formality. They abolished the feudal tenure of land, i.e., they got rid of all its obligations to the State, 'indemnified' the State by taxes on the peasantry and the rest of the mass of the people, vindicated for themselves the rights of modern private property in estates to which they had only a feudal title, and, finally, passed those laws of settlement,[81] which, *mutatis mutandis*, had the same effect on the English agricultural labourer, as the edict of the Tartar Boris Godunof on the Russian peasantry.

The 'Glorious Revolution'[82] brought into power, along with William of Orange, the landlord and capitalist appropriators of surplus-value. They inaugurated the new era by practicing on a colossal scale thefts of state lands. [...]

Communal property – always distinct from the State property just dealt with – was an old Teutonic institution which lived on under cover of feudalism. We have seen how the forcible usurpation of this, generally accompanied by the turning of arable into pasture land, begins at the end of the 15th and extends into the 16th century. But, at that time, the process was carried on by means of individual acts of violence against which legislation, for a hundred and fifty years, fought in vain. The advance made by the 18th century shows itself in this, that the law itself becomes now the instrument of the theft of the people's land, although the large farmers make use of their little independent methods as well. The parliamentary form of the robbery is that of Acts for enclosures of Commons, in other words, decrees by which the landlords grant themselves the people's land as private property, decrees of expropriation of the people.

[...]

In the 19th century, the very memory of the connection between the agricultural labourer and the communal property had, of course, vanished. To say nothing of more recent times, have the agricultural population received a farthing of compensation for the 3,511,770 acres of common land which between 1801 and 1831 were stolen from them and by parliamentary devices presented to the landlords by the landlords?

The last process of wholesale expropriation of the agricultural population from the soil is, finally, the so-called clearing of estates, i.e., the sweeping men off them. All the English methods hitherto considered culminated in 'clearing'. [...] What 'clearing of estates' really and properly signifies, we learn only in the promised land of modern romance, the Highlands of Scotland. There the process is distinguished by its systematic character, by the magnitude of the scale on which it is carried out at one blow (in Ireland landlords have gone to the length of sweeping away several villages at once; in Scotland areas as large as German principalities are dealt with), finally by the peculiar form of property, under which the embezzled lands were held {clan property}. [...] In the 18th century the hunted-out Gaels were forbidden to emigrate from the country, with a view to driving them by force to Glasgow and other manufacturing towns.

[...]

The spoliation of the church's property, the fraudulent alienation of the State's domains, the robbery of the common lands, the usurpation of feudal and clan property, and its transformation into modern private property under circumstances of reckless terrorism, were just so many idyllic methods of primitive accumulation. They conquered the field for capitalistic agriculture, made the soil part and parcel of capital, and created for the town industries the necessary supply of a 'free' and outlawed proletariat.

[...] This 'free' proletariat could not possibly be absorbed by the nascent manufactures as fast as it was thrown upon the world. On the other hand, these men, suddenly dragged from their wonted mode of life, could not as suddenly adapt themselves to the discipline of their new condition. They were turned *en masse* into beggars, robbers, vagabonds, partly from inclination, in most cases from stress of circumstances. Hence at the end of the 15th and during the whole of the 16th century, throughout Europe a bloody legislation against vagabondage. The fathers of the present working-class were chastised for their enforced transformation into vagabonds and paupers. Legislation treated them as 'voluntary' criminals, and assumed that it depended on their own good will to go on working under the old conditions that no longer existed.

[...]

Thus were the agricultural people, first forcibly expropriated from the soil, driven from their homes, turned into vagabonds, and then whipped, branded, tortured by laws grotesquely terrible, into the discipline necessary for the wage system.

It is not enough that the conditions of labour are concentrated in a mass, in the shape of capital, at one pole of society, while at the other are grouped masses of men, who have nothing to sell but their labour-power. Neither is it enough that they are compelled to sell it voluntarily. The advance of capitalist production develops a working-class, which by education, tradition, habit, looks upon the conditions of that mode of production as self-evident laws of Nature. The organisation of the capitalist process of production, once fully developed, breaks down all resistance. The constant generation of a relative surplus-population keeps the law of supply and demand of labour, and therefore keeps wages, in a rut that corresponds with the wants of capital. The dull compulsion of economic relations completes the subjection of the labourer to the capitalist. Direct force, outside economic conditions, is of course still used, but only exceptionally. In the ordinary run of things, the labourer can be left to the 'natural laws of production', i.e., to his dependence on capital, a dependence springing from, and guaranteed in perpetuity by, the conditions of production themselves. It is otherwise during the historic genesis of capitalist production. The bourgeoisie, at its rise, wants and uses the power of the state to 'regulate' wages, i.e., to force them within the limits suitable for surplus-value making, to lengthen the working-day and to keep the labourer himself in the normal degree of dependence. This is an essential element of the so-called primitive accumulation.[83]

[...]

Legislation on wage-labour (from the first, aimed at the exploitation of the labourer and, as it advanced, equally hostile to him), is started in England by the Statute of Labourers, of Edward III, 1349.[84] [...] {Marx goes on to detail legislation regulating wages and forbidding workers' combinations over the next half-millenium.} Only against its will and under the pressure of the masses did the English Parliament give up the laws against Strikes and Trades' Unions, after it had itself, for 500 years, held, with shameless egoism, the position of a permanent Trades' Union of the capitalists against the labourers.

[...]

The events that transformed the small peasants into wage-labourers, and their means of subsistence and of labour into material elements of capital, created, at the same time, a home-market for the latter. Formerly, the peasant family produced the means of subsistence and the raw materials, which they themselves, for the most part, consumed. These raw materials and means of subsistence have now become commodities; the large farmer sells them, he finds the market in manufactures. Yarn, linen, coarse woollen stuffs – things whose raw materials had been within the reach of every peasant family, had been spun and woven by it for its own use – were now transformed into articles of manufacture [...] Thus, hand in hand with the expropriation of the self-supporting peasants, with their separation from their means of production, goes the destruction of rural domestic industry, the process of separation between manufacture and agriculture. And only the destruction of rural domestic industry can give the internal market of a country that extension and consistence which the capitalist mode of production requires. Still the manufacturing period, properly so-called,[85] does not succeed in carrying out this transformation radically and completely. [...] Modern industry alone, and finally, supplies, in machinery, the lasting basis of capitalistic agriculture, expropriates radically the enormous majority of the agricultural population, and completes the separation between agriculture and rural domestic industry, whose roots – spinning and weaving – it tears up. It therefore also, for the first time, conquers for industrial capital the home market.

[...]

The genesis of the industrial capitalist did not proceed in such a gradual way as that of the farmer {which Marx sees as a process spanning the fourteenth to seventeenth centuries, and involving the gradual enrichment of tenant farmers at the expense of both their landlords and their labourers [1867a: 742–4]}. Doubtless many small guild-masters, and yet more independent small artisans, or even wage-labourers, transformed themselves into small capitalists, and (by gradually extending exploitation of wage-labour and corresponding accumulation) into full-blown capitalists. [...] The snail's pace of this method in no wise corresponded with the commercial requirements of the new world-market that the great discoveries at the end of the 15th century created. But the middle ages had handed down two distinct forms of capital, which mature in the most different economic and social formations [...] – usurer's capital and merchant's capital [...].

The money capital formed by means of usury and commerce was prevented from turning into industrial capital, in the country by the feudal constitution, in the towns by the guild organisation. These fetters vanished with the dissolution of feudal society, with the expropriation and partial eviction of the country population. The new manufactures were established at sea-ports, or at inland points beyond the control of the old municipalities and their guilds. Hence in England an embittered struggle of the corporate towns against these new industrial nurseries.

The discovery of gold and silver in America, the extirpation, enslavement and entombment in mines of the aboriginal population, the beginning of the conquest and looting of the East Indies, the turning of Africa into a warren for the commercial hunting of black-skins, signalised the rosy dawn of the era of capitalist production. These idyllic proceedings are the chief momenta of primitive accumulation. On their heels treads the commercial war of the European nations, with the globe for a theatre. It begins with the revolt of the Netherlands from Spain, assumes giant dimensions in England's Anti-Jacobin War, and is still going on in the opium wars against China, &c.

These different momenta of primitive accumulation distribute themselves now, more or less in chronological order, particularly over Spain, Portugal, Holland, France, and England. In England at the end of the 17th century, they arrive at a systematical combination, embracing the colonies, the national debt, the modern mode of taxation, and the protectionist system. These methods depend in part on brute force, e.g., the colonial system. But they all employ the power of the State, the concentrated and organised force of society, to hasten, hothouse fashion, the process of transformation of the feudal mode of production into the capitalist mode, and to shorten the transition. Force is the midwife of every old society pregnant with a new one. It is itself an economic power. {In the next few pages Marx elaborates on the historic role of colonialism, national debts, taxation, mercantile protectionism, and the slave trade, in 'primitive accumulation'.}

[...]

Tantae molis erat {So great was the effort required; Virgil, *Aeneid*, Book 1, line 33}, to establish the 'eternal laws of Nature' of the capitalist mode of production, to complete the process of separation between labourers and the conditions of production, to transform, at one pole, the social means of production and subsistence into capital, at the opposite pole, the mass of the population into wage-labourers, into 'free labouring poor', that artificial product of modern society. If money, according to Augier, 'comes into the world with a congenital blood-stain on one cheek', capital comes dripping from head to foot, from every pore, with blood and dirt.

[*Capital* 1, 1867; 1867a: from 717–60 (much condensed)][86]

6.4 The labour process {under capitalism} becomes the instrument of the valorization process, the process of the self-valorization of capital – the manufacture of surplus-value. The labour process is subsumed under capital (it is its *own* process) and the capitalist intervenes in the process as its director, manager. For him it also represents the direct exploitation of the labour of others. It is this that I refer to as the *formal subsumption of labour under capital*. It is the general form of every capitalist process of production; at the same time, however, it can be found as a *particular* form alongside the *specifically capitalist mode of production* in its developed form, because although the latter entails the former, the converse does not necessarily obtain.

The process of production has become the process of capital itself. It is a process involving the *factors of the labour process* into which the capitalist's money has been converted and which proceeds under his direction with the sole purpose of using money to make more money.

When a peasant who has always produced enough for his needs becomes a day-labourer working for a farmer; when the hierarchic order of guild production vanishes making way for the straightforward distinction between the capitalist and the wage-labourers he employs; when the former slave-owner engages his former slaves as paid workers, etc., then we find that what is happening is that production processes of varying social provenance have been transformed into capitalist production.

[...]

The mystification inherent in the *capital-relation* emerges at this point. The value-sustaining power of labour {i.e., its preservation of the value of means of production in the product}[87] appears as the self-supporting power of capital; the value-creating power of labour as the self-valorizing power of capital and, in general, in accordance with its concept, *living* labour appears to be put to work by *objectified* labour.

All this notwithstanding, this change does not in itself imply a fundamental modification in the real nature of the labour process, the actual process of production. On the contrary, the fact is that capital subsumes the labour process as it finds it, that is to say, it takes over an *existing labour process*, developed by different and more archaic modes of production. [...] For example, handicraft, a mode of agriculture corresponding to a small, independent peasant economy. If changes occur in these traditional established *labour processes* after their takeover by capital, these are nothing but the gradual consequences of that subsumption. The work may become more intensive, its duration may be extended, it may become more continuous or orderly under the eye of the interested capitalist, but in themselves these changes do not affect the character of the actual labour process, the actual mode of working. This stands in striking contrast to the development of a *specifically capitalist mode of production* (large-scale industry, etc.); the latter not only transforms the situations of the various agents of production, it also *revolutionizes* their actual mode of labour and the real nature of the labour process as a whole. It is in contradistinction to this last that we come to designate as the *formal subsumption of labour under capital* what we have discussed earlier, viz. the takeover by capital of a mode of labour developed before the emergence of capitalist relations. The latter as a form of *compulsion* by which surplus labour is exacted by extending the duration of labour-time – a *mode of compulsion* not based on personal relations of domination and dependency, but simply on differing economic functions – this is common to both forms. However, the specifically capitalist mode of production has yet other methods of exacting surplus value at its disposal.[88] But given a pre-existing mode of labour, i.e. an *established* development of the productive

power of labour and a mode of labour corresponding to this productive power, surplus-value can be created only by lengthening the working day, i.e. by increasing *absolute surplus-value*. In the *formal* subsumption of labour under capital, this is the *sole* manner of producing surplus-value.
[Results of the Immediate Process of Production, between 1863 and 1866; 1866: 1019–21]

Later Marx repeats that with formal subsumption 'There is no change as yet in the mode of production itself. *Technologically speaking*, the *labour process* goes on as before, with the proviso that it is now *subordinated* to capital' [p. 1026].

6.5 Apart from extremely elastic bounds, the nature of the exchange of commodities itself imposes no limit to the working-day, no limit to surplus-labour. The capitalist maintains his rights as a purchaser when he tries to make the working-day as long as possible, and to make, wherever possible, two working-days out of one. On the other hand, the peculiar nature of the commodity sold {labour-power} implies a limit to its consumption by the purchaser, and the labourer maintains his right as seller when he wishes to reduce the working-day to one of definite normal duration. There is here, therefore, an antinomy, right against right, both equally bearing the seal of the law of exchanges. Between equal rights force decides. Hence is it that in the history of capitalist production, the determination of what is a normal working-day, presents itself as the result of a struggle, a struggle between collective capital, i.e., the class of capitalists, and collective labour, i.e., the working-class.
[*Capital* 1, 1867: 1867a: 234–5]

6.6 Capital is reckless of the health or length of life of the labourer, unless under compulsion from society. To the out-cry as to the physical and mental degradation, the torture of overwork, it answers: Ought these to trouble us since they increase our profits? But looking at things as a whole, all this does not, indeed, depend on the good or ill will of the individual capitalist. Free competition brings out the inherent laws of capitalist production, in the shape of external coercive laws having power over every individual capitalist.
*We therefore find, e.g., that in the beginning of 1863, 26 firms owning extensive potteries in Staffordshire, amongst others, Josiah Wedgwood, & Sons, petition in a memorial for 'some legislative enactment'. Competition with other capitalists permits them no

voluntary limitation of working-time for children, &c. 'Much as we deplore the evils before mentioned, it would not be possible to prevent them by any scheme of agreement between the manufacturers ... Taking all these points into consideration, we have come to the conviction that some legislative enactment is wanted' (Children's Employment Comm., Rep. 1, 1863, p. 322). [...]*

The establishment of a normal working-day is the result of centuries of struggle between capitalist and labourer. The history of this struggle shows two opposed tendencies. Compare, e.g., the English factory legislation of our time with the English Labour Statutes from the 14th century to well into the middle of the 18th. Whilst the modern Factory Acts compulsorily shortened the working-day, the earlier statutes tried to lengthen it by compulsion. Of course the pretensions of capital in embryo – when, beginning to grow, it secures the right of absorbing a *quantum sufficit* of surplus-labour, not merely by the force of economic relations, but by the help of the State – appear very modest when put face to face with the concessions that, growling and struggling, it has to make in its adult condition. It takes centuries ere the 'free' labourer, thanks to the development of capitalistic production, agrees, i.e., is compelled by social conditions, to sell the whole of his active life, his very capacity for work, for the price of the necessaries of life, his birthright for a mess of pottage. Hence it is natural that the lengthening of the working-day, which capital, from the middle of the 14th to the end of the 17th century, tries to impose by State-measures on adult labourers, approximately coincides with the shortening of the working-day which, in the second half of the 19th century, has here and there been effected by the State to prevent the coining of children's blood into capital. That which today, e.g., in the State of Massachusetts, until recently the freest State of the North-American republic, has been proclaimed as the statutory limit of the labour of children under 12 {10 hours per day}, was in England, even in the middle of the 17th century, the normal working-day of able-bodied artisans, robust labourers, athletic blacksmiths.
[Ibid: 270–1; part of footnote incorporated into text between asterisks]

6.7 {The capitalist} shares with the miser the passion for wealth as wealth. But that which in the miser is a mere idiosyncrasy, is, in the capitalist, the effect of the social mechanism, of which he is but one of the wheels. Moreover, the development of capitalist production makes it constantly necessary to keep increasing the amount of the capital laid out in a given industrial undertaking, and competition

makes the immanent laws of capitalist production to be felt by each individual capitalist, as external coercive laws. It compels him to keep constantly extending his capital, in order to preserve it, but extend it he cannot, except by means of progressive accumulation.
[Ibid: 592]

6.8 In *competition*, this immanent tendency of capital {to overproduction} appears as a compulsion imposed upon it by *other* capital and driving it beyond the correct proportion {of output} with a constant *March, march*! [...] Conceptually, competition is nothing but the *inner nature of capital*, its essential character, manifested in and realised as the reciprocal action of many capitals upon each other; immanent tendency realised as external necessity. (Capital exists and can only exist as many capitals; hence its own character appears as their reciprocal action on each other.)
[*Grundrisse*, 1857–8; 1858a: 340–1]

6.9 After a thirty year's struggle, fought with most admirable perseverance, the English working classes, improving a momentous split between the landlords and the money-lords, succeeded in carrying the Ten Hours' Bill {of 1847}. The immense physical, moral, and intellectual benefits hence accruing to the factory operatives, half-yearly chronicled in the reports of the inspectors of factories, are now acknowledged on all sides. Most of the continental governments had to accept the English Factory Act in more or less modified forms, and the English Parliament itself is every year compelled to extend its sphere of action. But besides its practical import, there was something else to exalt the marvellous success of this working men's measure. Through their most notorious organs of science, such as Dr Ure, Professor Senior, and other sages of that stamp, the middle class had predicted, and to their heart's content proved, that any legal restriction of the hours of labour must sound the death knell of British industry, which, vampire-like, could but live by sucking blood, and children's blood, too. In olden times, child murder was a mysterious rite of the religion of Moloch, but it was practised on some very solemn occasions only, once a year perhaps, and then Moloch had no exclusive bias for the children of the poor. This struggle about the legal restriction of the hours of labour raged the more fiercely since, apart from frightened avarice, it told indeed upon the great contest between the blind rule of the supply and demand laws which form the political economy of the middle class, and social production controlled by social foresight, which forms the political economy of the working class. Hence the Ten Hours' Bill was not only a great practical success; it was the victory of a principle; it was the first time that in broad daylight the political economy of the middle class succumbed to the political economy of the working class.

[Inaugural Address to the IWMA, 1864; 1864: 10–11]

Marx discusses the history of factory legislation in England at length in *Capital* 1, Chapter 10. He also offers a slightly different emphasis there, on the advantages of Factory Acts to big capital.

6.10 If the general extension of factory legislation to all trades for the purpose of protecting the working-class both in mind and body has become inevitable, on the other hand [...] that extension hastens on the general conversion of numerous isolated small industries into a few combined industries carried on upon a large scale; it therefore accelerates the concentration of capital and the exclusive predominance of the factory system. It destroys both the ancient and the transitional forms, behind which the dominion of capital is still in part concealed, and replaces them by the direct and open sway of capital; but thereby it also generalises the direct opposition to this sway. While in each individual workshop it enforces uniformity, regularity, order, and economy, it increases by the immense spur which the limitation and regulation of the working-day give to technical improvement, the anarchy and the catastrophes of capitalist production as a whole, the intensity of labour, and the competition of machinery with the labourer. By the destruction of petty and domestic industries it destroys the last resort of the 'redundant population', and with it the sole remaining safety-valve of the whole social mechanism. By maturing the material conditions, and the combination on a social scale of the processes of production, it matures the contradictions and antagonisms of the capitalist form of production, and thereby provides, along with the elements for the formation of a new society, the forces for exploding the old one.

[*Capital* 1, 1867; 1867a: 503]

6.11 Capitalist production only then really begins [...] when each individual capital employs simultaneously a comparatively large number of labourers, when consequently the labour-process is carried on on an extensive scale and yields, relatively, large quantities of products. A greater number of labourers working together, at the same

time, in one place (or, if you will, in the same field of labour), in order to produce the same sort of commodity under the mastership of one capitalist, constitutes, both historically and logically, the starting-point of capitalist production. With regard to the mode of production itself, manufacture, in its strict meaning, is hardly to be distinguished, in its earliest stages, from the handicraft trades of the guilds, otherwise than by the greater number of workmen simultaneously employed by one and the same individual capital. The workshop of the mediaeval master handicraftsman is simply enlarged.
[Ibid: 322]

6.12 When numerous labourers work together side by side, whether in one and the same process, or in different but connected processes, they are said to co-operate, or to work in co-operation.

Just as the offensive power of a squadron of cavalry, or the defensive power of a regiment of infantry, is essentially different from the sum of the offensive or defensive powers of the individual cavalry or infantry soldiers taken separately, so the sum total of the mechanical forces exerted by isolated workmen differs from the social force that is developed, when many hands take part simultaneously in one and the same undivided operation, such as raising a heavy weight, turning a winch, or removing an obstacle. In such cases the effect of the combined labour could either not be produced at all by isolated individual labour, or it could only be produced by a great expenditure of time, or on a very dwarfed scale. Not only have we here an increase in the productive power of the individual, by means of co-operation, but the creation of a new power, namely, the collective power of masses.
[Ibid: 325–6]

6.13 The combined working-day produces, relatively to an equal sum of isolated working-days, a greater quantity of use-values, and, consequently, diminishes the labour-time necessary for the production of a given useful effect. Whether the combined working-day, in a given case, acquires this increased productive power, because it heightens the mechanical force of labour, or extends its sphere of action over a greater space, or contracts the field of production relatively to the scale of production, or at the critical moment sets large masses of labour to work, or excites emulation between individuals and excites their animal spirits, or impresses on the similar operations carried out by a number of men the stamp of continuity and many-sidedness, or

performs simultaneously different operations, or economises the means of production by use in common, or lends to individual labour the character of average social labour {Marx elaborates on these in the preceding pages} – whichever of these be the cause of the increase, the special productive power of the combined working-day is, under all circumstances, the social productive power of labour, or the productive power of social labour. This power is due to co-operation itself. When the labourer co-operates systematically with others, he strips off the fetters of his individuality, and develops the capabilities of his species.
[Ibid: 329]

Marx later adds that 'co-operation ever constitutes the fundamental form of the capitalist mode of production' [p. 335].

6.14 We [...] saw that at first, the subjection of labour to capital was only a formal result of the fact, that the labourer, instead of working for himself, works for and consequently under the capitalist. By the co-operation of numerous wage-labourers, the sway of capital develops into a requisite for carrying on the labour-process itself, into a real requisite of production. That a capitalist should command on the field of production, is now as indispensible as that a general should command on the field of battle.

All combined labour on a large scale requires, more or less, a directing authority, in order to secure the harmonious working of the individual activities, and to perform the general functions that have their origin in the action of the combined organism, as distinguished from the action of its separate organs. A single violin player is his own conductor; an orchestra requires a separate one. The work of directing, superintending, and adjusting, becomes one of the functions of capital, from the moment that the labour under the control of capital, becomes co-operative. Once a function of capital, it acquires special characteristics.

The directing motive, the end and aim of capitalist production, is to extract the greatest possible amount of surplus-value, and consequently to exploit labour-power to the greatest possible extent. As the number of co-operating labourers increases, so too does their resistance to the domination of capital, and with it, the necessity for capital to overcome this resistance by counter-pressure. The control exercised by the capitalist is not only a special function, due to the nature of the social labour-process, and peculiar to that process, but it is, at the same time, a function of the exploitation of a social

labour-process, and is consequently rooted in the unavoidable antagonism between the exploiter and the living and labouring raw material he exploits.
[Ibid: 330–1]

6.15 The labour of supervision and management, arising as it does out of an antithesis, out of the supremacy of capital over labour, and being therefore common to all modes of production based on class contradictions like the capitalist mode, is directly and inseparably connected, also under the capitalist system, with productive functions which all combined social labour assigns to individuals as their special tasks. [...] It has already been remarked by Mr Ure that it is not the industrial capitalists, but the industrial managers who are 'the soul of our industrial system' [...]

The capitalist mode of production has brought matters to a point where the work of supervision, entirely divorced from the ownership of capital, is always readily obtainable. It has, therefore, come to be useless for the capitalist to perform it himself. An orchestra conductor need not own the instruments of his orchestra, nor is it within the scope of his duties as conductor to have anything to do with the 'wages' of the other musicians. Co-operative factories furnish proof that the capitalist has become no less redundant as a functionary in production than he himself, looking down from his high perch, finds the landowner redundant. Inasmuch as the capitalist's work does not originate in the purely capitalistic process of production, and hence does not cease on its own when capital ceases; inasmuch as it therefore originates from the social form of the labour-process, from combination and co-operation of many in pursuance of a common result, it is just as independent of capital as that form itself as soon as it has burst its capitalistic shell. To say that this labour is necessary as capitalistic labour, or as a function of the capitalist, only means that the *vulgus* is unable to conceive the forms developed in the lap of capitalist production, separate and free from their antithetical capitalist character. [...] In a co-operative factory the antagonistic nature of the labour of supervision disappears, because the manager is paid by the labourers instead of representing capital counterposed to them. Stock companies in general – developed with the credit system – have an increasing tendency to separate this work of management as a function from the ownership of capital [...] Only the functionary remains and the capitalist disappears as superfluous from the production process.
[*Capital* 3, 1864–5; 1865a: 387–8][89]

6.16 That co-operation which is based on division of labour, assumes its typical form in manufacture, and is the prevalent characteristic form of the capitalist process of production throughout the manufacturing period properly so-called. That period, roughly speaking, extends from the middle of the 16th to the last third of the 18th century.

[...]

The mode in which manufacture arises, its growth out of handicrafts, is [...] two-fold. On the one hand, it arises from the union of various independent handicrafts, which become stripped of their independence and specialised to such an extent as to be reduced to mere supplementary partial processes in the production of one particular commodity {Marx exemplifies making of carriages in a single workshop, p. 336}. On the other hand, it arises from the co-operation of artificers of one handicraft; it splits up that particular handicraft into its various detail operations, isolating, and making these operations independent of one another up to the point where each becomes the exclusive function of a particular labourer {Marx exemplifies papermaking and needle-manufacture, p. 334}. On the one hand, therefore, manufacture either introduces division of labour into a process of production, or further develops that division; on the other, it unites together handicrafts that were formerly separate. But whatever may have been its particular starting-point, its final form is invariably the same – a productive mechanism whose parts are human beings.

[*Capital* 1, 1867: 1867a: 336, 338]

6.17 In manufacture, as well as in simple co-operation, the collective working organism is a form of existence of capital. The mechanism that is made up of numerous individual detail labourers belongs to the capitalist. Hence, the productive power resulting from a combination of labours appears to be the productive power of capital. Manufacture proper not only subjects the previously independent workmen to the discipline and command of capital, but, in addition, creates a hierarchic gradation of the workmen themselves. While simple co-operation leaves the mode of working by the individual for the most part unchanged, manufacture thoroughly revolutionises it, and seizes labour-power by its very roots. It converts the labourer into a crippled monstrosity, by forcing his detail dexterity at the expense of a world of productive capabilities and instincts; just as in the States of La Plata they butcher a whole beast for the sake of his hide or his tallow. Not only is the detail work distributed to the different individuals, but the individual himself is made the automatic motor of a fractional operation, and the absurd fable of Menenius Agrippa, which makes man a mere fragment of his own body, becomes realised. If, at first, the workman sells his labour-power to capital, because the material means of producing a commodity fail him, now his very labour-power refuses its services unless it has been sold to capital. Its functions can be exercised only in an environment that exists in the workshop of the capitalist after the sale. By nature unfitted to make anything independently, the manufacturing labourer develops productive activity as a mere appendage of the capitalist's workshop. As the chosen people bore in their features the sign manual of Jehovah, so division of labour brands the manufacturing workman as the property of capital.

The knowledge, the judgement, and the will, which, though in ever so small a degree, are practiced by the independent peasant or handicraftsman, in the same way as the savage makes the whole art of war consist in the exercise of his personal cunning – these faculties are now required only for the workshop as a whole. Intelligence in production expands in one direction, because it vanishes in many others. What is lost by the detail labourers, is concentrated in the capital that employs them. It is a result of the division of labour in manufactures, that the labourer is brought face to face with the intellectual potencies of the material process of production, as the property of another, and as a ruling power. This separation begins in simple co-operation, where the capitalist represents to the single workman, the oneness and the will of the associated labour. It is developed in manufacture which cuts down the labourer into a detail labourer. It is completed in modern industry, which makes science a productive force distinct from labour and presses it into the service of capital.

In manufacture, in order to make the collective labourer, and through him capital, rich in social productive power, each labourer must be made poor in individual productive powers.
[Ibid: 360–1]

6.18 Under the present system, if a crooked spine, twisted limbs, a one-sided development of certain muscles, etc., makes you more capable of working (more productive), then your crooked spine, your twisted limbs, your one-sided muscular movement are a productive force. If your intellectual vacuity is more productive than your abundant intellectual activity, then your intellectual vacuity is a productive force, etc., etc. If the monotony of an occupation makes

you better suited for that occupation, then monotony is a productive force.
[Draft of an article on Friedrich List, 1845; 1845a: 285]

6.19 By decomposition of handicrafts, by specialisation of the instruments of labour, by the formation of detail labourers, and by grouping and combining the latter into a single mechanism, division of labour in manufacture creates a qualitative gradation, and a quantitative proportion in the social process of production; it consequently creates a definite organisation of the labour of society, and thereby develops at the same time new productive forces in the society. In its specific capitalist form – and under the given conditions, it could take no other form than a capitalistic one – manufacture is but a particular method for begetting relative surplus-value, or of augmenting at the expense of the labourer the self-expansion of capital – usually called social wealth, 'Wealth of Nations', etc. It increases the social productive power of labour, not only for the benefit of the capitalist instead of for that of the labourer, but it does this by crippling the individual labourers. It creates new conditions for the lordship of capital over labour. If, therefore, on the one hand, it presents itself historically as a progress and as a necessary phase in the development of society, on the other hand, it is a refined and civilised method of exploitation.
[*Capital* 1, 1867; 1867a: 364]

6.20 At the same time manufacture was unable, either to seize upon the production of society to its full extent, or to revolutionise that production to its very core. It towered up as an economic work of art, on the broad foundation of the town handicrafts, and of the rural domestic industries. At a given stage in its development, the narrow technical basis on which manufacture rested, came into conflict with requirements of production that were created by manufacture itself.

One of its most finished creations was the workshop for the production of the instruments of labour themselves, including especially the complicated mechanical apparatus then already employed. [...] This workshop, the product of the division of labour in manufacture, produced in its turn – machines. It is they that sweep away the handicraftman's work as the regulating principle of social production. Thus, on the one hand, the technical reason for the life-long annexation of the workman to a detail function is removed.

On the other hand, the fetters that this same principle laid on the dominion of capital, fall away.
[Ibid: 368]

6.21 Only the capitalist production of commodities has become an epoch-making mode of exploitation which, in the course of its historical development, revolutionises, through the organisation of the labour-process and the enormous improvement of technique, the entire economic structure of society in a manner eclipsing all former epochs. [*Capital* 2, MS VI, 1877–8; 1878: 37]

6.22 We have demonstrated in detail {in Part 4 of *Capital* 1} the crucial importance of *relative surplus-value*. This arises when the individual capitalist is spurred on to seize the *initiative* by the fact that value = the socially necessary labour-time objectified in the product and that therefore *surplus-value* is created for him as soon as the *individual* value of his product falls *below* its social value {Marx means that it can be produced in less than the prevailing socially necessary labour-time} and can be sold accordingly at a price *above* its individual value {i.e., above what it actually costs the individual capital to produce}. With the production of relative surplus-value the entire real form of production is altered and a *specifically capitalist form of production* comes into being (at the technological level too). Based on this, and simultaneously with it, the corresponding *relations of production* between the various agents of production and above all between the capitalist and the wage labourer, come into being for the first time.

The *social* productive forces of labour, or the productive forces of directly social, *socialized* (i.e. collective) labour come into being through co-operation, division of labour within the workshop, the use of *machinery*, and in general the transformation of production through the conscious *use* of the sciences, of mechanics, chemistry, etc. for specific ends, technology, etc. and similarly, through the enormous increase of *scale* corresponding to such developments (for it is only socialized labour that is capable of applying the *general* products of human development, such as mathematics, to the immediate processes of production; and conversely, progress in these sciences presupposes a certain level of material production). This entire development of the productive forces of *socialized labour* (in contrast to the more or less isolated labour of individuals), and together with it the *use of science* (the *general* product of social development), in the *immediate process of production*, takes the form of the *productive power of capital*. It does not appear as the productive power of labour, or even of that part of it that is identical with capital. And least of all does it appear as the productive power either of the individual worker or of the workers joined together in the process of production. The mystification implicit in the relations of capital as a whole is greatly intensified here, far beyond the point it had reached or could have reached in the merely formal subsumption of labour under capital. On the other hand, we here find a striking illustration of the historic significance of capitalist production in its specific form – the transmutation of the immediate process of production itself and the development of the social forces of production of labour.

It has been shown {in *Capital* 1, Part 3} how not merely at the level of ideas, but also in reality, the social character of his labour confronts the worker as something not merely alien, but hostile and antagonistic, when it appears before him objectified and personified in capital.

If the production of absolute surplus-value was the material expression of the formal subsumption of labour under capital, then the production of relative surplus-value may be viewed as its real subsumption.
[Results of the immediate process of production, between 1863 and 1866; 1866: 1023–5]

6.23 The general features of the *formal subsumption* remain, viz. the direct *subordination of the labour process to capital*, irrespective of the state of its technological development. But on this foundation there now arises a technologically and otherwise *specific mode of production – capitalist production* – which transforms the nature *of the labour process and its actual conditions*. Only when that happens do we witness the *real subsumption of labour under capital*.
[...]
The real subsumption of labour under capital is developed in all the forms evolved by relative, as opposed to absolute surplus-value.

With the real subsumption of labour under capital a complete (and constantly repeated) revolution takes place in the mode of production, in the productivity of the workers and in the relations between workers and capitalists.

With the real subsumption of labour under capital, all the changes in the labour process already discussed now become a reality. The *social forces of production* of labour are now developed, and with large-scale production comes the direct application of science and

technology. On the one hand, *capitalist production* now establishes itself as a mode of production *sui generis* and brings into being a new mode of material production. On the other hand, the latter itself forms the basis for the development of capitalist relations whose adequate form, therefore, presupposes a definite stage in the evolution of the productive forces of labour.
[Ibid: 1034–5]

6.24 At any rate, if we consider the two forms of surplus-value, absolute and relative, separately, we shall see that absolute surplus-value always precedes relative. To these two forms of surplus-value there correspond two separate forms of the subsumption or subordination of labour under capital, or two distinct forms of capitalist production. And here too one form always precedes the other, although the second form, the more highly developed one, can provide the foundations for the introduction of the first in new branches of industry.
[Ibid: 1025]

A page later Marx underscores the point: formal subsumption of labour under capital, he says, is 'the premiss and precondition of its *real* subsumption'. Likewise in *Capital*:

6.25 The prolongation of the working-day beyond the point at which the labourer would have produced just an equivalent for the value of his labour-power, and the appropriation of that surplus-labour by capital, this is the production of absolute surplus-value. It forms the general groundwork of the capitalist system, and the starting-point for the production of relative surplus-value. The latter pre-supposes that the working-day is already divided into two parts, necessary labour, and surplus-labour. In order to prolong the surplus-labour, the necessary labour is shortened by methods whereby the equivalent for the wages is produced in less time. The production of absolute surplus-value turns exclusively upon the length of the working-day; the production of relative surplus-value, revolutionises out and out the technical processes of labour, and the composition of society. It therefore pre-supposes a specific mode, the capitalist mode of production, a mode which, along with its methods, means, and conditions, arises and develops itself spontaneously on the foundation afforded by the formal subjection of labour to capital. In the course of this development, the formal subjection is replaced by the real subjection of labour to capital.
[*Capital* 1, 1867; 1867a: 509–10]

6.26 The implements of labour, in the form of machinery, necessitate the substitution of natural forces for human force, and the conscious application of science, instead of rule of thumb. In Manufacture, the organisation of the social labour-process is purely subjective; it is a combination of detail-labourers; in the machinery system, Modern Industry has a productive organism that is purely objective, in which the labourer becomes a mere appendage to an already existing material condition of production. In simple co-operation, and even in that founded on division of labour, the suppression of the isolated, by the collective, workman still appears to be more or less accidental. Machinery [...] operates only by means of associated labour, or labour in common. Hence the co-operative character of the labour-process is, in the latter case, a technical necessity dictated by the instrument of labour itself.
[Ibid: 386]

6.27 Along with the tool, the skill of the workman in handling it passes over to the machine. The capabilities of the tool are emancipated from the restraints that are inseparable from human labour-power. Thereby the technical foundation on which is based the division of labour in Manufacture, is swept away. Hence, in the place of the hierarchy of specialised workmen that characterise manufacture, there steps, in the automatic factory, a tendency to equalise and reduce to one and the same level the work that has to be done by the minders of the machines [...]

Here as everywhere else, we must distinguish between the increased productiveness due to the development of the social process of production, and that due to the capitalist exploitation of that process. In handicrafts and manufacture, the workman makes use of a tool, in the factory, the machine makes use of him. There the movements of the instrument of labour proceed from him, here it is the movements of the machine that he must follow. In manufacture the workmen are parts of a living mechanism. In the factory we have a lifeless mechanism independent of the workman, who becomes its mere living appendage. [...] At the same time that factory work exhausts the nervous system to the uttermost, it does away with the many-sided play of the muscles, and confiscates every atom of freedom, both in bodily and intellectual activity. The lightening of the labour, even, becomes a sort of torture, since the machine does not free the labourer from work, but deprives the work of all interest. Every kind of capitalist production, in so far as it is not only a labour-process, but also a process of creating surplus-value, has this in common, that

it is not the workman that employs the instruments of labour, but the instruments of labour that employ the workman. But it is only in the factory system that this inversion for the first time acquires technical and palpable reality. By means of its conversion into an automaton, the instrument of labour confronts the labourer, during the labour-process, in the shape of capital, dead labour, that dominates, and pumps dry, living labour-power. The separation of the intellectual powers of production from the manual labourer, and the conversion of those powers into the might of capital over labour, is [...] finally completed by modern industry erected on the foundation of machinery. The special skill of each individual insignificant factory operative vanishes as an infinitesimal quantity before the science, the gigantic physical forces, and the mass of labour that are embodied in the factory mechanism, and, together with that mechanism, constitute the power of the 'master'.
[Ibid: 420, 422–3]

6.28 Capital's creation of *absolute surplus value* – more objectified labour – is conditional upon the expansion, indeed the constant expansion, of the periphery of circulation. The *surplus value* produced at one point requires the production of surplus value at *another* point, for which it may be exchanged. [...] A condition of production based on capital is therefore *the production of a constantly expanding periphery of circulation*, whether the sphere is directly expanded, *or whether* more points within it *become points of production*.

[...] Hence, just as capital has the tendency to produce ever more surplus labour, it has the complementary tendency to produce more points of exchange. With respect to *absolute* surplus value or surplus labour, this means that capital tends to generate more surplus labour as complement to itself; *au fond*, that it tends to propagate production based on capital or the mode of production corresponding to it. The tendency to create the *world market* is inherent directly in the concept of capital itself. [...]

On the other side, the production of *relative surplus value*, i.e. the production of surplus value based upon the increase and development of the productive forces, requires production of new consumption, so that the sphere of consumption within circulation is enlarged, as that of production [of absolute surplus value] was enlarged before. Firstly, quantitative increase in existing consumption; secondly, the creation of new needs by the propagation of existing ones over a wider area; *thirdly*, production of *new* needs and discovery and creation of new use values. In other words, it requires that the surplus labour obtained does not remain a merely quantitative surplus, but that at the same time the range of qualitatively distinct types of labour (including surplus labour) must be constantly extended, rendered more diverse, and internally differentiated.

[...]

Hence the exploration of the whole of nature in order to discover new useful properties of things; the universal exchange of the products coming from the most diverse climates and lands; new (artificial) modes of processing natural objects to give them new use values. [...] The all-round exploration of the earth to discover both new useful objects and new uses for old objects, such as their use as raw materials, etc.; hence the development of the natural sciences to their highest point; the discovery, creation and satisfaction of new needs arising from society itself; cultivating all the qualities of social man and producing him in a form as rich in possible in needs because rich in qualities and relations – producing man as the most total and universal product possible (for in order to enjoy many different kinds of things he must be capable of enjoyment, that is he must be cultivated to a high degree)[90] – all these are new branches of production based on capital. [...]

Thus, just as production based on capital produces universal industry, i.e. surplus labour, value-creating labour, on the one hand, so does it on the other produce a system of universal exploitation of natural and human qualities, a system of universal utility, whose bearer is science itself as much as all the physical and spiritual qualities, and under these conditions nothing appears as something *higher-in-itself*, as an end in itself, outside this circle of social production and exchange. Thus it is only capital which creates bourgeois society and the universal appropriation of nature and of the social nexus itself by the members of society. Hence the great civilising influence of capital; hence its production of a stage of society compared to which all previous stages seem merely *local developments* of humanity and *idolatry of nature*. For the first time, nature becomes purely an object for men, nothing more than a matter of utility. It ceases to be acknowledged as a power for itself, and even the theoretical cognition of its autonomous laws appears merely as a stratagem for its subjection to human needs, whether as object of consumption or means of production. It is this same tendency which makes capital drive beyond national boundaries and prejudices and, equally, beyond nature worship, as well as beyond the traditional satisfaction of existing needs and the reproduction of old ways of life confined within long-established and complacently accepted limits.

Capital is destructive towards, and constantly revolutionises, all this, tearing down all barriers which impede the development of the productive forces, the extension of the range of needs, the differentiation of production, and the exploitation and exchange of all natural and spiritual powers.

But from the fact that capital posits every such limit as a barrier which it has *ideally* already overcome, it does not at all follow that capital has *really* overcome it; and since every such limit contradicts the determination of capital, its production is subject to contradictions which are constantly overcome but just as constantly posited. Moreover, the universality for which capital constantly strives, comes up against barriers in capital's own nature, barriers which at a certain stage of its development will allow it to be recognised as being itself the greatest barrier in the way of this tendency, and will therefore drive towards its transcendence through itself.

[*Grundrisse*, 1857–8; 1858a: 334–7]

6.29 The bourgeoisie, historically, has played a most revolutionary part. [...] It has been the first to show what man's activity can bring about. It has accomplished wonders far surpassing Egyptian pyramids, Roman aqueducts, and Gothic cathedrals; it has conducted expeditions that put in the shade all former Exoduses of nations and crusades.

The bourgeoisie cannot exist without constantly revolutionising the instruments of production, and thereby the relations of production, and with them the whole relations of society. Conservation of the old modes of production in unaltered form was, on the contrary, the first condition of existence for all earlier industrial classes. Constant revolutionising of production, uninterrupted disturbance of all social conditions, everlasting uncertainty and agitation distinguish the bourgeois epoch from all earlier ones. All fixed, fast-frozen relations, with their train of ancient and venerable prejudices and opinions, are swept away, all new-formed ones become antiquated before they can ossify. All that is solid melts into air, all that is holy is profaned, and man is at last compelled to face with sober senses, his real conditions of life, and his relations with his kind.

The need of a constantly expanding market for its products chases the bourgeoisie over the whole surface of the globe. It must nestle everywhere, settle everywhere, establish connections everywhere.

The bourgeoisie has through its cosmopolitan character given a cosmopolitan character to production and consumption in every country. To the great chagrin of Reactionists, it has drawn from under the feet of industry the national ground on which it stood. All old-established national industries have been destroyed or are daily being destroyed. They are dislodged by new industries, whose introduction becomes a life and death question for all civilised nations, by industries that no longer work up indigenous raw materials, but raw material drawn from the remotest zones; industries whose products are consumed, not only at home, but in every quarter of the globe. In place of the old wants, satisfied by the productions of the country, we find new wants, requiring for their satisfaction the products of distant lands and climes. In place of the old local and national seclusion and self-sufficiency, we have intercourse in every direction, universal inter-dependence of nations. And as in material, so also in intellectual production. The intellectual creations of individual nations become common property. National one-sidedness and narrow-mindedness become more and more impossible, and from the numerous national and local literatures, there arises a world literature.

The bourgeoisie, by the rapid improvement of all instruments of production, by the immensely facilitated means of communication, draws all, even the most barbarian, nations into civilisation. The cheap prices of its commodities are the heavy artillery with which it batters down all Chinese walls, with which it forces the barbarians' obstinate hatred of foreigners to capitulate. It compels all nations, on pain of extinction, to adopt the bourgeois mode of production; it compels them to introduce what it calls civilisation into their midst, i.e., to become bourgeois themselves. In one word, it creates a world after its own image.

The bourgeoisie has subjected the country to the rule of the towns. It has created enormous cities, has greatly increased the urban population as compared with the rural, and has thus rescued a considerable part of the population from the idiocy of rural life. Just as it has made the country dependent on the towns, so it has made barbarian and semi-barbarian countries dependent on the civilised ones, nations of peasants on nations of bourgeois, the East on the West.

The bourgeoisie keeps more and more doing away with the scattered state of the population, of the means of production, and of property. It has agglomerated population, centralised means of production, and has concentrated property in a few hands. The necessary consequence of this was political centralisation. Independent, or but loosely connected provinces with separate interests, laws, governments and systems of taxation, became lumped together into one nation, with one government, one code of laws, one national class-interest, one frontier and one customs-tariff.

The bourgeoisie, during its rule of scarce one hundred years, has created more massive and more colossal productive forces than have all preceding generations together. Subjection of Nature's forces to man, machinery, application of chemistry to industry and agriculture, steam-navigation, railways, electric telegraphs, canalisation of rivers, whole populations conjured out of the ground – what earlier century had even a presentiment that such productive forces slumbered in the lap of social labour?
[Manifesto of the Communist Party, 1848; 1848b: 486–9]

6.30 On the one hand, the immediate effect of machinery is to increase the supply of raw material in the same way, for example, as the cotton gin augmented the production of cotton. On the other hand, the cheapness of the articles produced by machinery, and the improved means of transport and communication furnish the weapons for conquering foreign markets. By ruining handicraft production in other countries, machinery forcibly converts them into fields for the supply of its raw material. In this way East India was compelled to produce cotton, wool, hemp, jute, and indigo for Great Britain. By constantly making a part of the hands 'supernumerary', modern industry, in all countries where it has taken root, gives a spur to emigration and the colonisation of foreign lands, which are thereby converted into settlements for growing the raw material of the mother country, just as Australia, for example, was converted into a colony for growing wool. A new and international division of labour, a division suited to the requirements of the chief centres of modern industry springs up, and converts one part of the globe into a chiefly agricultural field of production, for supplying the other part which remains a chiefly industrial field.
[*Capital* 1, 1867; 1867a: 451]

In detailed discussions of Ireland, Marx makes clear the degree to which capitalist development may (forcibly) entail what would nowadays be called 'underdevelopment': England 'struck down the manufactures of Ireland, depopulated her cities, and threw her people back on the land'; 'every time Ireland was about to develop industrially, she was crushed and reconverted into a purely agricultural land'; one 'forced to contribute cheap labour and cheap capital to building up "the great works of Britain"' [MS of 1867; 1867c: 139, 142, 143]

6.31 Capital has not invented surplus-labour. Wherever a part of

society possesses a monopoly of the means of production, the labourer, free or not free, must add to the working-time necessary for his own maintenance an extra working-time in order to produce the means of subsistence for the owners of the means of production, whether this proprietor be the Athenian {aristocrat}, Etruscan theocrat, civis Romanus, Norman baron, American slave-owner, Wallachian Boyard, modern landlord or capitalist. It is, however, clear that in any given economic formation of society, where not the exchange-value but the use-value of the product predominates, surplus-labour will be limited by a given set of wants which may be greater or less and that here no boundless thirst for surplus-labour arises from the nature of the production itself. [...] But as soon as people, whose production still moves within the lower forms of slave-labour, corvée-labour, &c., are drawn into the whirlpool of an international market dominated by the capitalistic mode of production, the sale of their products for export becoming their principal interest, the civilised horrors of over-work are grafted onto the barbaric horrors of slavery, serfdom, &c. Hence the negro labour in the Southern States of the American Union preserved something of a patriarchal character, so long as production was chiefly directed to immediate local consumption. But in proportion, as the export of cotton became of vital interest to these states, the over-working of the negro and sometimes the using up of his life in 7 years of labour became a factor in a calculated and calculating system. It was no longer a question of obtaining from him a certain quantity of useful products. It was now a question of production of surplus-labour itself. So was it also with the corvee, e.g., in the Danubian Principalities (now Roumania).
[*Capital* 1, 1867; 1867a: 235–6]

6.32 Direct slavery is as much the pivot of bourgeois industry as machinery, credits, etc. Without slavery you have no cotton; without cotton you have no modern industry. It is slavery that gave the colonies their value; it is the colonies that created world trade, and it is world trade that is the pre-condition of large-scale industry. Thus slavery is an economic category of the greatest importance.
[*The Poverty of Philosophy*, 1847; 1847a: 167]

In *Capital* Marx argues that 'there is not the least doubt that the rapid strides in cotton spinning, not only pushed on with tropical luxuriance the growth of cotton in the United States, and with it the African slave trade, but also made the breeding of slaves the chief business of the border slave-states' (1867a: 443–4). Likewise in a

Die Presse article: 'The cotton monopoly of the slave states of the American Union is not a natural, but an historical monopoly. It grew and developed simultaneously with the monopoly of the English cotton industry on the world market [...] the industry in Lancashire and Yorkshire {rested} on the sovereignty of the slave-whip in Georgia and Alabama' (1861b: 84–5).

6.33 The exchange of living labour for objectified labour – i.e. the positing of social labour in the form of the contradiction of capital and wage labour – is the ultimate development of the *value-relation* and of production resting on value. Its presupposition is – and remains – the mass of direct labour time, the quantity of labour employed, as the determinant factor in the production of wealth. But to the degree that large industry develops, the creation of real wealth comes to depend less on labour time and on the amount of labour employed than on the power of the agencies set in motion during labour time, whose 'powerful effectiveness' is itself in turn out of all proportion to the direct labour time spent on their production, but depends rather on the general state of science and on the progress of technology, or the application of this science to production. [...] Real wealth manifests itself, rather – and large industry reveals this – in the monstrous disproportion between the labour time applied, and its product, as well as in the qualitative imbalance between labour, reduced to a pure abstraction, and the power of the production process it superintends. Labour no longer appears so much to be included within the production process; rather, the human being comes to relate more as watchman and regulator of the production process itself. (What holds for machinery holds likewise for the combination of human activities and the development of human intercourse.) [...] In this transformation, it is neither the direct human labour he himself performs, nor the time during which he works, but rather the appropriation of his own general productive power, his understanding of nature and his mastery over it by virtue of his presence as a social body – it is, in a word, the development of the social individual which appears as the great foundation-stone of production and of wealth. The *theft of alien labour time, on which the present wealth is based*, appears as a miserable foundation in the face of this new one, created by large-scale industry itself. As soon as labour in the direct form has ceased to be the great well-spring of wealth, labour time ceases and must cease to be its measure, and hence exchange value [must cease to be the measure] of use value. The *surplus labour of the mass* has ceased to be the condition for the development of the general wealth, just as the *non-labour of* *the few*, for the development of the general powers of the human head. With that, production based on exchange value breaks down, and the direct, material production process is stripped of the form of penury and antithesis. The free development of individualities, and hence not the reduction of necessary labour time so as to posit surplus labour, but rather the general reduction of the necessary labour of society to a minimum, which then corresponds to the artistic, scientific etc. development of the individuals in the time set free, and with the means created, for all of them. Capital itself is the moving contradiction, [in] that it presses to reduce labour time to a minimum, while it posits labour time, on the other side, as sole measure and source of wealth. Hence it diminishes labour time in the necessary form so as to increase it in the superfluous form; hence posits the superfluous in growing measure as a condition – question of life and death – for the necessary. On the one side, then, it calls to life all the powers of science and of nature, as of social combination and social intercourse, in order to make the creation of wealth independent (relatively) of the labour time employed upon it. On the other side, it wants to use labouring time as the measuring rod for the giant social forces thereby created, and to confine them within the limits required to maintain the already created value as value. Forces of production and social relations – two different sides of the development of the social individual – appear to capital as mere means, and are merely means for it to produce on its limited foundation. In fact, however, they are the material conditions to blow this foundation sky-high.

[*Grundrisse*, 1857–8; Nicolaus: 705–6]

7

Civil society

E. P. Thompson has argued that Marx's focus, after the 1840s, on political economy had the effect of limiting his sociology.[91] His wholesale critique of bourgeois *society* became caught up in the snares of an 'anti-political economy'. I believe Thompson overstates his case. But it is certainly true that Marx treated some issues much more fully in earlier writings than ever again. These include individualism, the modern state, law, morality and religion: the 'surface' forms of modern society.[92] I give particular attention to Marx's analysis of the relation between a 'civil society' of 'abstract individuals', and the 'political state'.[93] Although this chapter rests largely on Marx's early writings, I have included several later passages, particularly 7.30, from the first draft of *The Civil War in France*,[94] to indicate the continuity of his thinking on these issues. We might also note Marx's anticipations of some central concerns of a later generation of sociologists: Durkheim, on the peculiar paradox of that division of labour which both individualizes and interlinks; Weber, on both bureaucracy and the Protestant ethic; Simmel, on the enduringly transitory quality of modern life.

7.1 With money every form of intercourse, and intercourse itself, becomes fortuitous for the individuals. Thus money implies that all intercourse up till now was only intercourse of individuals under particular conditions, not of individuals as individuals [...]. On the other hand, the individuals themselves are entirely subordinated to the division of labour and hence are brought into the most complete dependence on one another.

[*The German Ideology*, 1845–6; 1846a: 85–6]

7.2 When we consider social conditions which produce an undeveloped system of exchange, of exchange-values and of money, or to which these correspond only in an undeveloped form, it is clear from the outset that individuals, although their relationships appear to be more personal, only enter into relations with each other as individuals in a particular determination, as feudal lord and vassal, lord of the manor and serf, etc., or as members of castes, etc., or as members of an estate, etc. In money relations, in a developed system of exchange (and this appearance leads democracy astray), the ties of personal dependence, distinctions of birth, education, etc. (all the personal ties at least appear as *personal* relationships), are in fact broken, abolished. The individuals *appear* to be independent (this independence, which altogether is merely an illusion and should more correctly be called unconcern, in the sense of indifference), appear to collide with each other freely, and to exchange with each other in this freedom; but they appear independent only to those who abstract from the *conditions*, the *conditions of existence*, in which those individuals come into contact with each other (and these in turn are independent of the individuals and appear, though produced by society, as it were, as *natural conditions*, i.e. beyond the control of the individuals).

The determinateness which in the first case appears as a personal limitation of one individual by another, appears in the second case, in its developed form, as an objective limitation of the individual by relationships which are independent of him and self-sufficient. (Since the single individual cannot shed his personal determinateness but can overcome external relationships and subordinate them to himself, his freedom *appears* greater in the second case. A closer examination of those external relationships and conditions shows, however, that it is impossible for the individuals of a class, etc., to overcome them *en masse* without abolishing them. A single individual may by chance cope with them; the mass of individuals dominated by them cannot do so, since the very existence of that mass expresses the subordination, and the necessary subordination, of the individuals to it.)

These external relationships, far from abolishing the 'relationships of dependence', merely dissolve them into a general form; they are rather the elaboration of the general *foundation* of relationships of personal dependence. Here, too, individuals enter into relation with each other only as determinate individuals. These *objective* relationships of dependence, in contrast to the *personal* ones, also appear in such a way that the individuals are now ruled by *abstractions* whereas previously they were dependent on one another. (The objective relationship of dependence is nothing but the social relations independently confronting the seemingly independent individuals, i.e. their own reciprocal relations of production which have acquired an existence independent of and separate from them.) Yet the abstraction or idea is nothing but the theoretical expression of those material relationships which dominate the individuals.

Relationships can naturally be expressed only in ideas, and so philosophers have seen the peculiarity of modern times in the individuals' being dominated by ideas, and have identified the birth of free individuality with the overthrow of this domination of ideas.[95] From the ideological standpoint, this mistake was the easier to make because that domination of relationships (that objective dependence, which incidentally is transformed into certain personal relationships of dependence, only divested of all illusion) appears in the consciousness of individuals themselves to be the rule of ideas, and the belief in the eternal validity of these ideas, i.e. of those objective relationships of dependence, is of course in every way reinforced, sustained, drummed into people by the ruling classes.

(With regard to the illusion of the 'purely personal relationships' of feudal times, etc., we must not of course for a moment forget: (1) that in a certain phase, these relationships themselves acquired within their sphere an objective character, as is shown by the development of landed property relationships, for example, out of purely military subordination.[96] But, (2) the objective relationship in which they founder has itself a restricted, naturally determined character and thus *appears* as personal, whereas in the modern world personal relationships emerge purely as the outcome of the relationships of production and exchange.)

[*Grundrisse*, 1857–8; 1858a: 100–2; compare passage 3.8, p.20]

7.3 Individuals have always proceeded from themselves, but of course from themselves within their given historical conditions and relations, not from the 'pure' individual in the sense of the ideologists. But in the course of historical development, and precisely through the fact that within the division of labour social relations inevitably take on an independent existence, there appears a cleavage in the life of each individual, insofar as it is personal and insofar as it is determined by some branch of labour and the conditions pertaining to it. (We do not mean it to be understood from this that, for example, the rentier, the capitalist, etc., cease to be persons; but their personality is conditioned and determined by quite definite class relations, and the cleavage appears only in their opposition to another class and, for themselves, only when they go bankrupt.) In the estate (and even more in the tribe) this is as yet concealed: for instance, a nobleman always remains a nobleman, a commoner always a commoner, a quality inseparable from his individuality irrespective of his other relations. The difference between the private individual and the class individual, the accidental nature of the conditions of life for the individual, appear only with the emergence of the class, which is itself a product of the bourgeoisie. This accidental character as such is only engendered and developed by competition and the struggle of individuals among themselves. Thus, in imagination, individuals seem freer under the dominance of the bourgeoisie than before, because their conditions of life seem accidental; in reality, of course, they are less free, because they are to a greater extent governed by material forces.

[*The German Ideology*, 1845–6; 1846a: 78–9]

7.4 Thus two facts are here revealed. First the productive forces appear as a world for themselves, quite independent of and divorced from the individuals, alongside the individuals; the reason for this is that the individuals, whose forces they are, exist split up and in opposition to one another, whilst, on the other hand, these forces are only real forces in the intercourse and association of these individuals. Thus, on the one hand, we have a totality of productive forces, which have, as it were, taken on a material form and are for the individuals themselves no longer the forces of the individuals but of private property, and hence of the individuals only insofar as they are owners of private property. Never, in any earlier period, have the productive forces taken on a form so indifferent to the intercourse of individuals *as* individuals, because their intercourse itself was still a restricted one. On the other hand, standing against these productive forces, we have the majority of the individuals from whom these forces have been wrested away, and who, robbed thus of all real life-content, have become abstract individuals, who are, however, by this very fact put into a position to enter into relation with one another *as individuals*.

[Ibid: 86–7]

7.5 Maine[97] ignores the much deeper point: that the seeming supreme independent existence of the State is itself only seeming and that it is in all its forms an excrescence of society; just as its appearance itself arises only at a certain stage of social development, it disappears again as soon as society has reached a stage not yet attained. First the tearing of the individuality loose from the originally not despotic chains (as blockhead Maine understands it), but rather satisfying and agreeable bonds of the group, of the primitive community – and therewith the one-sided elaboration of the individuality.
[Ethnological Notebooks, 1880–1; 1881a: 39][98]

7.6 It is obvious that the political constitution as such is brought into being only where the private spheres have won an independent existence. Where trade and landed property are not free and have not yet become independent, the political constitution too does not yet exist. The Middle Ages were the *democracy of unfreedom*.

The abstraction of the *state as such* belongs only to modern times, because the abstraction of private life belongs only to modern times. The abstraction of the *political state* is a modern product.

In the Middle Ages there were serfs, feudal estates, merchant and trade guilds, corporations of scholars, etc.: that is to say, in the Middle Ages property, trade, society, man are *political*; every private sphere has a political character or is a political sphere; that is, politics is a characteristic of the private spheres too. In the Middle Ages the political constitution is the constitution of private property, but only because the constitution of private property is a political constitution. In the Middle Ages the life of the nation and the life of the state are identical. Man is the actual principle of the state – but *unfree* man. It is thus the *democracy of unfreedom* – estrangement carried to completion. The abstract reflected antithesis belongs only to the modern world. The Middle Ages are the period of *actual* dualism; modern times, one of *abstract* dualism.

[...]

In the spontaneously evolved monarchy, democracy or aristocracy there is as yet no political constitution as distinct from the actual, material state or the other content of the life of the nation. The political state does not yet appear as the *form* of the material state. Either, as in Greece, the *res publica* is the real private affair of the citizens, their real content, and the private individual is a slave; the political state, *qua* political state, being the true and only content of the life and will of the citizens; or, as in an Asiatic despotism, the political state is nothing but the personal caprice of a single individual; or the political

state, like the material state, is a slave. What distinguishes the modern state from these states characterised by the substantial unity between people and state is not, as Hegel[99] would have it, that the various elements of the constitution have been developed into a *particular* actuality, but that the constitution itself has been developed into a *particular* actuality alongside the actual life of the people – that the political state has become the *constitution* of the rest of the state.
[Critique of Hegel's *Rechtsphilosophie*, 1843; 1843b: 31–3]

7.7 Civil society and state are separated. Hence the citizen of the state is also separated from the citizen as a member of civil society. He must therefore effect a *fundamental division* with himself. As an *actual citizen* he finds himself in a twofold organization: the *bureaucratic* organization, which is an external, formal feature of the distant state, the executive, which does not touch him or his independent reality, and the *social* organization, the organization of civil society. But in the latter he stands as a *private person* outside the state; this social organization does not touch the political state as such. The former is a state organization for which he always provides the *material*. The second is a *civil organization* the material of which is not the state. In the former the state stands as formal antithesis to him, in the second he stands as material antithesis to the state. Hence, in order to behave as an *actual citizen of the state*, and to attain political significance and effectiveness, he must step out of his civil reality, disregard it, and withdraw from this whole organization into his individuality; for the sole existence which he finds for his citizenship of the state is his sheer, blank *individuality*, since the existence of the state as executive is complete without him, and his existence in civil society is complete without the state. He can be a *citizen of the state* only in contradiction to these *sole available communities*, only as an *individual*. His existence as a citizen of the state is an existence outside his *communal* existences and is therefore purely *individual* [...] The separation of civil society and political state necessarily appears as a separation of the *political* citizen, the citizen of the state, from civil society, from his own, actual, empirical reality, for as an idealist of the state he is *quite another being*, a *different*, distinct, opposed being. Civil society here effects within itself the relationship of state and civil society which already exists on the other side as *bureaucracy*.
[Ibid: 77–8]

7.8 Hegel proceeds from the *separation* of the 'state' and 'civil' society, from 'particular interests' and the 'intrinsically and explicitly general'; and indeed bureaucracy is based on *this separation*.

[...]

The 'bureaucracy' is the '*state formalism*' of civil society. It is the 'state consciousness', the 'state will', the 'state power', as *one corporation* – and thus a *particular*, *closed* society within the state [...]

The 'state formalism' which bureaucracy is, is the 'state as formalism'; and it is as a formalism of this kind that Hegel has described bureaucracy. Since this 'state formalism' constitutes itself as an actual power and itself becomes its own *material* content, it goes without saying that the 'bureaucracy' is a web of *practical* illusions, or the 'illusion of the state'. The bureaucratic spirit is a jesuitical, theological spirit through and through. The bureaucrats are the jesuits and theologians of the state. The bureaucracy is *la république prêtre* {the religious republic}.

Since by its *very nature* the bureaucracy is the 'state as formalism', it is also this as regards its *purpose*. The actual purpose of the state therefore appears to the bureaucracy as an objective *hostile* to the state. The spirit of the bureaucracy is the 'formal state spirit'. The bureaucracy therefore turns the 'formal state spirit' or the *actual* spiritlessness of the state into a categorical imperative. The bureaucracy takes itself to be the ultimate purpose of the state. Because the bureaucracy turns its 'formal' objectives into its content, it comes into conflict everywhere with 'real' objectives. It is therefore obliged to pass off the form for the content and the content for the form. State objectives are transformed into objectives of the department, and department objectives into objectives of the state. The bureaucracy is a circle from which no one can escape. Its hierarchy is a *hierarchy of knowledge*. The top entrusts the understanding of detail to the lower levels, whilst the lower levels credit the top with understanding of the general, and so all are mutually deceived.

The bureaucracy is the imaginary state alongside the real state – the spiritualism of the state. Each thing has therefore a double meaning, a real and a bureaucratic meaning, just as knowledge (and also the will) is both real and bureaucratic. The really existing, however, is treated in the light of its bureaucratic nature, its other-worldly, spiritual essence. The bureaucracy has the state, the spiritual essence of society, in its possession, as its *private property*. The general spirit of the bureaucracy is the *secret*, the mystery, preserved within itself by the hierarchy and against the outside world by being a closed corporation. Avowed political spirit, as also political-mindedness, therefore appear to the bureaucracy as *treason* against its mystery. Hence, *authority* is the basis of its knowledge, and the deification of authority is its *conviction*. Within the bureaucracy itself, however, *spiritualism* becomes *crass materialism*, the materialism of passive obedience, of faith in authority, of the *mechanism* of fixed and formalistic behaviour, and of fixed principles, views and traditions. In the case of the individual bureaucrat, the state objective turns into his private objective, into a *chasing after higher posts*, the *making of a career*. In the first place, he looks on actual life as something *material*, for the *spirit of this life has its distinctly separate existence* in the bureaucracy. The bureaucracy must therefore proceed to make life as material as possible. Secondly, actual life is material for the bureaucrat himself, i.e., so far as it becomes an object of bureaucratic manipulation; for his spirit is prescribed for him, his aim lies beyond him, and his existence is the existence of the department. The state only continues to exist as various fixed bureaucratic minds, bound together in subordination and passive obedience. *Actual* knowledge seems devoid of content, just as actual life seems dead; for this imaginary knowledge and this imaginary life are taken for the real thing. The bureaucrat must therefore deal with the actual state jesuitically, whether this jesuitry is conscious or unconscious. However, once its antithesis is knowledge, this jesuitry is likewise bound to achieve self-consciousness and then become deliberate jesuitry.

Whilst the bureaucracy is on the one hand this crass materialism, it manifests its crass spiritualism in the fact that it wants to *do everything*, i.e., by making the *will* the *causa prima*. For it is purely an *active* form of existence and receives its content from without and can prove its existence, therefore, only by shaping and restricting this content. For the bureaucrat the world is a mere object to be manipulated by him.

When Hegel calls the executive the *objective* aspect of the sovereignty dwelling in the monarch, that is right in the same sense in which the Catholic Church was the *real presence* of the sovereignty, substance and spirit of the Holy Trinity. In the bureaucracy the identity of state interest and particular private aim is established in such a way that the *state interest* becomes a *particular* private aim over against other private aims.

The abolition of the bureaucracy is only possible by the general interest *actually* – and not, as with Hegel, merely in thought, in *abstraction* – becoming the particular interest, which in turn is only possible as a result of the *particular* interest actually becoming the *general* interest.
[Ibid: 45–8][100]

7.9 In the genuine state it is not a question of the opportunity of every citizen to devote himself to the general estate as one particular estate, but the capacity of the general estate to be really general – that is, to be the estate of every citizen. But Hegel proceeds from the premise of the pseudo-general, illusory-general estate – the premise of generality as a particular estate {the bureaucracy}.

The identity which he has constructed between civil society and the state is the identity of *two hostile armies*, where every soldier has the 'opportunity' to become, by 'desertion', a member of the 'hostile' army; and indeed Hegel herewith correctly describes the present empirical position.

It is the same with his construction of the 'examinations'. In a rational state, to sit an examination should be demanded of a shoemaker rather than an executive civil servant. For shoemaking is a skill without which one can be a good citizen of the state and a social human being; whereas the necessary 'political knowledge' is a requirement without which a person in the state lives outside the state, cut off from himself, from the air. The 'examination' is nothing but a Masonic rite, the legal recognition of a knowledge of citizenship as a privilege.

The *examination* – this 'link' between the 'office of state' and the 'individual', this objective bond between the knowledge of civil society and the knowledge of the state – is nothing but the *bureaucratic baptism of knowledge*, the official recognition of the *transubstantiation* of profane into sacred knowledge (in every examination, it goes without saying, the examiner knows all). One does not hear that the Greek or Roman statesmen passed examinations. But of course, what is a Roman statesman against a Prussian government official!
[Ibid: 50–1]

7.10 The transformation of *state activities* into *official posts* presupposes the separation of the state from society.
[Ibid: 52]

7.11 It is an historical advance which has transformed the *political estates* {of medieval society} into *social* estates, so that, just as the Christians are equal in heaven, but unequal on earth, so the individual members of the nation are *equal* in the heaven of their political world, but unequal in the earthly existence of *society*. The real transformation of the *political* estates into *civil* estates took place in the *absolute monarchy*. The bureaucracy maintained the notion of unity against the various estates within the state. Nevertheless, the *social difference* of the estates, even alongside the bureaucracy of the absolute executive power, remained a political difference, *political within* and alongside the bureaucracy of the absolute executive power. Only the French Revolution completed the transformation of the *political* into *social* estates, or changed the *differences of estate* of civil society into mere *social* differences, into differences of civil life which are without significance in political life. With that the separation of political life from civil society was completed.

The estates of civil society were likewise transformed in the process: civil society was changed by its separation from political society. *Estate* in the medieval sense continued only within the bureaucracy itself, where civil and political position are directly identical. As against this stands civil society as *civil estate*. Difference of estate here is no longer a difference of *needs* and of *work* as independent bodies. The only general, *superficial and formal* difference still remaining here is that of *town* and *country*. Within society itself, however, the difference was developed in mobile and not fixed circles, of which *free choice* is the principle. *Money* and *education* are the main criteria. [...] The estate of civil society has for its principle neither need, that is, a natural element, nor politics. It consists of separate masses which form fleetingly and whose very formation is fortuitous and does *not* amount to an organisation.

Only one thing is characteristic, namely, that *lack of property* and the *estate of direct* labour, of concrete labour, form not so much an estate of civil society as the ground upon which its circles rest and move. The estate proper is confined to the *members of the executive authority*. The present-day estate of society already shows its difference from the earlier estate of civil society in that it does not hold the individual as it formerly did as something communal, as a community, but that it is partly accident, partly the work and so on of the individual which does, or does not, keep him in his estate, an *estate* which is itself only an *external* quality of the individual, being neither inherent in his labour nor standing to him in fixed relationships as an objective community organised according to rigid laws. It stands, rather, in no sort of *real* relation to his material actions, to his *real standing*. The physician does not form a special estate within civil society. One merchant belongs to a different estate from another, to a different *social position*. For just as civil society is separated from political society, so civil society has within itself become divided into *estate* and *social* position, however many relations may occur between them. The principle of the civil estate or of civil society is *enjoyment* and the *capacity to enjoy.* In his political significance the member of civil society frees himself from his estate, his true civil position; it is only here that he acquires importance as a *human being*, or that his quality as member of the state, as social being, appears as his *human* quality. For all his other qualities in civil society *appear inessential* to the human being, the individual, as *external* qualities which indeed are necessary for his existence in the whole, i.e., as a link with the whole, but a link that he can just as well throw away again. (Present-day civil society is the realised principle of *individualism*; the individual existence is the final goal; activity, work, content, etc., are *mere* means.)

[...]

The *real human being* is the *private individual* of the present-day state constitution.

In general, the *estate* has the significance that *difference* and *separation* constitute the *very existence* of the individual. His way of life, activity, etc., instead of turning him into a member, a function of society, make of him an *exception* to society, are his privilege. That this *difference* is not merely *individual* but is established as a *community*, estate or corporation, not only does not cancel its exclusive nature but is rather an expression of it. Instead of the individual function being a function of society, it turns, on the contrary, the individual function into a society for itself.

Not only is the *estate* based on the *separation* of society as the prevailing law; it separates the human being from his general essence, it turns him into an animal that is directly identical with its function. The Middle Ages are the *animal history* of human society, its zoology.

The modern era, *civilisation*, makes the opposite mistake. It separates the *objective* essence of the human being from him as merely something *external*, material. It does not accept the content of the human being as his true reality.

[Ibid: 79–81]

Three years later, in *The German Ideology*, Marx was to write bluntly that 'the *modern* state, the rule of the bourgeoisie, is based on *freedom of labour*' [1846a: 205].

7.12 The state abolishes, in its own way, distinctions of *birth*, *social rank*, *education*, *occupation*, when it declares that birth, social rank, education, occupation, are *non-political* distinctions, when it proclaims, without regard to these distinctions, that every member of the nation is an *equal* participant in national sovereignty, when it treats all elements of the real life of the nation from the standpoint of the state. Nevertheless, the state allows private property, education, occupation, to *act* in *their* way, i.e., as private property, as education, as occupation, and to exert the influence of their *special* nature. Far from abolishing these *real* distinctions, the state only exists on the presupposition of their existence; it feels itself to be a *political state* and asserts its *universality* only in opposition to these elements of its being [...]

The perfect political state is, by its nature, man's *species-life*, as *opposed* to his material life. All the preconditions of this egoistic life continue to exist in *civil society outside* the sphere of the state, but as qualities of civil society. Where the political state has attained its true development, man – not only in thought, in consciousness, but in *reality*, in *life* – leads a twofold life, a heavenly and an earthly life: life in the *political community*, in which he considers himself a *communal being*, and life in *civil society*, in which he acts as a *private individual*, regards other men as a means, degrades himself into a means, and becomes the plaything of alien powers. The relation of the political state to civil society is just as spiritual as the relation of heaven to earth. The political state stands in the same opposition to civil society, and it prevails over the latter in the same way as religion prevails over the narrowness of the secular world, i.e., by likewise always having to acknowledge it, to restore it, and allow itself to be dominated by it. In his *most immediate* reality, in civil society, man is a secular being. Here, where he regards himself as a real individual, and is so regarded by others, he is a *fictitious* phenomenon. In the state, on the other hand, where man is regarded as a species-being, he is the imaginary member of an illusory sovereignty, is deprived of his real individual life and endowed with an unreal universality.
[On the Jewish question, 1843; 1843c: 153–4]

7.13 Political emancipation is at the same time the *dissolution* of the old society on which the state alienated from the people, the sovereign power, is based. Political revolution is a revolution of civil society. What was the character of the old society? It can be described in one word – *feudalism*. The character of the old civil society was *directly political*, that is to say, the elements of civil life, for example, property, or the family, or the mode of labour, were raised to the level of elements of political life in the form of seignority, estates, and corporations. In this form they determined the relation of the individual to the *state as a whole*, i.e., his *political* relation, that is, his relation of separation and exclusion from the other components of society. For that organization of national life did not raise property or labour to the level of social elements; on the contrary, it completed their *separation* from the state as a whole and constituted them as *discrete* societies within society. Thus, the vital functions and conditions of life of civil society remained nevertheless political, although political in the feudal sense, that is to say, they secluded the individual from the state as a whole and they converted the *particular* relation of his corporation to the state as a whole into his general relation to the life of the nation, just as they converted his particular civil activity and situation into his general activity and situation. As a result of this organization, the unity of the state, and also the consciousness, will and activity of this unity, the general power of the state, are likewise bound to appear as the *particular* affair of a ruler isolated from the people, and of his servants.

The political revolution which overthrew this sovereign power and raised state affairs to become affairs of the people, which constituted the political state as a matter of *general* concern, that is, as a real state, necessarily smashed all estates, corporations, guilds, and privileges, since they were all manifestations of the separation of the people from the community. The political revolution thereby *abolished* the *political character of civil society*. It broke up civil society into its simple component parts; on the one hand, the *individuals*; on the other hand, the *material* and *spiritual elements* constituting the content of the life and social position of these individuals. It set free the political spirit, which had been, as it were, split up, partitioned and dispersed in the various blind alleys of feudal society. It gathered the dispersed parts of the political spirit, freed it from its intermixture with civil life, and established it as the sphere of the community, the *general* concern of the nation, ideally independent of those *particular* elements of civil life. A person's *distinct* activity and distinct situation in life were reduced to a merely individual significance. They no longer constituted the general relation of the individual to the state as a whole. Public affairs as such, on the other hand, became the general affair of each individual, and the political function became the individual's general function.

But the completion of the idealism of the state was at the same time the completion of the materialism of civil society. Throwing off the political yoke meant at the same time throwing off the bonds which restrained the egoistic spirit of civil society. Political emancipation was at the same time the emancipation of civil society from politics, from even having the *semblance* of a universal content.

Feudal society was resolved into its basic element – *man*, but man as he really formed its basis – *egoistic* man.

This *man*, the member of civil society, is thus the basis, the precondition, of the *political* state. He is recognised as such by this state in the rights of man.[101]

The liberty of egoistic man and the recognition of this liberty, however, is rather the recognition of the *unrestrained* movement of the spiritual and material elements which form the content of his life.

Hence man was not freed from religion, he received religious freedom. He was not freed from property, he received freedom to own property. He was not freed from the egoism of business, he received freedom to engage in business.

The *establishment of the political state* and the dissolution of civil society into independent *individuals* – whose relations with one another depend on *law*, just as the relations of men in the system of estates and guilds depended on *privilege* – is accomplished by *one and the same act*. Man as a member of civil society, *unpolitical* man, inevitably appears, however, as the *natural* man. The *droits de l'homme* {rights of man} appear as *droits naturels* {natural rights}, because *conscious activity* is concentrated on the *political act*. *Egoistic* man is the *passive* result of this dissolved society, a result that is simply *found in existence*, an object of *immediate certainty*, therefore a *natural* object. The *political revolution* resolves civil life into its component parts, without *revolutionising* these components themselves or subjecting them to criticism. It regards civil society, the world of needs, labour, private interests, civil law, as the *basis of its existence*, as a *precondition* not requiring further substantiation and therefore as its *natural basis*. Finally, man as a member of civil society is held to be man in the proper sense, *homme* as distinct from the *citoyen*, because he is man in his sensuous, individual, *immediate* existence, whereas *political* man is only abstract, artificial man, man as an *allegorical, juridical* person. The real man is recognised only in the shape of the *egoistic* individual, the *true* man is recognised only in the shape of the *abstract citoyen*.

[...]

All emancipation is a *reduction* of the human world and relationships to *man himself*.

Political emancipation is the reduction of man, on the one hand, to a member of civil society, to an *egoistic, independent* individual, and, on the other hand, to a *citizen*, a juridical person.

Only when the real, individual man re-absorbs in himself the abstract citizen, and as an individual human being has become a *species-being* in his everyday life, in his particular work, and in his particular situation, only when man has recognised and organized his '*forces propres*' {own powers} as *social* forces, and consequently no longer separates social power from himself in the shape of *political* power, only then will human emancipation have been accomplished. [Ibid: 165–8][102]

7.14 The *contradiction* between the purpose and goodwill of the administration, on the one hand, and its means and possibilities, on the other hand, cannot be abolished by the state without the latter abolishing itself, for it is *based* on this contradiction. The state is based on the contradiction between *public* and *private life*, on the contradiction between *general interests* and *private interests*. Hence the *administration* has to confine itself to a *formal* and *negative* activity, for where civil life and its labour begin, there the power of the administration ends. Indeed, confronted by the consequences which arise from the unsocial nature of this civil life, this private ownership, this trade, this industry, this mutual plundering of the various circles of citizens, confronted by all these consequences, *impotence* is the *law of nature* of the administration. For this fragmentation, this baseness, this *slavery of civil society* is the natural foundation on which the *modern* state rests, just as the *civil society of slavery* was the natural foundation on which the *ancient* state rested. The existence of the state and the existence of slavery are inseparable. The ancient state and ancient slavery – these straightforward *classic* opposites – were not more intimately *riveted* to each other than are the modern state and the modern commercial world, these hypocritical *Christian* opposites. If the modern state wanted to abolish the *impotence* of its administration, it would have to abolish the *private life* of today. But if it wanted to abolish private life, it would have to abolish itself, for it exists *only* in the contradiction to private life.
[Critical notes on the article 'The king of Prussia and social reform', 1844; 1844a: 198]

7.15 In the Middle Ages the citizens in each town were compelled to unite against the landed nobility to defend themselves. The extension of trade, the establishment of communications, led separate towns to establish contact with other towns, which had asserted the same interests in the struggle with the same antagonist. Out of the many local communities of citizens in the various towns there arose only gradually the middle *class*. The conditions of life of the individual citizens became – on account of their contradiction to the existing relations and of the mode of labour determined by this – conditions which were common to them all and independent of each individual. The citizens created these conditions insofar as they had torn themselves free from feudal ties, and were in their turn created by them insofar as they were determined by their antagonism to the feudal system which they found in existence. With the setting up of intercommunications between the individual towns, these common conditions developed into class conditions. The same conditions, the same contradiction, the same interests were bound to call forth on the whole similar customs everywhere. The bourgeoisie itself develops only gradually together with its conditions, splits according to the division of labour into various sections and finally absorbs all propertied classes it finds in existence (while it develops the majority of the earlier propertyless and a part of the hitherto propertied classes into a new class, the proletariat) in the measure to which all property found in existence is transformed into industrial or commercial capital.

The separate individuals form a class only insofar as they have to carry on a common battle against another class; in other respects they are on hostile terms with each other as competitors. On the other hand, the class in its turn assumes an independent existence as against the individuals, so that the latter find their conditions of life predetermined, and have their position in life and hence their personal development assigned to them by their class, thus being subsumed under it. This is the same phenomenon as the subjection of the separate individuals to the division of labour and can only be removed by the abolition of private property and of labour itself. We have already indicated several times that this subsuming of individuals under the class brings with it their subjection to all kinds of ideas, etc.

[*The German Ideology*, 1845–6; 1846a: 76–77]

7.16 Further, the division of labour also implies the contradiction between the interest of the separate individual or the individual family and the common interest of all individuals who have intercourse with one another. And indeed, this common interest does not exist merely in the imagination, as the 'general interest', but first of all in reality, as the mutual interdependence of the individuals among whom the labour is divided.

*Out of this very contradiction between the particular and the common interests, the common interest assumes an independent form as the *state*, which is divorced from the real individual and collective interests, and at the same time as an illusory community, always based, however, on the real ties existing in every family conglomeration and tribal conglomeration – such as flesh and blood, language, division of labour on a larger scale, and other interests – and especially [...] on the classes, already implied by the division of labour, which in every such mass of men separate out, and one of which dominates all the others. It follows from this that all struggles within the state, the struggle between democracy, aristocracy, and monarchy, the struggle for the franchise, etc., etc., are merely the illusory forms – altogether the general interest is the illusory form of common interests – in which the real struggles of the different classes are fought out among one another [...] Further, it follows that every class which is aiming at domination, even when its domination, as is the case with the proletariat, leads to the abolition of the old form of society in its entirety and of domination in general, must first conquer political power in order to represent its interest in turn as the general interest, which in the first moment it is forced to do.*

Just because individuals seek *only* their particular interest, which for them does not coincide with their common interest, the latter is asserted as an interest 'alien' to them, and 'independent' of them, as in its turn a particular and distinctive 'general' interest; or they themselves must remain within this discord, as in democracy. On the other hand, too, the *practical* struggle of these particular interests, which *actually* constantly run counter to the common and illusory common interests, necessitates *practical* intervention and restraint by the illusory 'general' interest in the form of the state.

[Ibid: 46–7. Paragraph between asterisks added to the MS by Engels.]

7.17 [...] the ruling class constitutes its joint domination as public power, as the state [...] the bourgeois do not allow the state to interfere in their private interests and give it only as much power as is necessary for their own safety and the maintenance of competition [...] the bourgeois in general act as citizens only to the extent that their private interests demand it [...] the bourgeois, and in general all the members of civil society, are forced to constitute themselves as 'we', as a juridical person, as the state, in order to safeguard their common interests and – if only because of the division of labour – to delegate the collective power thus created to a few persons.

[Ibid: 355–7]

7.18 In actual history, those theoreticians who regarded *might* as the basis of right were in direct contradiction to those who looked on *will* as the basis of right [...] If power is taken as the basis of right, as Hobbes, etc., do, then right, law, etc., are merely the symptom, the expression of *other* relations upon which state power rests. The material life of individuals, which by no means depends merely on their 'will', their mode of production and form of intercourse, which mutually determine each other – this is the real basis of the state and remains so at all the stages at which division of labour and private property are still necessary, quite independently of the *will* of individuals. These actual relations are in no way created by the state power; on the contrary they are the power creating it. The individuals who rule in these conditions – leaving aside the fact that their power must assume the form of the *state* – have to give their will, which is determined by these definite conditions, a universal expression as the will of the state, as law, an expression whose content is always determined by the relations of this class, as the civil and criminal law demonstrates in the clearest possible way. Just as the weight of their bodies does not depend on their idealistic will or on their arbitrary decision, so also the fact that they enforce their own will in the form of law, and at the same time make it independent of the personal arbitrariness of each individual among them, does not depend on their idealistic will. Their personal rule must at the same time assume the form of average rule. Their personal power is based on conditions of life which as they develop are common to many individuals, and the continuance of which they, as ruling individuals, have to maintain against others and, at the same time, to maintain that they hold good for everybody. The expression of this will, which is determined by their common interests, is the law. It is precisely because individuals who are independent of one another assert themselves and their own will, and because on this basis their attitude to one another is bound to be egoistical, that self-denial is made necessary in law and right, self-denial in the exceptional case, and self-assertion of their interests in the average case [...] The same applies to the classes which are ruled, whose will plays just as small a part in determining the existence of law and the state. For example, so long as the productive forces are still insufficiently developed to make competition superfluous, and therefore would give rise to competition over and over again, for so long the classes which are ruled would be wanting the impossible if they had the 'will' to abolish competition and with it the state and the law. Incidentally, too, it is only in the imagination of the ideologist that this 'will' arises before relations have developed far enough to make the emergence of such a will possible. After relations have developed sufficiently to produce it, the ideologist is able to imagine this will as being purely arbitrary and therefore as conceivable at all times and in all circumstances.

Like right, so crime, i.e., the struggle of the isolated individual against the predominant relations, is not the result of pure arbitrariness. On the contrary, it depends on the same conditions as that domination. The same visionaries who see in right and law the domination of some independently existing general will can see in crime the mere violation of right and law. Hence the state does not exist owing to the dominant will, but the state, which arises from the material mode of life of individuals, has also the form of a dominant will. If the latter loses its domination, it means that not only the will has changed but also the material existence and life of the individuals, and only for that reason has their will changed. It is possible for rights and laws to be 'inherited', but in that case they are no longer dominant, but nominal, of which striking examples are furnished by the history of ancient Roman law and English law.
[Ibid: 329–30]

One of the themes in this passage is tersely glossed in some notes written by Marx at the end of the MS of the first chapter of *The German Ideology*: 'It is precisely because the bourgeoisie rules as a class that in the law it must give itself a general expression' [Ibid: 92].[103] He makes a similar point *vis-à-vis* representative democracy:

7.19 The question regarding 'the importance of each man, the individual', can [...] only arise in a democratically elected representative body, and during the {French} revolution it only came up for discussion in the Convention [...] A problem which the Constituent Assembly decided *also* theoretically was the distinction between the representative body of a ruling *class* and that of the ruling *estates*; and this political rule of the bourgeois *class* was determined by each individual's position, since it was determined by the relations of production prevailing at the time. The representative system is a very specific product of modern bourgeois society which is as inseparable from the latter as is the isolated individual of modern times.
[Ibid: 199–200]

In his earlier Critique of Hegel's *Rechtsphilosophie*, Marx had dismissed 'the representative system' thus: 'The real antithesis between nation and government is overcome when the nation attains existence as a *notion*, as a fantasy, an illusion, a *representation* – as the *represented* nation, or the estates, which straightaway finds itself, as a *particular power*, cut off from the real nation' [1843b: 69–70].

7.20 The first form of property, in the ancient world as in the Middle Ages, is tribal property, determined with the Romans chiefly by war, with the Germans by the rearing of cattle. In the case of the ancient peoples, since several tribes live together in one city, tribal property appears as state property, and the right of the individual to it as mere 'possession' which, however, like tribal property as a whole, is confined to landed property only. Real private property began with the ancients, as with modern nations, with moveable property. (Slavery and community) (*dominium ex jure Quiritum* {ownership in accordance with the law applying to full Roman citizens}). – In the case of the nations which grew out of the Middle Ages, tribal property evolved through various stages – feudal landed property, corporative moveable property, capital invested in manufacture – to modern capital, determined by large-scale industry and universal competition, i.e., pure private property, which has cast off all semblance of a communal institution and has shut out the state from any influence on the development of property. To this modern private property corresponds the modern state, which, purchased gradually by the owners of property by means of taxation, has fallen entirely into their hands through the national debt, and its existence has become wholly dependent on the commercial credit which the owners of property, the bourgeois, extend to it, as reflected in the rise and fall of government securities on the stock exchange. By the mere fact that it is a *class* and no longer an *estate*, the bourgeoisie is forced to organize itself no longer locally, but nationally, and to give a general form to its average interests. Through the emancipation of private property from the community, the state has become a separate entity, alongside and outside civil society; but it is nothing more than the form of organization which the bourgeois are compelled to adopt, both for internal and external purposes, for the mutual guarantee of their property and interests. The independence of the state is only found nowadays in those countries where the estates have not yet completely developed into classes, where the estates, done away with in more advanced countries, still play a part and there exists a mixture, where consequently no section of the population can achieve dominance over the others. This is the case particularly in Germany. The most perfect example of the modern state is North America. The modern French, English and American writers all express the opinion that the state exists only for the sake of private property, so that this view has also been generally accepted by the average man.

Since the state is the form in which the individuals of a ruling class assert their common interests, and in which the whole civil society of an epoch is epitomised, it follows that all common institutions are set up with the help of the state and are given a political form. Hence the illusion that law is based on the will, and indeed on the will divorced from its real basis – on *free* will. Similarly, justice is in its turn reduced to statute law.

Civil law develops simultaneously with private property out of the disintegration of the natural community. With the Romans the development of private property and civil law had no further industrial and commercial consequences, because their whole mode of production did not alter. With modern peoples, where the feudal community was disintegrated by industry and trade, there began with the rise of private property and civil law a new phase, which was capable of further development. The very first town which carried on an extensive maritime trade in the Middle Ages, Amalfi, also developed maritime law. As soon as industry and trade developed private property further, first in Italy and later in other countries, the highly developed Roman civil law was immediately adopted again and raised to authority. When later the bourgeoisie had acquired so much power that the princes took up its interests in order to overthrow the feudal nobility by means of the bourgeoisie, there began in all countries – in France in the sixteenth century – the real development of law, which in all countries except England proceeded on the basis of the Roman code of laws. In England, too, Roman legal principles had to be introduced to further the development of civil law (especially in the case of moveable property). (It must not be forgotten that law has just as little an independent history as religion.)

In civil law the existing property relations are declared to be the result of the general will. The *jus utendi et abutendi* {right of use and disposal} itself asserts on the one hand the fact that private property has become entirely independent of the community, and on the other the illusion that private property itself is based solely on the private will, the arbitrary disposal of the thing. In practice, the *abuti* has very definite economic limitations for the owner of private property, if he does not wish to see his property and hence his *jus abutendi* pass into other hands, since actually the thing, considered merely with reference to his will, is not a thing at all, but only becomes a thing, true property, in intercourse, and independently of the law (a *relationship*, which philosophers call an idea. *For the *philosophers relationship* = *idea*. They only know the relation of 'Man' to himself and hence for them all relations become ideas.*) This juridical illusion, which reduces law to the mere will, necessarily leads, in the further development of property relations, to the position that a man may have a legal title to a thing without really having the thing. If, for instance, the income from a piece of land disappears owing to competition, then the proprietor has certainly his legal title to it along with the *jus utendi et abutendi*. But he can do nothing with it: he owns nothing as a landed proprietor if he has not enough capital elsewhere to cultivate his land. This illusion of the jurists also explains the fact that for them, as for every code, it is altogether fortuitous that individuals enter into relations among themselves (e.g., contracts); it explains why they consider that these relations [can] be entered into or not at will and that their content [rests] purely on the individual free will of the contracting parties.

Whenever, through the development of industry and commerce, new forms of intercourse have been evolved (e.g., insurance companies, etc.), the law has always been compelled to admit them among the modes of acquiring property.

[*The German Ideology*, 1845–6; 1846a: 89–92; marginal note (by Marx) incorporated into text between asterisks]

7.21 With {Adolph Wagner} there is, first, the law, and then commerce; in reality it's the other way round: at first there is *commerce*, and then a *legal order* develops out of it. In the analysis of the circulation of commodities I have demonstrated that in a developed trade the exchangers recognise each other tacitly as equal persons and owners of the goods to be exchanged respectively by them; they *do* this while they offer the goods to one another and agree to trade with one another. This *practical* relation, arising through and in exchange itself, only later attains a *legal form* in contracts etc.; but this form produces neither its content, the exchange, nor the relationship, existing in it, of persons to one another, but vice versa.

[Marginal notes on Wagner, 1880; 1880b: 210]

7.22 The act of exchange is both the positing and the confirmation of exchange values as well as of the subjects as exchangers. The content falling outside the act of exchange, outside the specific economic form, can only consist of: (1) the natural particularity of the commodities exchanged; (2) the particular natural need of the exchangers. Or, combining both aspects, the different use value of the commodities to be exchanged. So far from compromising the social equality of individuals, this content of exchange, which lies wholly outside the specific economic form, turns their natural difference into the basis of their social equality. If individual A had the same need as individual B, and had realised his labour in the same object as individual B, no relation at all would exist between them [...] Only the difference of their needs and their production is the occasion for exchange and for their being socially equated in it. Hence this natural difference is the precondition of their social equality in the act of exchange and of this relationship in general, in which they relate to each other as productive agents [...]

More: the fact that the need of the one individual can be satisfied by the product of the other and vice versa, and that the one is able to produce the object for the other's need, and that each confronts the other as possessor of the object of the other's need, shows that as a *human being* each transcends his own particular needs, etc., that they are behaving towards each other as men, that their common species being is known by all. This is unique. Elephants do not produce for tigers, or animals for other animals. A swarm of bees, for instance, *au fond* constitutes only one bee, and all the bees produce the same thing.

Moreover, in so far as this natural difference between individuals and their commodities constitutes the motivation for their integration, for their social relationship as exchangers, in which they are *presupposed* as and *prove* themselves to be equals, *freedom* comes to play a role in addition to equality. Although individual A may feel a need for the commodity of individual B, he does not seize it by force, or vice versa; A and B recognise each other as owners, as persons, whose commodities are permeated by their will. Accordingly, the juridical concept of the person comes in here, as well as that of freedom in so far as it is contained therein. Neither forcibly takes possession of the property of the other; each disposes of it voluntarily.

But this is not all. Individual A satisfies individual B's need by means of the commodity *a* only to the extent that and because individual B satisfies individual A's need by means of commodity *b*, and vice versa. Each serves the other in order to serve himself; and makes reciprocal use of the other as his means. Each individual is now conscious that (1) each attains his end only in so far as he serves the other as means; (2) each becomes a means for the other (being for another) only as end for himself (being for himself); (3) this reciprocity whereby each is at once means and end [...] is a necessary fact, presupposed as a natural condition of exchange, but that it is as such a matter of indifference for each of the two subjects of exchange, and is of interest to each of them only in so far as it satisfies his own interest as excluding that of the other, without relation to it.

This means that the social interest which appears as the motive of the act as a whole, is certainly recognised as a fact on both sides, but as such it is not the motive, but goes on, as it were, merely behind the back of the self-reflected particular interests, behind the back of an individual's interest in contrast to that of the other. In this latter respect, the individual can at most have the consoling awareness that the satisfaction of his individual interest as opposed to that of the other is precisely the realisation of the transcended antithesis, of the general social interest. From the act of exchange itself, the individual, each of them, is reflected in himself as the exclusive and dominant (determining) subject of the exchange. With that the complete freedom of the individual is posited: voluntary transaction; force on neither side; positing of oneself as a means, or as serving, only as a means to posit oneself as an end in oneself, as the dominating and transcending element; ultimately realising the selfish interest, not an interest standing above it. The other party to the exchange is also recognised and known as likewise realising his own selfish interest, so that both know that the social interest is nothing but the exchange of the selfish interest in its duality, many-sidedness and autonomy. The general interest is nothing but the generality of selfish interests.

Thus, if the economic form, exchange, in every respect posits the equality of the subjects, the content, the material, both individual and objective, which impels them to exchange, posits *freedom*. Hence equality and freedom are not only respected in exchange which is based on exchange values, but the exchange of exchange values is the real productive basis of all *equality* and *freedom*. As pure ideas, equality and freedom are merely idealised expressions of this exchange; developed in juridical, political and social relations, they are merely this basis at a higher level. And indeed this has been confirmed by history. Equality and freedom at the higher level are the exact opposite of freedom and equality in the ancient world, which were not based on developed exchange value, but which on the contrary perished through its development. They presuppose relations of production not yet realised in the ancient world, nor indeed in the Middle Ages. Direct forced labour was the foundation of the ancient world; it was on this existing basis that the community rested. Labour itself regarded as a privilege, as still particularised, not labour generally producing exchange value, was the foundation of the Middle Ages. [Modern] labour is neither forced labour, nor, as in the second case, is it carried on with reference to something common, as something higher (corporations).

[...]

In Roman Law the *servus* {slave} is therefore correctly defined as one who can acquire nothing for himself by means of exchange (see *Institutiones* {of Justinian}). It is therefore clear that this *law*, although

it corresponds to a state of society in which exchange was by no means developed, nevertheless, inasmuch as it was developed in a certain sphere, could evolve *the definitions of the legal person, i.e. the individual engaged in exchange*, and could thus (at least in basic principle) anticipate the legal system of industrial society. Above all, it could be upheld as the law of emerging bourgeois society as against the Middle Ages. It is significant that its development coincides exactly with the dissolution of the Roman community.
[*Grundrisse*, 1857–8; 1858a: 174–7][104]

7.23 To speak here {with regard to interest on capital} of natural justice [...] is nonsense. The justice of the transactions between agents of production rests on the fact that these arise as natural consequences out of the production relationships. The juristic forms in which these economic transactions appear as wilful acts of the parties concerned, as expressions of their common will and as contracts which may be en- forced at law against some individual party, cannot, being mere forms, determine this content. They merely express it. This content is just whenever it corresponds, is appropriate, to the mode of production. It is unjust whenever it contradicts that mode. Slavery on the basis of capitalist production is unjust; likwise fraud in the quality of commodities.
[*Capital* 3, 1864–5; 1865a: 339–40]

Two brief general remarks of Marx's are worth noting here: 'the opposition between political economy and ethics is only an *apparent* opposition [...] political economy expresses moral laws *in its own way*' [Economic and philosophic manuscripts of 1844; 1844c: 311]; and 'every *social form* of property has "morals" of its own' [*Civil war*, first draft, 1871; 1871b: 505]. Marx's approving quotation of Linguet's riposte to Montesquieu, '*L'ésprit des lois, c'est la propriété*' {'the spirit of the laws is property'} [1867a: 615n] is also germane.

7.24 For Germany the *criticism of religion* is in the main complete, and criticism of religion is the premise of all criticism.

The *profane* existence of error is discredited after its *heavenly oratio pro aris et focis* {speech for altars and hearths} has been disproved. Man, who looked for a superhuman being in the fantastic reality of heaven and found nothing there but the *reflection* of himself, will no longer be disposed to find but the *semblance* of himself, only an inhuman being, where he seeks and must seek his true reality.

The basis of irreligious criticism is: *Man makes religion*, religion does not make man. Religion is the self-consciousness and self-esteem of man who has either not yet found himself or has already lost himself again. But *man* is no abstract being encamped outside the world. Man is *the world of man*, the state, society. This state, this society, produce religion, an *inverted world-consciousness*, because they are an *inverted world*. Religion is the general theory of that world, its encyclopaedic compendium, its logic in a popular form, its spiritualistic *point d'honneur*, its enthusiasm, its moral sanction, its solemn complement, its universal source of consolation and justification. It is the *fantastic realisation* of the human essence because the *human essence* has no true reality. The struggle against religion is therefore indirectly a fight against *the world* of which religion is the spiritual *aroma*.

Religious distress is at the same time the *expression* of real distress and also the *protest* against real distress. Religion is the sigh of the oppressed creature, the heart of a heartless world, just as it is the spirit of spiritless conditions. It is the *opium* of the people.

To abolish religion as the *illusory* happiness of the people is to demand their *real* happiness. The demand to give up illusions about the existing state of affairs is the *demand to give up a state of affairs which needs illusions*. The criticism of religion is therefore *in embryo the criticism of the vale of tears*, the *halo* of which is religion.

Criticism has torn up the imaginary flowers from the chain not so that man shall wear the unadorned, bleak chain but so that he will shake off the chain and pluck the living flower. The criticism of religion disillusions man to make him think and act and shape his reality like a man who has been disillusioned and has come to reason, so that he will revolve round himself and therefore round his true sun. Religion is only the illusory sun which revolves round man as long as he does not revolve round himself.

The *task of history*, therefore, once the *world beyond the truth* has disappeared, is to establish the *truth of this world*. The immediate *task of philosophy*, which is at the service of history, once the *holy form* of human self-estrangement has been unmasked, is to unmask self-estrangement in its *unholy forms*. Thus the criticism of heaven turns into the criticism of the earth, the *criticism of religion* into the *criticism of law* and the *criticism of theology* into the *criticism of politics*.

[Critique of Hegel's *Rechtsphilosophie*: introduction, 1843; 1843d: 175–6]

7.25 The cult of money has its corresponding asceticism, its renunciation, its self-sacrifice – thrift and frugality, contempt for the worldly, temporary and transient pleasures; the pursuit of *eternal* treasure. Hence the connection of English Puritanism or also Dutch Protestantism with money-making.
[*Grundrisse*, 1857–8; 1858a: 164]

A propos the recommendations for restricting domestic consumption by the early school of political economy known as 'mercantilism', Marx observes in *Capital* 2 that 'these sermons frequently remind one in form and content of analogous ascetic expostulations of the fathers of the church' [this section from MS 5, 1877; 1878: 60].

7.26 The religious world is but the reflex of the real world. And for a society based upon the production of commodities, in which the producers in general enter into social relations with one another by treating their products as commodities and values, whereby they reduce their individual private labour to the standard of homogeneous human labour – for such a society, Christianity with its *cultus* of abstract man, more especially in its bourgeois developments, Protestantism, deism, etc., is the most fitting form of religion. In the ancient Asiatic and other ancient forms of production, we find that the conversion of products into commodities, and therefore the conversion of men into producers of commodities, holds a subordinate place, which, however, increases in importance as the primitive communities approach nearer and nearer to their dissolution. Trading nations, properly so-called, exist in the ancient world only in its interstices, like the gods of Epicurus in the Intermundia, or like Jews in the pores of Polish society. Those ancient social organisms of production are, as compared with bourgeois society, extremely simple and transparent. But they are founded either on the immature development of man individually, who has not yet severed the umbilical cord that unites him with his fellowmen in a primitive tribal community, or upon direct relations of subjection. They can arise and exist only when the development of the productive powers of labour has not risen beyond a low stage, and when, therefore, the social relations within the sphere of material life, between man and man, and between man and Nature, are correspondingly narrow. This narrowness is reflected in the ancient worship of Nature, and in the other elements

of the popular religions. The religious reflex of the real world can, in any case, only then finally vanish, when the practical relations of everyday life offer to man none but perfectly intelligible and reasonable relations with regard to his fellowmen and to Nature.
[*Capital* 1, 1867; 1867a: 79]

7.27 In the face of the habitual mode of life of the old feudal nobility, which, as Hegel rightly says, 'consists in consuming what is in hand', and more especially displays itself in the luxury of personal retainers, it was extremely important for bourgeois economy to promulgate the doctrine that accumulation of capital is the first duty of every citizen, and to preach without ceasing, that a man cannot accumulate, if he eats up all his revenue, instead of spending a good part of it in the acquisition of additional productive labourers, who bring in more than they cost.
[...]
But original sin is at work everywhere. As capitalist production, accumulation, and wealth, become developed, the capitalist ceases to be the mere incarnation of capital. He has a fellow-feeling for his own Adam, and his education gradually enables him to smile at the rage for asceticism, as a mere prejudice of the old-fashioned miser. While the capitalist of the classical type brands individual consumption as a sin against his function, and as 'abstinence' from accumulating, the modernised capitalist is capable of looking on accumulation as 'abstinence' from pleasure.

Two souls, alas, do dwell within his breast;
The one is ever parting from the other.

At the historical dawn of capitalist production – and every capitalist upstart has personally to go through this historical stage – avarice, and desire to get rich, are the ruling passions. But the progress of capitalist production not only creates a world of delights; it lays open, in speculation and the credit system, a thousand sources of sudden enrichment. When a certain stage of development has been reached, a conventional degree of prodigality, which is also an exhibition of wealth, and consequently a source of credit, becomes a business necessity to the 'unfortunate' capitalist. Luxury enters into capital's expenses of representation. Moreover, the capitalist gets rich, not like the miser, in proportion to his personal labour and restricted consumption, but at the same rate as he squeezes out the labour-power of others, and enforces on the labourer abstinence from all life's

enjoyments. Although, therefore, the prodigality of the capitalist never possesses the bona fide character of the open-handed feudal lord's prodigality, but, on the contrary, has always lurking behind it the most sordid avarice and the most anxious calculation, yet his expenditure grows with his accumulation, without the one necessarily restricting the other. But along with that growth, there is at the same time developed in his breast, a Faustian conflict between the passion for accumulation, and the desire for enjoyment.
[Ibid: 588, 593–4. Marx's quotation is from Goethe's *Faust*]

7.28 Although the bourgeoisie was originally very thrifty, with the growing productivity of capital, i.e., of the labourers, it imitates the retainer system of the feudal lords. According to the latest report (1861 or 1862) on the factories, the total number of persons (managers included) employed in the factories properly so-called of the United Kingdom was only 775,534, while the number of female servants in England alone amounted to 1 million. What a convenient arrangement it is that makes a factory girl to sweat twelve hours in a factory, so that the factory proprietor, with a part of her unpaid labour, can take into his personal service her sister as maid, her brother as groom and her cousin as soldier or policeman!
[*Theories of Surplus Value*, 1861–3; 1863a: 200–1]

Commenting on the same growth of 'flunkeys, Jenkinses, etc., in short the whole train of retainers' in *Grundrisse*, Marx also notes 'in relation to the whole of society, the production of *disposable time* [can] also [be considered] as the creation of time for the production of science, art, etc.' [1858a: 328]

7.29 Bentham is a purely English phenomenon. Not even excepting our philosopher, Christian Wolff,[105] in no time and in no country has the most home-spun commonplace ever strutted about in so self-satisfied a way. The principle of utility was no discovery of Bentham. He simply reproduced in his dull way what Helvetius and other Frenchmen had said with esprit in the 18th century. To know what is useful for a dog, one must study dog-nature. This nature itself is not to be deduced from the principle of utility. Applying this to man, he that would criticise all human acts, movements, relations, etc., by the principle of utility, must first deal with human nature in general, and then with human nature as modified in each historical epoch. Bentham makes short work of it. With the dryest naivete he takes the modern shopkeeper, especially the English shopkeeper, as the normal man. Whatever is useful to this queer normal man, and to his world, is absolutely useful. This yard-measure, then, he applies to past, present, and future. The Christian religion, e.g., is 'useful', because it forbids in the name of religion the same faults that the penal code condemns in the name of the law. Artistic criticism is 'harmful', because it disturbs worthy people in their enjoyment of Martin Tupper, etc. With such rubbish has the brave fellow, with his motto, *'nulla dies sine linea'* {'no day without its line': ascribed to the painter Apelles, who let no day go by without adding something to a painting}, piled up mountains of books. Had I the courage of my friend, Heinrich Heine, I should call Mr Jeremy a genius in the way of bourgeois stupidity. [*Capital* 1, 1867; 1867a: 609n][106]

7.30 The centralized state machinery[107] which, with its ubiquitous and complicated military, bureaucratic, clerical and judiciary organs, entoils (inmeshes) the living civil society like a boa-constrictor, was first forged in the days of absolute monarchy as a weapon of nascent modern society in its struggle of emancipation from feudalism. The seignorial privileges of the medieval lords and cities and clergy were transformed into the attribute of a unitary state power, displacing the feudal dignitaries by salaried state functionaries, transferring the arms from medieval retainers of the landlords and the corporations of townish citizens to a standing army, substituting for the checkered (party coloured) anarchy of conflicting medieval powers the regulated plan of a state power, with a systematic and hierarchic division of labour. The first French Revolution {1789} with its task to found national unity (to create a nation) had to break down all local, territorial, townish and provincial independences. It was, therefore, forced to develop, what absolute monarchy had commenced, the centralization and organization of state power, and to expand the circumference and the attributes of the state power, the number of its tools, its independence of, and its supernaturalist sway of real society which in fact took the place of the medieval supernaturalist heaven with its saints. Every minor solitary interest engendered by the relations of social groups was separated from society itself, fixed and made independent of it and opposed to it in the form of state interest, administered by state priests with exactly determined hierarchical functions.

This parasitical [excrescence upon] civil society, pretending to be its ideal counterpart, grew to its full development under the sway of the first Bonaparte. The restoration and the monarchy of July added nothing to it but a greater division of labour, growing at the same measure in which the division of labour in civil society created new groups of interest, and, therefore, new material for state action. In their struggle against the Revolution of 1848, the parliamentary republic of France and the governments of all continental Europe, were forced to strengthen, with their measures of repression against the popular movement, the means of action and the centralization of that governmental power. All revolutions thus perfected the state machinery instead of throwing off this deadening incubus. The fractions and parties of the ruling classes which alternately struggled for supremacy, considered the occupancy (Control) (seizure) and the direction of this immense machinery of government as the main booty of the victor. It centred in the creation of immense standing armies, a host of state vermin, and huge national debts. During the time of the absolute monarchy it was a means of the struggle of modern society against feudalism, crowned by the French revolution, and under the first Bonaparte it served not only to subjugate the Revolution and annihilate all popular liberties, it was an instrument of the French revolution to strike abroad, to create for France on the Continent instead of feudal monarchies more or less states after the image of France. Under the Restoration and the Monarchy of July it became not only a means of the forcible class domination of the middle class, and a means of adding to the direct economic exploitation a second exploitation of the people by assuring to their families all the rich places of the State household. During the time of the Revolutionary struggle of 1848 at last it served as a means of annihilating that Revolution and all aspirations at the emancipation of the popular masses. But the state parasite received only its last development during the second Empire. The governmental power with its standing army, its all directing bureaucracy, its stultifying clergy and its servile tribunal hierarchy, had grown so independent of society itself, that a grotesquely mediocre adventurer {Napoleon III} with a hungry band of desperadoes behind him sufficed to wield it. It did no longer want the pretext of an armed Coalition of old Europe against the modern world founded by the Revolution of 1789. It appeared no longer as a means of class domination, subordinate to its parliamentary ministry or legislature. Humbling under its sway even the interests of the ruling classes, whose parliamentary show-work it supplanted by self-elected Corps Legislatifs and self-paid senates, sanctioned in its absolute sway by universal suffrage, the acknowledged necessity for keeping up 'order', that is the rule of the capitalist and the landlord over the producer, cloaking under the tatters of a maskerade of the past, the orgies of the corruption of the present and the victory of the most parasitic faction, the financial swindler, the *debauchery* of all the reactionary influences of the past let loose – a pandemonium of infamies – the state power had received its last and supreme expression in the Second Empire. Apparently the final victory of this governmental power over society, it was in fact the orgy of all the corrupt elements of that society. To the eye of the uninitiated it appeared only as the victory of the Executive over the legislative, as the final defeat of the form of class rule pretending to be the autocracy of society under its form pretending to be a superior power to society. But in fact it was only the last degraded and the only possible form of that class rule, as humiliating to those classes themselves as to the working classes which they kept fettered by it.

The 4th of September {1870: the proclamation of the republic, following Napoleon III's defeat and capture by the Prussians at Sedan} was only the vindication of the Republic against the grotesque adventurer that had assassinated it. The true antithesis to the *Empire itself* – that is to the state power, the centralized executive, of which the Second Empire was only the exhausting formula – was *the Commune*. This state power forms in fact the creation of the middle class, first a means to break down feudalism, then a means to crush the emancipatory aspirations of the producers, of the working class. All reactions and all revolutions had only served to transfer that organised power – the organised force of the slavery of labour – from one hand to the other, from one fraction of the ruling classes to the other. It had served the ruling classes as a means of subjugation and of pelf. It had sucked new forces from every new change. It had served as the instrument of breaking down every popular rise and served it to crush the working classes after they had fought and been ordered to secure its transfer from one part of its oppressors to the others. This was, therefore, a Revolution not against this or that, legitimate, constitutional, republican or Imperialist form of State Power. It was a revolution against the *State* itself, this supernaturalist abortion of society, a resumption by the people for the people, of its own social life. It was not a revolution to transfer it from one fraction of the ruling classes to the other, but a Revolution to break down this horrid machinery of Class domination itself [...]

It was only the working class that could formulate by the word 'Commune' and initiate by the fighting Commune of Paris – this new aspiration. Even the last expression of that state power in the Second Empire although humbling for the pride of the ruling classes and casting to the winds their parliamentary pretentions of self-government, had been only the last possible form of their class rule. While politically dispossessing them, it was the orgy under which all the economic and social infamies of their regime got full sway. The middling bourgeoisie and the petty middle class were by their economical conditions of life excluded from initiating a new revolution and induced to follow in the tracks of the ruling classes or [be] the followers of the working class. The peasants were the passive economical basis of the Second Empire, of that last triumph of a *State* separate of and independent from society. Only the Proletarians, fired by a new social task to accomplish by them for all society, to do away with all classes and class rule, were the men to break the instrument of that class rule – the State, the centralized and organized governmental power usurping to be the master instead of .the servant of society. In the active struggle against them by the ruling classes, supported by the passive adherence of the peasantry, the Second Empire, the last crowning at the same time as the most signal prostitution of the State – which had taken the place of the medieval church – had been engendered. It had sprung into life against them. By them it was broken, not as a peculiar form of centralized governmental power, but as its most powerful, elaborated into seeming independence from society expression, and, therefore, also its most prostitute reality, covered by infamy from top to bottom, having centred in absolute corruption at home and absolute powerlessness abroad.

[...]

The *Commune* – the reabsorption of the State power by society, as its own living forces instead of as forces controlling and subduing it, by the popular masses themselves, forming their own force instead of the organized force of their suppression – the political form of their social emancipation, instead of the artificial force (appropriated by their oppressors) (their own force opposed to and organized against them) of society wielded for their oppression by their enemies. The form was simple like all great things [...] {The Commune} first displaced the army by the National Guard [...] (the people had only to organize this militia on a national scale to have done away with the Standing armies; the first economical *conditio sine qua non* for all social improvements, discarding at once this source of taxes and state debt, and this constant danger to government usurpation of class rule – of the regular class rule or an adventurer pretending to save all classes); at the same time the safest guarantee against Foreign aggression and making in fact the costly military apparatus impossible in all other states; the emancipation of the peasant from the bloodtax and the most fertile source of all state taxation and state debts. Here already the point in which the Commune is a *bait for the peasant*, the first word of his emancipation. With the 'independent police' abolished, and its ruffians supplanted by servants of the Commune. The general suffrage, till now abused either for the parliamentary sanction of the Holy State Power, or a play in the hands of the ruling classes, only employed by the people to choose the instruments of parliamentary class rule once in many years, adapted to its real purposes, to choose by the communes their own functionaries of administration and initiation. [Gone is] the Delusion as if administration and political governing were mysteries, transcendent functions only to be trusted to the hands of a trained caste, state parasites, richly paid sycophants and sinecurists, in the higher posts, absorbing the intelligences of the masses and turning them against themselves in the lower places of the hierarchy. Doing away with the state hierarchy altogether and replacing the haughteous masters of the people by its always removable servants, a mock responsibility by a real responsibility, as they act continuously under public supervision. Paid like skilled workmen, 12 pounds a month [...] The whole sham of state mysteries and state pretensions was done away with by a Commune, mostly consisting of simple working men, organizing the defence of Paris, carrying war against the Pretorians of Bonaparte, securing the *approvisionment* of that immense town, filling all the posts hitherto divided between Government, police, and Prefecture, doing their work publicly, simply, under the most difficult and complicated circumstances, and doing it, as Milton did his *Paradise Lost*, for a few pounds, acting in bright daylight, with no pretensions to infallibility, not hiding itself behind circumlocution office,[108] not ashamed to confess blunders by correcting them. Making in one order the public functions – military, administrative, political – *real workmen's functions*, instead of the hidden attributes of a trained caste; (keeping order in the turbulence of civil war and revolution) (initiating measures of general regeneration). Whatever the merits of the single measures of the Commune, its greatest measure was its own organization [...]

With all the great towns organized into Communes after the model of Paris no government could repress the movement by the surprise of sudden reaction [...] All France organized into self-working and self-governing communes, the standing army replaced by the popular militias, the army of state parasites removed, the clerical hierarchy displaced by the schoolmaster, the state judges transformed into Communal organs, the suffrage for the National representation not a matter of sleight of hand for an allpowerful government, but the deliberate expression of organized communes, the state functions reduced to a few functions for general national purposes.

Such is the *Commune – the political form of the social emancipation*, of the liberation of labour from the usurpation of the (slaveholding) monopolists of the means of labour, created by the labourers themselves or forming the gift of nature. As the state machinery and parliamentarism are not the real life of the ruling classes, but only the organized general organs of their dominion, the political guarantees and forms and expressions of the old order of things, so the Commune is not the social movement of the working class and therefore of a general regeneration of mankind but the organized means of action. The Commune does not [do] away with the class struggles, through which the working classes strive for the abolition of all classes and, therefore, of all class rule (because it does not represent a particular interest. It represents the liberation of 'labour', that is the fundamental and natural condition of individual and social life which only by usurpation, fraud, and artificial contrivances can be shifted from the few upon the many), but it affords the rational medium in which that class struggle can run through its different phases in the most rational and human way. It could start violent reactions and as violent revolutions. It begins the *emancipation of labour* – its great goal – by doing away with the unproductive and mischievous work of the state parasites, by cutting away the springs which sacrifice an immense portion of the national produce to the feeding of the state-monster, on the one side, by doing, on the other, the real work of administration, local and national, for workingmen's wages. It begins therefore with an immense saving, with economical reform as well as political transformation.

[...]

The working class know that they have to pass through different phases of class struggle. They know that the superseding of the economical conditions of the slavery of labour by the conditions of free and associated labour can only be the progressive work of time, (that economical transformation) that they require not only a change of distribution, but a new organization of production, or rather the delivery (setting free) of the social forms of production in present organized labour (engendered by present industry) of the trammels of slavery, of their present class character, and their harmonious national and international coordination. They know that this work of regeneration will be again and again relented and impeded by the resistances of vested interests and class egotisms. They know that the present 'spontaneous action of the natural laws of capital and landed property' – can only be superseded by 'the spontaneous action of the

laws of the social economy of free and associated labour', by a long
process of development of new conditions, as was the 'spontaneous
action of the economic laws of slavery' and the 'spontaneous action of
the economical laws of serfdom'. But they know at the same time that
great strides may be taken at once through the Communal form of
political organization and that the time has come to begin that
movement for themselves and mankind.
[*The Civil War in France*, 1871, first draft; 1871b: 483–92. The MS
was written in English.]

It is worth comparing this text with the corresponding passages in
the second draft, and the final version of *The Civil War*. Two
differences of emphasis in the second draft are especially worth
noting. First, Marx describes the Second Empire as '*professing* to
rest upon the producing majority of the nation, the peasants' (1871c:
535, my emphasis). Second, he explicitly draws, and several times
reiterates, the conclusion that 'the working class cannot simply lay
hold on the ready-made state machinery and wield it for their own
purpose. The political instrument of their enslavement cannot serve
as the political instrument of their emancipation' (1871c: 533).
Marx repeats this in the Preface to the 1872 German edition of the
Manifesto (1872c), and on this ground distances himself from the
famous 'revolutionary measures' which he had advocated in the
earlier text. These measures hinged on 'centralization [...] in the
hands of the State [1848b: 505]. Compare this passage also with the
analysis of the French state given in the concluding section of the
18th Brumaire (1852a).

8

Precapitalist societies

Marx's sociology of pre-capitalist societies is sketchy compared
with his work on capitalism. But it is unfailingly interesting, not
least because of what it reveals about his methodology. His
discussions of property in primitive communes, or of relations of
production in feudal society, for instance, display a far subtler
handling of these concepts than is often attributed to him. Similarly,
his analysis of the 'millenial stagnation' of Asiatic society (wrong
as it might very well be) suggests that, contrary to what is often
asserted, Marx did not believe in a universal tendency for society's
productive forces to develop.[109] Such issues affect our entire
reading of his social theory. This chapter contains a long extract
from Marx's best known foray into precapitalist societies, in the
Grundrisse; a substantial section of the drafts of the letter to
Zasulich, on the Russian peasant commune; and a number of shorter
passages on the 'Asiatic mode of production' and European
feudalism.[110]

8.1 One of the prerequisites of wage labour and one of the historical
conditions for capital is free labour and the exchange of free labour
for money, in order to reproduce money and to valorize it, in order to
be consumed by money, not as use value for enjoyment, but as use

value for money. Another prerequisite is the separation of free labour from the objective conditions of its realisation – from the means and material of labour. This means above all separation of the worker from the land, which functions as his natural workshop, hence the dissolution both of free small holdings and of communal landed property, based on the Oriental commune.

In both these forms the labourer relates to the objective conditions of his labour as to his property; this is the natural unity of labour with its physical prerequisites. Hence the labourer has an objective existence independent of his labour. The individual relates to himself as proprietor, as master of the conditions of his reality. He relates in the same way to the others, and – depending on whether this *prerequisite* derives from the community or from the individual families constituting the community – he relates to the others as co-proprietors, as so many incarnations of the common property, or as independent proprietors coexisting with him, independent private proprietors, beside whom the common property which formerly absorbed everything and embraced them all subsists as a special *ager publicus* {state land} separate from the numerous private landed proprietors.

In both forms, the individuals relate not as workers but as proprietors – as members of a community who work. The purpose of this labour is not the *creation of value*, although they may perform surplus labour in order to exchange it for *alien*, i.e., surplus, products. Its purpose is the maintenance of the individual proprietor and his family as well as of the community as a whole. The positing of the individual as a *worker*, who is stripped of all qualities except this one, is itself a *historical* product.

In the earliest form of this landed property, a naturally evolved community is the first prerequisite: the family, and the family expanded into a tribe [*Stamm*], or [formed] through intermarriage between families, or a combination of tribes. Since we may assume that *pastoralism*, or more generally a *nomadic way of life*, is the first form of existence; that the tribe does not settle on a certain site but that it grazes off what it finds there and moves on – men are not settled by nature [...] the *tribal community*, the natural community, is not the *result* but the *precondition of the common* (temporary) *appropriation* and *use of the soil*.

When men finally do settle down, the degree of change which this original community will undergo, will depend partly on various external, climatic, geographical, physical, etc., conditions and partly on their particular natural dispositions, etc. – their tribal character. The naturally evolved tribal community, or, if you wish, the herd – common ties of blood, language, custom, etc. – is the first precondition for the *appropriation of the objective conditions* of their life, and of the life activity reproducing and objectifying itself (activity as herdsmen, hunters, agriculturalists, etc.).

The earth is the great workshop, the arsenal which provides both the means and the materials of labour, as well as the location, the *basis* of the community. Men relate naively to it as the *property of the community*, and of the community which produces and reproduces itself in living labour. Each individual regards himself as a *proprietor* or *owner* only *qua* member of such a community.

The real *appropriation* through the process of labour takes place under these *preconditions*, which are not themselves the *product* of labour but appear as its natural or *divine* preconditions. This form, where the fundamental relationship is the same [common property in land], may realise itself in a variety of ways. It does not contradict it at all, for instance, that, as in most *Asiatic* fundamental forms, the *all-embracing unity* which stands above all these small communities may appear as the *higher* or as the *sole proprietor*, and the real communities, therefore, merely as *hereditary* occupiers. Since the *unity* is the real proprietor, and the real precondition of common property, it is quite possible for it to appear as something *distinct* over and above the many real, particular communities. The individual is then in fact propertyless, or property – i.e. the relation of the individual to his natural conditions of labour as belonging to him, as the objective body of his subjectivity present in the form of inorganic nature – appears to be mediated for him through a concession from the total unity – a unity realised in the despot as the father of the many communities – to the individual via the particular commune. It therefore follows that the surplus product (which, incidentally, is legally determined in consequence of the real appropriation through labour) belongs to this highest unity.

Hence, in the midst of Oriental despotism and the absence of property which it juridically appears to imply, there in fact exists as its foundation this tribal or communal property, mostly produced through a combination of manufacture and agriculture within the small community, which thereby becomes completely self-sustaining and comes to contain within itself all the conditions necessary for reproduction and extended production. Part of its surplus labour belongs to the higher community, which ultimately exists as a *person*, and this surplus labour is expressed both in tribute, etc., and in common labours performed for the glorification of the unity, which is in part the real despot and in part the imagined tribal being, the god.

In so far as it is actually realised in labour, this type of communal property can appear in two ways: either the small communities vegetate independently side by side, and within each the individual labours independently with his family on the plot assigned to him. (A certain amount of labour will also be performed for the *communal reserve* – for insurance, so to speak – on the one hand; and [on the other] for *defraying the costs of the community as such*, i.e. for war, religious worship, etc.; lordly dominion, in its most original sense, emerges only at this point, e.g. in the Slavonic and Romanian communities, etc. Herein lies the transition to labour services, etc.) Or the unity can extend to the communality of labour itself, which may be systematically organized, as in Mexico and especially Peru, among the ancient Celts, and among some tribes in India.

Furthermore, the communality within the tribal body may appear either in such a way that its unity is represented in one head of the tribal kinship group, or else as a relationship between the heads of families. The former will produce a more despotic, the latter a more democratic form of this community. The communal conditions for real appropriation through labour, such as *irrigation systems* (very important among the Asian peoples), means of communication, etc., then appear as the work of the higher unity – of the despotic government poised above the lesser communities. Cities in the proper sense arise alongside these villages only where the location is especially favourable to foreign trade, or where the head of State and his satraps exchange their revenue (the surplus product) for labour, spend it as labour funds.

The second form [of property] has, like the first, given rise to substantial local, historical, etc., variations. It is the product of a more dynamic historical life, of the fate and modification of the original tribes. It also assumes the *communal system* as the first presupposition, but not, as in the first case, as the substance of which the individuals are mere accidental factors, or of which they are only naturally evolved parts. It does not presuppose land as its basis, but the city as already constructed seat [centre] of the rural population (landowners). The cultivated fields are the territory of a city, whereas [in the first form of property] the village was a mere appendage to the land.

However great the obstacles the land may put in the way of those who till it and really appropriate it, it offers no resistance to the people relating to it as the inorganic nature of the living individual, as his workshop, his means of labour, the object of his labour, and the means of subsistence of the subject. The difficulties encountered by the organized community can arise only from other communities which either have already occupied the territory or disturb the community in its occupation of it. War is therefore the great all-embracing task, the great communal labour, which is required either for the occupation of the objective conditions of being alive, or for the protection and perpetuation of this occupation. The community consisting of families is therefore organized above all on military lines, for purposes of war, and this is one of the conditions of its being there as proprietor. Concentration of settlement in the city is the foundation of this warlike organization.

The nature of the tribal system leads to the differentiation of kinship groups into higher and lower, and this differentiation is developed further through intermixture with subjugated tribes, etc.

Communal property – as State property, *ager publicus* – is here separate from private property. The property of the individual is here not itself direct communal property, as in our first case, where the individual is not a proprietor in separation from the community, but rather merely the occupier [of the plot of communal land allotted to him].

The less it is the case that individual property can only be utilised through communal labour (such as e.g. the irrigation systems of the Orient); the more the purely naturally evolved character of the tribe breaks down through the movement of history or migration; the more the tribe moves away from its original place of settlement and occupies *foreign* territory, thus entering into essentially new conditions of labour and stimulating the development of the energies of the individual; and the more the communal character of the tribe appears, and must appear, rather as a negative unity as against the outside world – the more are the conditions given under which the individual can become a *private proprietor of land* – of a particular plot – whose particular cultivation falls to himself and his family.

The community as a State is on the one hand the relationship of those free and equal private proprietors to each other, their combination against the outside world – and it is at the same time their safeguard. Communal life is here based as much on the fact that its members are working landed proprietors, smallholding peasants, as the peasants' independence is based on their mutual relations as members of the community, on safeguarding the *ager publicus* for the communal needs and the communal glory, etc. To be a member of the community remains the precondition for the appropriation of land, but as a member of the community the individual is a private proprietor. He relates to his private property as to land but at the same time as to his being as a member of the community, and his maintenance as such is just as much the maintenance of the community, and vice versa, etc. Since the community, though here already a *product of history*, not only *de facto*, but also in its own consciousness, is therefore conceived as *having come into being*, we have here the precondition for *property in land* – i.e. for the relation of the working subject to the natural preconditions of labour as belonging to him. But this belonging is mediated through his being a member of the State, through the existence of the State – i.e. through a *presupposition* which is regarded as divine, etc.

Concentration in the city, with the land as its territory; small-scale agriculture producing for direct consumption; manufacture as the domestic sideline of wives and daughters (spinning and weaving), or made independent only in a few individual branches (*fabri* {ancient Roman artisans}, etc.).

The precondition for the survival of this community is the maintenance of equality among its free self-sustaining peasants, and their own labour as the condition for the continued existence of their property. They relate as proprietors to the natural conditions of labour; but their personal labour must constantly posit these conditions as real conditions and objective elements of the personality of the individual, of his personal labour.

On the other hand, the tendencies of this small warlike community drives it beyond these limits, etc. (Rome, Greece, the Jews, etc.). [...]

The individual is placed in such conditions of gaining his life as to make not the acquiring of wealth his object, but self-sustenance, his own reproduction as a member of the community; the reproduction of himself as proprietor of the parcel of ground and, in that quality, as a member of the commune.

The continuation of the commune is the reproduction of all its members as self-sustaining peasants, whose surplus time belongs precisely to the commune, to the labour of war, etc. Property in one's own labour is mediated through property in the conditions of labour – the hide of land, which is itself guaranteed by the existence of the community, which in turn is safeguarded by the surplus labour of its members in the form of military service, etc. The member of the community reproduces himself not by cooperation in wealth-producing labour, but by cooperation in labour for the (real or imaginary) communal interests aimed at maintaining the union against external and internal stress. Property is *quiritarium* {property of the citizens of ancient Rome}, property of the Romans; the private owner of land is such only by virtue of being a Roman, but as a Roman he *is* a private landowner.

A third form of the property of working individuals, self-sustaining members of the community, in the natural conditions of their labour, is the *Germanic*. Here it is not the case, as in the specifically oriental form, that the member of the community is as such co-holder of the communal property. The Germanic form also differs from the Roman, Greek (in short, the ancient classical) form, where the land is occupied by the community, Roman land; where part of the land remains with the community as such, as distinct from its members, *ager publicus* in its various forms; and where the remainder is distributed, and each plot is Roman by virtue of the fact that it is the private property, the domain, of a Roman, the part of the workshop which belongs to him, but he is a Roman only by virtue of the fact that he enjoys this sovereign right over part of the Roman soil. [...] Since the patrician represents the community to a higher degree, he is the possessor of the *ager publicus*, and uses it through his clients, etc. (also, gradually appropriates it).

The Germanic commune is not concentrated in the city; by means of such a concentration – the city as centre of rural life, residence of the agricultural labourers, as also the centre of warfare – the commune as such gains an outward existence, distinct from that of the individual. Ancient classical history is the history of cities, but cities based on landed property and agriculture; Asiatic history is a kind of indifferent unity of town and country (the really large cities must be regarded here merely as royal camps, as an artificial excrescence upon the actual economic structure); the Middle Ages (Germanic period) begins with the land as the locus of history, whose further development then proceeds through the contradiction between town and country; modern [history] is the urbanisation of the countryside, not, as in ancient times, the ruralisation of the city.

With its coming together in the city, the commune as such acquires an economic existence; the very *presence* of the city as such distinguishes it from a mere multiplicity of separate houses. The whole here is not merely a collection of its separate parts. It is a kind of independent organism. Among the Germanic peoples where the individual family chiefs settled in forests, separated by long distances, the commune exists even *outwardly* merely by virtue of the periodic gatherings of its members, although their unity *in-itself* is posited in descent, language, common past and history, etc.

The *commune* therefore appears as an *assembly*, not an *association*, as a unification whose independent subjects are the landed proprietors, and not as a unity. In fact, the community therefore does not exist as a *State*, as a *State system*, as among the ancients, because it does not exist as a *city*. For the community to come into real existence, the free landed proprietors must hold an *assembly*, whereas, e.g. in Rome, it *exists* apart from such assemblies, in the presence of the *city itself* and in the persons of the officials put in charge of it, etc.

True, the *ager publicus*, the communal land or people's land, occurs among the Germanic peoples also, as distinct from the property of the individual. It consists of hunting grounds, pastures, woodlands, etc., that part of the land which cannot be partitioned, if it is to serve as a means of production in this specific form. However, the *ager publicus* does not, as among e.g. the Romans, embody the specific economic being of the State, as against the private owners – so that they were *private* owners properly speaking in so far as they were *excluded* from, i.e. deprived of the use of, the *ager publicus*, like the plebeians.

The *ager publicus* is rather a mere supplement to individual property among the Germanic peoples, and figures as property only in so far as it is defended against hostile tribes as the common property of one particular tribe. The property of the individual is not mediated through the community, but the existence of the community and of communal property is mediated, i.e. it appears as a relation of the independent subjects to one another. *Au fond*, each individual household contains an entire economy, forming as it does an independent centre of production (manufacture merely the domestic sideline of the women, etc.).

In the ancient world, it is the city with its attached territory that forms the economic totality, in the Germanic world, it is the individual home, which itself appears merely as a small dot in the land belonging to it; which is not a concentration of many proprietors, but the family as an independent unit. In the Asiatic form (at least in its predominant variant), there is no property, but only occupation by individuals; the commune is properly speaking the real proprietor – hence property only as *communal property* in land.

Among the ancients (Romans as the classical example, the thing in its purest, most fully developed form), there is a contradiction between the form of State landed property and private landed property, so that the latter is mediated through the former, or the former itself exists in this dual form. The private landed proprietor is thus simultaneously an urban citizen. Economically, citizenship may be expressed in the simple statement that the tiller of the soil is a city dweller.

In the Germanic form, the tiller of the soil is not a citizen, i.e. not a city dweller; the foundation of this form is the isolated, independent family settlement, guaranteed by its bond with the other settlements of the same tribe, and their occasional assembly for the purposes of war, religion, adjudication, etc., which establishes their mutual surety. Individual landed property does not appear here as a contradictory form as against communal landed property, nor as mediated by the community, but the other way round. The community exists only in the mutual relation of the individual landed proprietors as such. Communal property as such appears only as a communal appendage to the individual kin settlements and land appropriations.

The [Germanic] community is neither the substance, of which the individual appears merely as the accident [as in the Oriental community], nor is it the general, which exists as such and has a *unified being* [as with the ancients] either in the mind or in the reality of the city and its urban requirements as distinct from those of the individual, or in the urban territory as its separate being as distinct from the particular economic being of the member of the community. The community is, rather, on the one hand, presupposed in itself to the individual proprietor as the common element in language, blood, etc.; but on the other hand it has being only in its *real assembly* for communal purposes. In so far as it has a separate economic existence in the communally used hunting grounds, pastures, etc., it is used in these ways by every individual proprietor as such, and not in his capacity as a representative of the State (as in Rome). It is therefore genuinely the common property of the individual proprietors, and not of the union of these proprietors as an entity endowed with an existence of its own in the city, distinct from themselves as individuals.

The crucial point here is this: in all these forms, in which landed property and agriculture constitute the basis of the economic order, and hence the economic object is the production of use values, i.e. the *reproduction of the individual* in his particular relationships to his community, in which he forms its basis, we find the following elements:

(1) Appropriation of the natural condition of labour, of the *earth* as the original instrument of labour, both as workshop and repository of raw materials; however, appropriation not by means of labour but as the prerequisite for labour. The individual relates simply to the objective conditions of labour as his own, as the inorganic nature of his subjectivity, which realises itself through them. The chief objective condition of labour does not itself appear as the *product* of labour, but is already there as *nature*. On the one hand the living individual, on the other the earth, as the objective condition of his reproduction.

(2) However, this *relation* to the land, to the soil, as the property of the working individual, who therefore right from the outset does not appear merely as a working individual in this abstraction, but who has an *objective mode of existence* in his ownership of the land, an existence which is *presupposed* to his activity and is not a mere result of it, and which is as much a precondition of his activity as his skin, his sense organs, which, though he also reproduces and develops these in his life process, are nevertheless presupposed to this reproduction process – this relation is instantly mediated by the naturally evolved and more or less historically developed and modified being of the individual as a *member of a community* – his naturally evolved being as part of a tribe, etc.

An isolated individual could no more have property in land than he could speak. True, he could live off the land, as animals do. But the relation to the soil as property always arises from the peaceful or violent occupation of the land by the tribe, the community in a form more or less naturally evolved or already historically developed. The individual here can never appear so thoroughly isolated as he does as a mere free worker. If the objective conditions of his labour are presupposed as belonging to him, he himself is subjectively presupposed as belonging to a community, through which his relationship to the land is mediated. His relation to the objective conditions of labour is mediated by his being as a member of a community. Conversely, the real being of the community is determined by the particular form of his ownership of the objective conditions of labour. Whether this property mediated by his being within a community is *communal property*, where the individual is merely occupier and where there is no private property in land, – or whether property has the dual form of state and private property, but in such a way that the latter appears as posited by the former, so that only the citizen is and has to be a private proprietor, while on the other hand his property as a citizen also has a separate existence, – or whether, finally, communal property appears as merely supplementary to individual property, the latter, however, as the basis, and the community does not exist for itself at all outside the *assembly* of its members and their association for common purposes – these different forms of relation of the members of the commune or tribe to the tribal land – to the territory on which it has settled – depend partly on the natural character of the tribe, partly on the economic conditions under which it now actually relates itself to the soil as proprietor, i.e. appropriates its fruits by means of labour, and this, in turn, depends on the climate, the physical properties of the soil, the physically conditioned mode of its utililisation, the relationship to hostile or neighbouring tribes, and the modifications brought about by migrations, historical events, etc.

For the commune to continue to exist as such in the old way, the reproduction of its members under the objective conditions presupposed is necessary. In time, production itself, the increase in population (which also belongs to production) necessarily transcends these conditions, destroys them instead of reproducing them, etc., and as a result of this the communal system decays and dies along with the property relations on which it was based.

The Asiatic form necessarily survives longest and most stubbornly. This is inherent in its presupposition, namely that the individual does not become independent vis-à-vis the commune; that there is a self-sustaining circle of production, a unity of agriculture and handicrafts, etc.

If the individual changes his relationship to the community, he thereby changes and undermines the community and its economic premiss. On the other hand, the modification of this economic premiss, which is brought about by its own dialectic, impoverishment, etc., particularly the impact of war and conquest, which, e.g. in Rome, belongs essentially to the economic conditions of the community itself, transcends the real bond on which the community rests.

In all these forms, the basis of development is the *reproduction of presupposed* relationships between the individual and his commune – relationships more or less naturally evolved or else historically developed, but become traditional – and a *specific objective* existence, *predetermined* for the individual, both as regards his relation to the conditions of labour and his relation to his co-workers, fellow-tribesmen, etc. The development is therefore from the outset a *limited* one, but once the limit is transcended, decay and ruin ensue. The development of slavery, the concentration of landed property, exchange, a monetary economy, conquest, etc., had this effect among the Romans, though all these elements seemed up to a certain point compatible with the basis, in part a mere harmless extension of it, in part mere abuses flowing out of it. Considerable developments are possible here within a particular sphere. Individuals may appear great. But free and full development, either of the individual or of society, is inconceivable here, since such a development stands in contradiction to the original relation.

Among the ancients, we never come across an investigation into which form of landed property, etc., is the most productive, creates the greatest wealth. Wealth does not appear as the purpose of production, although Cato may well investigate which way of field cultivation is the most profitable, or even Brutus may lend his money at the highest rate of interest. The enquiry is always about which form of property creates the best citizens. Wealth as an end-in-itself appears only among a few trading peoples – monopolists of the carrying trade – who live in the pores of the ancient world like the Jews in medieval society. Now, wealth is on the one hand a thing, embodied in things, in material products, which man commands as subject. On the other hand, wealth as value is simply command over alien labour, not for the purpose of domination but of private consumption, etc. In all its forms it appears in physical shape, whether as a thing or as a relationship mediated by a thing, located outside the individual, somewhere near him.

In this way, the old view according to which man always appears in however narrowly national, religious or political a determination as the end of production, seems very exalted when set against the modern world, in which production is the end of man, and wealth the end of production. In fact, however, if the narrow bourgeois form is peeled off, what is wealth if not the universality of the individual's needs, capacities, enjoyments, productive forces, etc., produced in universal exchange; what is it if not the full development of human control over the forces of nature – over the forces of so-called Nature, as well as those of his own nature? What is wealth if not the absolute unfolding of man's creative abilities, without any precondition other than the preceding historical development, which makes the totality of this development – i.e. the development of all human powers as such, not measured by any *previously given* yardstick – an end-in-itself, through which he does not reproduce himself in any specific character, but produces his totality, and does not seek to remain something he has already become, but is in the absolute movement of becoming?

In the bourgeois economy – and in the epoch of production to which it corresponds – this complete unfolding of man's inner potentiality turns into his total emptying-out. His universal objectification becomes his total alienation, and the demolition of all determined one-sided aims becomes the sacrifice of the [human] end-in-itself to a wholly external purpose. That is why, on the one hand, the childish world of antiquity appears as something superior. On the other hand, it *is* superior, wherever fixed shape, form and established limits are being looked for. It is satisfaction from a narrow standpoint; while the modern world leaves us unsatisfied or, where it does appear to be satisfied with itself, is merely *vulgar*.

[...]*

The original conditions of production cannot initially be *themselves produced*, cannot be the results of production. (Instead of original conditions of production we might also say: the conditions for the reproduction of an increasing number of human beings by means of the natural process of the two sexes. For if this reproduction appears on one side as the appropriation of the objects by the subjects, it equally appears on the other as the shaping and the subjection of the objects by and to a subjective purpose; the transformation of the objects into results and repositories of subjective activity.) What requires explanation is not the *unity* of living and active human beings with the natural, inorganic conditions of their exchange of matter with nature, and therefore their appropriation of nature; nor of course is this the result of an historical process. What we must explain is the *separation* between these inorganic conditions of human existence and this active being, a separation which is posited in its complete form only in the relationship between wage labour and capital.

In the relation of slavery and serfdom there is no such separation; rather, one part of society is treated by another as the mere *inorganic and natural* condition of its own reproduction. The slave stands in no relation whatsoever to the objective conditions of his labour; rather, *labour* itself, both in the form of the slave and of the serf, is placed along with the other natural beings such as cattle *as an inorganic condition* of production, as an appendage of the soil.

In other words: the original conditions of production appear as natural presuppositions, *natural conditions of the existence of the producer*, just as his living body, even though he reproduces and develops it, is not originally posited by himself, but appears as his own *presupposition*; his own (corporeal) being is a natural presupposition not posited by himself. These *natural conditions of existence*, to which he relates as to his own inorganic body, have a dual character: they are (1) subjective and (2) objective. The producer becomes aware of himself as member of a family, a tribe, a clan, etc. – which then, in the process of intermixture and conflict with others, assume historically different shapes; and, as such a member, he relates to a specific nature (we can still call it land, earth, soil) as his own inorganic being, as the condition of his production and reproduction. As the natural member of a community, he participates in the communal property and takes a particular share of it into his own possession; just so, as a native Roman citizen, he has (at least) a notional claim to the *ager publicus* and a real claim to a specified number of *jugera* of land, etc.

His *property*, i.e. his relation to the natural presuppositions of his production as belonging to himself, as *his own*, is mediated by his natural membership of a community. (The abstraction of a community whose members have nothing in common but e.g. language, etc., and barely even that, is plainly the product of much later historical circumstances.) With regard to the individual, for instance, it is evident that he himself relates to his language as *his own* only as the natural member of a human community. Language as the product of an individual is an absurdity. But this is equally true of property.

Language itself is just as much the product of a community as in another respect it is the being of the community, its articulate being, as it were.

(Communal production and communal property, as found e.g. in Peru, is evidently a *secondary* form, introduced and transmitted by conquering tribes, who had been familiar at home with communal property and communal production in the older and simpler form, as it occurs in India and among the Slavs. Similarly, the form found e.g. among the Celts in Wales appears to have been transmitted to them, a *secondary* form, introduced by conquerors among the less developed conquered tribes. The perfection and systematic elaboration of these systems by *supreme central authority* indicate their later origins. Just as the feudalism introduced into England was formally more complete than the feudalism which had evolved naturally in France.)

[...]

Thus originally *property* means nothing more than man's relating to his natural conditions of production as belonging to him, as his own, as *presupposed along with his own being*; his relating to them as *natural presuppositions* of himself, which constitute, as it were, only an extension of his body. Actually, he does not relate to his conditions of production, but has a dual being, both subjectively as himself, and objectively in these natural inorganic conditions of his existence.

The forms of these *natural conditions of production* are dual: (1) his being as member of a community, hence the being of this community which in its original form is a *tribal community*, more or less modified; (2) his relation to the *land* by means of the community, as to *his own*; communal landed property, at the same time *individual occupation* for the individual, or in such a manner that the soil itself and its cultivation remain communal, and only its fruits are divided [...] Membership of a *naturally evolved society*, a tribe, etc., is a natural condition of production for the living individual. His own productive being can only have existence under this condition. His subjective being as such is conditioned by it as much as it is conditioned by his relating to the land as to his workshop.

[...]

Property therefore means *belonging to a tribe* (community) (having one's subjective/objective existence within it), and, mediated by the relationship of this community to the land, to the earth as its inorganic body, [it also means] the relation of the individual to the land, to the external primary condition of production – since the earth is at the same time raw material, tool and fruit – as the preconditions belonging to his individuality, as its modes of being. We *reduce this property to the relation to the conditions of production.* [...]

The fundamental condition of property based on tribalism (which is what communalism originally amounts to) is to be a member of the tribe. This makes a tribe conquered and subjugated by another *propertyless* and places it among the *inorganic conditions* of the conquering tribe's reproduction, to which that community relates as its own. Slavery and serfdom are therefore only further developments of property based on tribalism. They necessarily modify all its forms. They are least able to do this in the Asiatic form. In the self-sustaining unity of manufacture and agriculture on which this form is based, conquest is not so essential a condition as where *landed property*, *agriculture*, predominate exclusively. On the other hand, since the individual in this form never becomes a proprietor but only an occupier, he is *au fond* himself the property, the slave of that [in] which the unity of the community exists. Here slavery neither puts an end to the conditions of labour, nor does it modify the essential relation.

It is now further evident that:

In so far as property is only a conscious relation to the conditions of production as one's *own* – and, with respect to the individual, a relation posited by the community and proclaimed and guaranteed as law, the being of the producer thus appearing as a being within the objective conditions *belonging to him* – it is realised only through production. Real appropriation does not occur through the establishment of a notional relationship to these conditions, but takes place in the active, real relationship to them, when they are really posited as the conditions of man's subjective activity.

In the light of this it is also clear that *these conditions change.* Only when a tribe hunts, does a particular region of the earth become a hunting ground; only when the soil is tilled, is the land posited as the extension of the body of the individual. Once the *city of Rome* was built, and its surrounding land cultivated by its citizens, the conditions of the community were different from what they had been before. The object of all these communities is preservation, i.e. *the reproduction of their individual members as proprietors, i.e. in the same objective mode of existence,* which *also constitutes the relationship of the members to each other, and therefore constitutes the community itself. But this reproduction is at the same time necessarily new production and the destruction of the old form.* For instance, where each individual is supposed to possess a certain amount of land, the increase in population already presents a problem. If it is to be coped with, colonisation and with it wars of conquest have to be undertaken. Hence slaves, etc., also e.g. the enlargement of the *ager publicus,* and hence more patricians, who represent the community, etc.

Thus the preservation of the old community implies the destruction of the conditions on which it rests, and turns into its opposite. For instance, if it were to be argued that productivity could be increased within the same territory, through a development of the productive forces, etc. (which in traditional agriculture is precisely what develops more slowly than anything else), this would imply new methods and combinations of labour, a high proportion of the day being devoted to agriculture, etc., and, once again, the old economic conditions of the community would be transcended. In the act of reproduction itself are changed not only the objective conditions – e.g. village becomes city, the wilderness becomes cultivated clearings, etc. – but also the producers, who transform themselves in that they evolve new qualities from within themselves, develop through production new powers and new ideas, new modes of intercourse, new needs, and new speech.

The more traditional the mode of production itself – and it persists for a long time in agriculture and even longer in the Oriental mutual complementation of agriculture and manufacture – i.e. the more the *real process* of appropriation remains the same, the more unchanging will be the old forms of property and therefore also the community as a whole.

Where the members of the community have already developed a separate identity as private proprietors from their collective entity as an urban community and owners of the urban territory, conditions already arise in which the individual may *lose* his property, i.e. the dual relationship which makes him both a citizen with equal status, belonging to the community, and a *proprietor.* In the Oriental form, this *loss* is hardly possible, except as a result of wholly external influences, since the individual member of the commune never enters into so independent a relation to it that he could lose his (objective, economic) tie with it. He is firmly rooted. This is also inherent in the union of manufacture and agriculture, of town (in this instance the village) and country.

Among the ancients [Greeks and Romans], manufacture already

appears as degeneration (an occupation fit only for freedmen, clients and foreigners), etc. This development of productive labour (its emancipation from total subordination to agriculture, as domestic labour, labour of freedmen, manufacture devoted only to agricultural purposes and war, or to religious observances and communal requirements such as the construction of houses, roads and temples), this development, which necessarily arises from intercourse with foreigners, from slaves, from the desire to exchange the surplus product, etc., destroys the mode of production on which the community rests, and with it the *objective individual* – i.e. the individual Greek, Roman, etc. Exchange has the same effect, and so has indebtedness, etc.

The original unity between a specific form of communal or tribal entity and the property in nature corresponding to it, or relation to the objective conditions of production as natural, as the objective being of the individual mediated by the community – this unity, which in one sense appears as the particular form of property, has its living reality in a specific *mode of production* itself, and this mode is as much the relationship of the individuals to one another as it is their specific active relationship towards inorganic nature, a specific mode of working (which is always family labour and often communal labour). The community itself appears as the first great force of production; particular conditions of production ([favouring] e.g. stock-breeding or agriculture) give rise to particular modes of production and particular forces of production, both subjective ones, i.e. those which appear as qualities of the individuals, and objective ones.

In the final analysis the community, as well as the property based upon it, comes down to a certain stage in the development of the productive forces of the working subjects, to which correspond certain relations of these subjects to each other and to nature. Up to a certain point, reproduction. Then this turns into dissolution.

Property – and this applies to its Asiatic, Slavonic, ancient [classical] and Germanic forms – therefore originally means the relation of the working (producing) subject (or the subject reproducing himself) to the conditions of his production or reproduction as his own. Hence it will take different forms depending on the conditions of production. The object of production itself is to reproduce the producer in and together with these objective conditions of his being. This relation as a proprietor – not as the result but as the presupposition of labour, i.e. of production – presupposes in turn a particular existence of the individual as member of a tribal or communal entity (whose property he himself is up to a certain point).

Slavery, serfdom, etc., where the labourer himself appears among the natural conditions of production for a third individual or community (this does *not* apply e.g. to the general slavery of the Orient, [or does] *only* from the European point of view) – and where property therefore is no longer the relation of the independently working individual to the objective conditions of labour – is always secondary, never original, although it is the necessary and logical result of property based on the community and on labour in the community.

It is of course very simple to imagine a powerful, physically superior individual, who starts by catching animals and proceeds to capture men in order to make them catch animals for him; in other words, uses man as a naturally occurring condition for his reproduction as he uses any other natural living being. His own labour then is reduced to domination, etc. But such a view is absurd, even though it may be correct from the standpoint of some particular tribal or communal entity, because it starts from the development of *isolated* individuals.

Man becomes individualised only through the process of history. Originally he is a *species being, a tribal being, a herd animal* – though by no means a *zoon politikon* in the political sense. Exchange itself is a major agent of this individuation. It makes herd-like existence superfluous and dissolves it. This occurs when matters have changed in such a way that man as an isolated individual relates only to himself, but that the means of positing himself as an isolated individual have become precisely what gives him his general and communal character. It is in the community that the objective being of the individual as a proprietor (e.g. a landed proprietor) is presupposed, and is so, moreover, under certain conditions which chain him to the community, or rather constitute a link in his chain. In bourgeois society, e.g., the worker stands there purely subjectively, without object; but the thing which *confronts* him has now become the *true community*, which he tries to make a meal of and which makes a meal of him.

All forms (more or less naturally evolved, but all at the same time results of historical processes) in which the community presupposes its subjects in a specific objective unity with the conditions of their production, or in which a specific subjective mode of being presupposes the communities themselves as condition of production, necessarily correspond only to a development of the productive forces which is limited, and indeed limited in principle. The development of the productive forces dissolves them, and their dissolution is itself a development of the human productive forces. Labour is only undertaken on a certain basis – first naturally evolved – then an historical presupposition. Later, however, this basis or presupposition is itself transcended, or posited as a transient one, which has become too narrow for the unfolding of the progressive human pack.

[*Grundrisse*, 1857–8; 1858a: 399–420. One passage omitted here, denoted by an asterisk, is given above as 3.17.][111]

8.2 Leaving aside all questions of a more or less theoretical nature, I do not have to tell you that the very existence of the Russian commune is now threatened by a conspiracy of powerful interests.[112] A certain type of capitalism, fostered by the state at the peasants' expense, has risen up against the commune and found an interest in stifling it. The landowners, too, have an interest in forming the more or less well-off peasants into an agricultural middle class, and in converting the poor farmers – that is, the mass – into mere wage labourers – that is to say, cheap labour. How can a commune resist, pounded as it is by state exactions, plundered by trade, exploited by landowners, and undermined from within by usury!

What threatens the life of the Russian commune is neither a historical inevitability nor a theory; it is state oppression, and exploitation by capitalist intruders whom the state has made powerful at the peasants' expense.

[...]

From a historical point of view, only one serious argument has been given for *the inevitable dissolution* of the Russian peasant commune: If we go far back, it is said, a more or less archaic type of communal property may be found everywhere in Western Europe. But with the progress of society it has everywhere disappeared. Why should it escape the same fate only in Russia?

My answer is that, thanks to the unique combination of circumstances in Russia, the rural commune, which is still established on a national scale, may gradually shake off its primitive characteristics and directly develop as an element of collective production on a national scale. Precisely because it is contemporaneous with capitalist production, the rural commune may appropriate all its positive achievements without undergoing its (terrible) frightful vicissitudes. Russia does not live in isolation from the modern world, and nor has it fallen prey, like the East Indies, to a conquering foreign power.

Should the admirers of the capitalist system deny that such a development is *theoretically* possible, then I would ask them the following question. Did Russia have to undergo a long Western-style incubation of mechanical industry before it could make use of machinery, steamships, railways, etc.? Let them also explain how they managed to introduce, in the twinkling of an eye, that whole machinery of exchange (banks, credit companies, etc.) which was the work of centuries in the West.

If, at the time of the emancipation {1861},[113] the rural commune had been initially placed under conditions of normal prosperity, if, moreover, the huge public debt, mostly financed at the peasants' expense, along with the enormous sums which the state (still at the peasants' expense) provided for the 'new pillars of society', transformed into capitalists – if all these expenses had served for the further development of the rural commune, no one would be dreaming today of the 'historical inevitability' of the annihilation of the commune. Everyone would see the commune as the element in the regeneration of Russian society, and an element of superiority over the countries still enslaved by the capitalist regime.

[...]

Also favourable to the maintenance of the Russian commune (on the path of development) is the fact not only that it is contemporary with capitalist production (in the Western countries), but that it has survived the epoch when the social system stood intact. Today, it faces a social system which, both in Western Europe and the United States, is in conflict with science, with the popular masses, and with the very productive forces that it generates [...] In short, the rural commune finds it in a state of crisis that will end only when the social system is eliminated through the return of modern societies to the 'archaic' type of communal property [...] We should not, then, be too frightened by the word 'archaic'.

But at least we should be thoroughly acquainted with all the historical twists and turns. We know nothing about them. *The history of the decline of the primitive communities has still to be written (it would be wrong to put them all on the same plane; in historical as in geological formations, there is a whole series of primary, secondary, tertiary and other types). So far, only very rough sketches have been made. Still, the research is sufficiently advanced to warrant the assertion that: (1) the primitive communities had incomparably greater vitality than the Semitic, Greek, Roman and a fortiori the modern capitalist societies; and (2) the causes of their decline lie in economic factors which prevented them from going beyond a certain degree of development, and in historical contexts quite unlike that of the present-day Russian commune [...].* In one way or another, this commune perished in the midst of never-ending foreign and intestine warfare. It probably died a violent death when the Germanic tribes came to conquer Italy, Spain, Gaul, and so on. The commune of the archaic type had already ceased to exist. And yet, its *natural vitality* is proved by two facts. Scattered examples survived all the vicissitudes of the Middle Ages and have maintained themselves up to the present-day – e.g. in my own home region of Trier. More importantly, however, it so stamped its own features on the commune that supplanted it (a commune in which arable land became private property, while the forests, pastures, waste ground, etc., remained communal property), that Maurer was able to reconstruct the archaic prototype while deciphering the commune (of more recent origin) of secondary formation. Thanks to the characteristic features inherited from the prototype, the new commune which the Germans introduced into every conquered region became the only focus of liberty and popular life throughout the Middle Ages.

We know nothing of the life of the (Germanic) (rural) (archaic) commune after Tacitus, nor how and when it actually disappeared. Thanks to Julius Caesar, however, we do at least know its point of departure. In Caesar's time, the (arable) land was already distributed on an annual basis – not yet, however, among individual members of a commune, but among the gentes and tribes of the (various) Germanic confederations. The agricultural *rural commune* therefore emerged in Germania from a more archaic type; it was the product of spontaneous development rather than being imported ready-made from Asia. It may also be found in Asia – in the East Indies – always as the *final term* or last period of the archaic formation.

If I am (now) to assess the possible destinies (of the 'rural commune') from a purely theoretical point of view – that is, always supposing conditions of normal life – I must now refer to certain characteristics which differentiate the 'agricultural commune' from the more archaic type.

Firstly, the earlier primitive communities all rested on the natural kinship of their members. In breaking this strong yet narrow tie, the agricultural commune proved more capable of adapting and expanding, and of undergoing contact with strangers.

Secondly, within the commune, the house and its complementary yard were already the farmer's private property, whereas the communal house was one of the material bases of previous communities, long before agriculture was even introduced.

Finally, although the arable land remained communal property, it was periodically divided among the members of the agricultural commune, so that each farmer tilled on his own behalf the various fields allocated to him and individually appropriated their fruits. In the more archaic communities, by contrast, production was a common activity, and only the final produce was distributed among individual members. Of course, this primitive type of collective or co-operative production stemmed from the weakness of the isolated individual, not from socialization of the means of production.

It is easy to see that the dualism inherent in the 'agricultural commune' may give it a sturdy life: for communal property and all the resulting social relations provide it with a solid foundation, while the privately owned houses, fragmented tillage of the arable land and private appropriation of its fruits all permit a development of individuality incompatible with conditions in the more primitive communities. It is just as evident, however, that the very same dualism may eventually become a source of disintegration. Apart from the influence of a hostile environment, the mere accumulation over time of movable property, beginning with wealth in livestock and even extending to wealth in serfs, combines with the ever more prominent role played by movables in agriculture itself and with a host of other circumstances, inseparable from such accumulation, which would take me too far from the central theme. All these factors, then, serve to dissolve economic and social equality, generating within the commune itself a conflict of interests which leads, first, to the conversion of arable land into private property, and ultimately to the private appropriation of forests, pastures, waste ground, etc., already no more than communal appendages of private property. Accordingly, the 'agricultural commune' everywhere presents itself as *the most recent type* of the archaic formation of societies; and the period of the agricultural commune appears in the historical course of Western Europe, both ancient and modern, as a period of transition from communal to private property, from the primary to the secondary formation. But does this mean that the development of the 'agricultural commune' must follow this route in every circumstance (in every historical context)? Not at all. Its constitutive form allows of the following alternative: either the element of private property which it implies gains the upper hand over the collective element, or the reverse takes place. Everything depends upon the historical circumstance in which it is situated. Both solutions are *a priori* possibilities, but each one naturally requires a completely different historical context.

Coming now to the 'agricultural commune' in Russia [...] On the one hand, communal land ownership allows it directly and gradually to transform fragmented, individualist agriculture into collective agriculture [...] and the Russian peasants already practice it in the jointly-owned meadows; the physical configuration of the land makes it suitable for huge-scale mechanised cultivation; the peasant's familiarity with the *artel* relationship[114] can help him to make the transition from augmented to co-operative labour; and, finally, Russian society, which has for so long lived at his expense, owes him the credits required for such a transition. (To be sure, the first step should be to create normal conditions for the commune *on its present basis*, for the peasant is above all hostile to any abrupt change.) On the other hand, the *contemporaneity* of Western (capitalist) production, which dominates the world market, enables Russia to build into the commune all the positive achievements of the capitalist system, without having to pass under its harsh tribute.

[...]

One debilitating feature of the 'agricultural commune' in Russia is inimical to it in every way. This is its isolation, the lack of connection between the lives of different communes. It is not an immanent or universal characteristic of this type that the commune should appear as a *localised microcosm*. But wherever it does so appear, it leads to the formation of a more or less central despotism above the communes. The federation of North Russian republics proves that such isolation, which seems to have been originally imposed by the huge size of the country, was largely consolidated by Russia's political changes of fortune after the Mongol invasion. Today, it is an obstacle that could be removed with the utmost ease. All that is necessary is to replace the *'volost'*,[115] a government institution, with a peasant assembly chosen by the peasants themselves – an economic and administrative body serving their own interests.

[...]

The historical situation of the Russian 'rural commune' is without parallel! Alone in Europe, it has preserved itself not as scattered debris (like the rare and curious miniatures of an archaic type that were recently to be found in the West), but as the more or less dominant form of popular life spread over a vast empire. While it has in common land ownership the (natural) basis of collective appropriation, its historical context – the contemporaneity of capitalist production – provides it with ready-made material conditions for huge-scale common labour. It is therefore able to incorporate the positive achievements of the capitalist system, without having to pass under its harsh tribute. The commune may gradually replace fragmented agriculture with large-scale, machine-assisted agriculture particularly suited to the physical configuration of Russia. It may thus become the *direct starting-point* of the economic system towards which modern society is tending; it may open a new chapter that does not begin with its own suicide.

[Drafts of a letter to Vera Zasulich, 1881; 1881b: 104–12. Marginal note incorporated into text between asterisks.]

8.3 If, in a society with capitalist production, anarchy in the social division of labour and despotism in that of the workshop are mutual conditions the one of the other, we find, on the contrary, in those earlier forms of society in which the separation of trades has been spontaneously developed, then crystallized, and finally made permanent by law, on the one hand, a specimen of the organization of the labour of society, in accordance with an approved and authoritative plan, and on the other, the entire exclusion of division of labour in the workshop, or at all events a mere dwarf-like or sporadic and accidental development of the same.

Those small and extremely ancient Indian communities, some of which have continued down to this day, are based on possession in common of the land, on the blending of agriculture and handicrafts, and on an unalterable division of labour, which serves, whenever a new community is started, as a plan and scheme ready cut and dried. Occupying areas of from 100 up to several thousand acres, each forms a compact whole producing all it requires. The chief part of the products is destined for direct use by the community itself, and does not take the form of a commodity. Hence, production here is independent of that division of labour brought about, in Indian society as a whole, by means of the exchange of commodities. It is the surplus alone that becomes a commodity, and a portion of even that, not until it has reached the hands of the State, into whose hands from time immemorial a certain quantity of these products has found its way in the shape of rent in kind. The constitution of these communities varies in different parts of India. In those of the simplest form, the land is tilled in common, and the produce divided amongst the members. At the same time, spinning and weaving are carried on in each family as subsidiary industries. Side by side with the masses thus occupied with one and the same work, we find the 'chief inhabitant', who is judge, police, and tax-gatherer in one; the book-keeper, who keeps the accounts of the tillage and registers everything relating thereto; another official, who prosecutes criminals, protects strangers travelling through and escorts them to the next village; the boundary man, who guards the boundaries against neighbouring communities; the water-overseer,

who distributes the water from the common tanks for irrigation; the Brahmin, who conducts the religious services; the schoolmaster, who on the sand teaches the children reading and writing; the calendar-Brahmin, or astrologer, who makes known the lucky or unlucky days for seed-time and harvest, and for every other kind of agricultural work; a smith and a carpenter, who make and repair all the agricultural implements; the potter, who makes all the pottery of the village; the barber, the washerman, who washes clothes, the silversmith, here and there the poet, who in some communities replaces the silversmith, in others the schoolmaster. This dozen of individuals is maintained at the expense of the whole community. If the population increases, a new community is founded, on the pattern of the old one, on unoccupied land. The whole mechanism discloses a systematic division of labour; but a division like that in manufactures is impossible, since the smith and the carpenter, etc., find an unchanging market, and at the most there occur, according to the size of the villages, two or three of each, instead of one. The law that regulates the division of labour in the community acts with the irresistible authority of a law of nature, at the same time that each individual artificer, the smith, the carpenter, and so on, conducts in his workshop all the operations of his handicraft in the traditional way, but independently, and without recognising any authority over him. The simplicity of the organization for production in these self-sufficing communities that constantly reproduce themselves in the same form, and when accidentally destroyed, spring up again on the same spot and with the same name – this simplicity supplies the key to the secret of the unchangeableness of Asiatic societies, an unchangeableness in such striking contrast with the never-ceasing changes of dynasty. The structure of the economic elements of society remains untouched by the storm-clouds of the political sky.
[*Capital* 1, 1867; 1867a: 357–8]

In a famous article of 1853, Marx wrote that 'however changing the political aspect of India's past must appear, its social condition has remained unaltered since its remotest antiquity, until the first decennium of the 19th century'; 'English interference [...] produced the greatest, and to speak the truth, the only *social* revolution ever heard of in Asia' [1853a: 128, 132]. He concluded:

8.4 Now, sickening as it must be to human feeling to witness those myriads of industrious patriarchal and inoffensive social organizations disorganized and dissolved into their units, thrown into a sea of woes, and their individual members losing at the same time their ancient form of civilization, and their hereditary means of subsistence, we must not forget that these idyllic village-communities, inoffensive as they may appear, had always been the solid foundation of oriental despotism, that they restrained the human mind within the smallest possible compass, making it the unresisting tool of superstition, enslaving it beneath traditional rules, depriving it of all grandeur and historical energies. We must not forget the barbarian egotism which, concentrating on some miserable patch of land, had quietly witnessed the ruin of empires, the perpetuation of unspeakable cruelties, the massacre of the populations of large towns, with no other consideration bestowed upon them than on natural events, itself the helpless prey of any aggressor who deigned to notice it at all. We must not forget that this undignified, stagnatory, and vegetative life, that this passive sort of existence evoked on the other part, in contradistinction, wild, aimless, unbounded forces of destruction and rendered murder itself a religious rite in Hindostan. We must not forget that these little communities were contaminated by distinctions of caste and by slavery, that they subjugated man to external circumstances instead of elevating man the sovereign of circumstances, that they transformed a self-developing social state into never changing natural destiny, and thus brought about a brutalizing worship of nature, exhibiting its degradation in the fact that man, the sovereign of nature, fell down on his knees in adoration of Kanuman, the monkey, and Sabbala, the cow. [The British Rule in India, 1853; 1853a: 132; see also 1853b]

8.5 There have been in Asia, generally, from immemorial times, but three departments of Government; that of Finance, or the plunder of the interior; that of War, or the plunder of the exterior; and, finally, the department of Public Works. Climate and territorial conditions, especially the vast tracts of desert, extending from the Sahara, through Arabia, Persia, India, and Tartary, to the most elevated Asiatic highlands, constituted artificial irrigation by canals and waterworks the basis of Oriental agriculture. As in Egypt and India, inundations are used for fertilizing the soil in Mesopotamia, Persia, etc.; advantage is taken of a high level for feeding irrigative canals. This prime necessity of an economical and common use of water, which, in the Occident, drove private enterprise to voluntary association, as in Flanders and Italy, necessitated, in the Orient where civilization was too low and the territorial extent too vast to call into life voluntary association, the centralizing power of Government. Hence an economical function devolved upon all Asiatic Governments, the function of providing

public works. This artificial fertilization of the soil, dependent on a Central Government, and immediately decaying with the neglect of irrigation and drainage, explains the otherwise strange fact that we now find whole territories barren and desert that were once brilliantly cultivated, as Palmyra, Petra, the ruins in Yemen, and large provinces of Egypt, Persia, and Hindostan; it also explains how a single war of devastation has been able to depopulate a country for centuries, and to strip it of all its civilization.
[1853a: 127]

In *Capital* Marx repeats the point, with a cutting addition: 'One of the material bases of the power of the State over the small disconnected producing organisms in India, was the regulation of the water supply. The Mahometan rulers of India understood this better than their English successors. It is enough to recall to mind the famine of 1866, which cost the lives of more than a million Hindus in the district of Orissa, in the Bengal presidency' [1867a: 514n].

8.6 Even this first work on *rent*[116] is distinguished by what has been lacking in all English economists since Sir James Steuart, namely, a sense of the *historical* differences in modes of production [...]

Jones traces rent throughout all its changes, from its crudest form, performance of labour services, to modern farmer's rent. He finds that everywhere a specific form of rent, i.e., of landed property, corresponds to a definite form of labour and of the conditions of labour. Thus, labour rents or serf rents, the change from labour rent to produce rent, metayer rents, ryot rents, etc., are examined in turn, a development the details of which do not concern us here. In all previous forms, it is the landed proprietor, not the capitalist, who directly appropriates the *surplus labour* of other people. *Rent* (as the Physiocrats[117] conceive it by *reminiscence* [of feudal conditions]) appears historically (and still on the largest scale among the Asiatic peoples) as the general form of *surplus labour*, of labour performed without payment in return. The appropriation of this surplus labour is here not mediated by exchange, as is the case in capitalist society, but its basis is the forcible domination of one section of society over another. (There is, accordingly, direct slavery, serfdom or political dependence.)
[*Theories of Surplus Value*, 1861–3; 1863c: 399–400]

8.7 If we consider ground-rent in its simplest form, that of *labour* *rent*, where the direct producer, using instruments of labour (plough, cattle, etc.) which actually or legally belong to him, cultivates soil actually owned by him during part of the week, and works during the remaining days upon the estate of the feudal lord without any compensation from the feudal lord, the situation here is quite clear, for in this case rent and surplus-value are identical. Rent, not profit, is the form here through which unpaid surplus-labour expresses itself. To what extent the labourer (a self-sustaining serf) can secure in this case a surplus above his indispensible necessities of life, i.e., a surplus above that which we would call wages under the capitalist mode of production, depends, other circumstances remaining unchanged, upon the proportion in which his labour-time is divided into labour-time for himself and enforced labour-time for his feudal lord. This surplus above the indispensible requirements of life, the germ of what appears as profit under the capitalist mode of production, is therefore wholly determined by the amount of ground-rent, which in this case is not only directly unpaid surplus-labour, but also appears as such. It is unpaid surplus-labour for the 'owner' of the means of production, which here coincide with the land, and so far as they differ from it, are mere accessories to it. [...] It is furthermore evident that in all forms in which the direct labourer remains the 'possessor' of the means of production and labour conditions necessary for the production of his own means of subsistence, the property relationship must simultaneously appear as a direct relationship of lordship and servitude, so that the direct producer is not free; a lack of freedom which may be reduced from serfdom with enforced labour to a mere tributary relationship. The direct producer, according to our assumption, is to be found here in possession of his own means of production, the necessary material labour conditions required for the realisation of his labour and the production of his means of subsistence. He conducts his agricultural activity and the rural home industries connected with it independently. This independence is not undermined by the circumstance that the small peasants may form among themselves a more or less natural production community, as they do in India, since it is here merely a question of independence from the nominal lord of the manor. Under such conditions the surplus-labour for the nominal owner of the land can only be extorted from them by other than economic pressure, whatever the form assumed may be. This differs from slave or plantation economy in that the slave works under alien conditions of production and not independently. Thus, conditions of personal dependence are requisite, a lack of personal freedom, no matter to what extent, and

being tied to the soil as its accessory, bondage in the true sense of the word.
[*Capital* 3, 1864–5; 1865a: 790–1]

In *Capital* 1 Marx reiterates that 'we must never forget that even the serf was not only the owner, if but a tribute-paying owner, of the piece of land attached to his house, but also a co-possessor of the common land' [1867a: 717n].

8.8 The relation of retainers to their lords, or that of personal service, is essentially different.[118] For personal service constitutes *au fond* merely the mode of existence of the landowner who no longer works for himself but whose property includes the workers themselves as serfs, etc., among the conditions of production. Here the *relationship of domination* exists as an essential relation of appropriation. *Au fond* there can be no relationship of dominion to animals, to the soil, etc., by virtue of appropriation, even though the animal serves. The appropriation of another's *will* is presupposed in the relationship of dominion. Creatures without will, like animals for instance, may indeed render services, but this doesn't make the owner their *lord*. However, what we see here is how the *relationships of dominion and servitude* also belong to this formula of the appropriation of the instruments of production; and they constitute a necessary ferment in the development and decay of all primitive relations of property and production, just as they express their limitations.
[*Grundrisse*, 1857–8; 1858a: 424–5]

8.9 Let us now transport ourselves from Robinson's island bathed in light to the European middle ages shrouded in darkness. Here, instead of the independent man, we find everyone dependent, serfs and lords, vassals and suzerains, laymen and clergy. Personal dependence here characterises the social relations of production just as much as it does the other spheres of life organized on the basis of that production. But for the very reason that personal dependence forms the groundwork of society, there is no necessity for labour and its products to assume a fantastic form different from their reality. They take the shape, in the transactions of society, of services in kind and payments in kind. Here the particular and natural form of labour, and not, as in a society based on the production of commodities, its general abstract form is the immediate social form of labour. Compulsory labour is just as properly measured by time, as commodity-producing labour; but every serf knows that what he expends in the service of his lord, is a definite quantity of his own personal labour-power. The tithe to be rendered to the priest is more matter of fact than his blessing. No matter, then, what we may think of the parts played by the different classes of people themselves in this society, the social relations between individuals in the performance of their labour, appear at all events as their own mutual personal relations, and are not disguised under the shape of social relations between the products of labour.

[*Capital* 1, 1867; 1867a: 77]

9

Guiding principles?

This chapter contains two main selections. Each, in different ways, has been hailed as providing the master-key to all Marx's thought. The first is the famous section of the Economic and Philosophical Manuscripts of 1844 on 'estranged labour', in which Marx outlines the concept of alienation. The second (to which I have appended a clarificatory footnote from *Capital* 1) is the Preface to the 1859 *Critique of Political Economy*, in which Marx provides a brief sketch of his own intellectual development, and summarizes what he calls the 'guiding principle' of his studies. Both texts have never ceased to generate controversy. The final passage in this anthology is from the Foreword to Marx's doctoral dissertation. As a 'guiding principle' to reading Marx, it is, to my mind at least, hard to better.

9.1 We have proceeded from the premises of political economy. We have accepted its language and its laws. We presupposed private property, the separation of labour, capital and land, and of wages, profit of capital and rent of land – likewise division of labour, competition, the concept of exchange-value, etc. On the basis of political economy itself, in its own words, we have shown that the worker sinks to the level of a commodity and becomes indeed the most wretched of commodities; that the wretchedness of the worker is in inverse proportion to the power and magnitude of his production; that the necessary result of competition is the accumulation of capital in a few hands, and thus the restoration of monopoly in a more terrible form; and that finally the distinction between capitalist and land rentier, like that between the tiller of the soil and the factory worker, disappears and that the whole society must fall apart into the two classes – the *property owners* and the propertyless *workers*.

Political economy starts with the fact of private property; it does not explain it to us. It expresses in general, abstract formulas the *material* process through which private property actually passes, and these formulas it then takes for *laws*. It does not *comprehend* these laws, i.e., it does not demonstrate how they arise from the very nature of private property. Political economy throws no light on the cause of the division between labour and capital, and between capital and land. When, for example, it defines the relationship of wages to profit, it takes the interest of the capitalist to be the ultimate cause, i.e., it takes for granted what it is supposed to explain. Similarly, competition comes in everywhere. It is explained from external circumstances. As to how far these external and apparently accidental circumstances are but the expression of a necessary course of development, political economy teaches us nothing. We have seen how exchange itself appears to it as an accidental fact. The only wheels which political economy sets in motion are *greed* and the *war amongst the greedy – competition*.

Precisely because political economy does not grasp the way the movement is connected, it was possible to oppose, for instance, the doctrine of competition to the doctrine of monopoly, the doctrine of the freedom of the crafts to the doctrine of the guild, the doctrine of the division of landed property to the doctrine of the big estate – for competition, freedom of the crafts and the division of landed property were explained and comprehended only as accidental, premeditated and violent consequences of monopoly, of the guild system, and of feudal property, not as their necessary, inevitable and natural consequences.

Now, therefore, we have to grasp the intrinsic connection between private property, avarice, the separation of labour, capital, and landed property; the connection of exchange and competition, of value and the devaluation of men, of monopoly and competition, etc. – we have to grasp this whole estrangement connected with the *money* system.

Do not let us go back to a fictitious primordial condition as the political economist does, when he tries to explain. Such a primordial condition explains nothing; it merely pushes the question away into a grey nebulous distance. The economist assumes in the form of a fact, of an event, what he is supposed to deduce – namely, the necessary relationship between two things – between, for example, division of labour and exchange. Thus the theologian explains the origin of evil by the fall of man; that is, he assumes as a fact, in historical form, what has to be explained.

We proceed from an *actual* economic fact.

The worker becomes all the poorer the more wealth he produces, the more his production increases in power and size. The worker becomes an ever cheaper commodity the more commodities he creates. The *devaluation* of the world of men is in direct proportion to the *increasing value* of the world of things. Labour produces not only commodities: it produces itself and the worker as a *commodity* – and this at the same rate at which it produces commodities in general.

This fact expresses merely that the object which labour produces – labour's product – confronts it as *something alien*, as a *power independent* of the producer. The product of labour is labour which has been embodied in an object, which has become material: it is the *objectification* of labour. Labour's realisation is its objectification. Under these economic conditions this realisation of labour appears as *loss of realisation* for the workers; objectification as *loss of the object and bondage to it*; appropriation as *estrangement, as alienation*.

So much does labour's realisation appear as loss of realisation that the worker loses realisation to the point of starving to death. So much does objectification appear as loss of the object that the worker is robbed of the objects most necessary not only for his life but for his work. Indeed, labour itself becomes an object which he can obtain only with the greatest effort and with the most irregular interruptions. So much does the appropriation of the object appear as estrangement that the more objects the worker produces the less he can possess and the more he falls under the sway of his product, capital.

All these consequences are implied in the statement that the worker is related to the *product of his labour* as to an *alien* object. For on this premise it is clear that the more the worker spends himself, the more powerful becomes the alien world of objects which he creates over and against himself, the poorer he himself – his inner world – becomes, the less belongs to him as his own. It is the same in religion. The more man puts into God, the less he retains in himself. The worker puts his life into the object; but now his life no longer belongs to him but to the object. Hence, the greater this activity, the more the worker lacks objects. Whatever the product of his labour is, he is not. Therefore the greater this product, the less is he himself. The *alienation* of the worker in his product means not only that his labour becomes an object, an *external* existence, but that it exists *outside him*, independently, as something alien to him, and that it becomes a power on its own confronting him. It means that the life which he has conferred on the object confronts him as something hostile and alien.

Let us now look more closely at the *objectification*, at the production of the worker; and in it at the *estrangement*, the *loss* of the object, of his product.

The worker can create nothing without *nature*, without the *sensuous external world*. It is the material on which his labour is realised, in which it is active, from which and by means of which it produces.

But just as nature provides labour with [the] *means of life* in the sense that labour cannot *live* without objects on which to operate, on the other hand, it also provides the *means of life* in the more restricted sense, i.e., the means for the physical existence of the *worker* himself.

Thus the more the worker by his labour *appropriates* the external world, sensuous nature, the more he deprives himself of *means of life* in two respects: first, in that the sensuous external world more and more ceases to be an object belonging to his labour – to be his labour's *means of life*; and secondly, in that it more and more ceases to be *means of life* in the immediate sense, means for the physical subsistence of the worker.

In both respects, therefore, the worker becomes a servant of his object, first, in that he receives an *object of labour*, i.e., in that he receives *work*; and secondly, in that he receives *means of subsistence*. This enables him to exist, first, as a *worker*; and, second, as a *physical subject*. The height of this servitude is that it is only as a *worker* that he can maintain himself as a *physical subject*, and that it is only as a *physical subject* that he is a worker.

(According to the economic laws the estrangement of the worker in his object is expressed thus: the more the worker produces, the less he has to consume; the more values he creates, the more valueless, the more unworthy he becomes; the better formed his product, the more deformed becomes the worker; the more civilised his object, the more barbarous becomes the worker; the more powerful labour becomes, the more powerless becomes the worker; the more ingenious labour becomes, the less ingenious becomes the worker and the more he becomes nature's servant.)

Political economy conceals the estrangement inherent in the nature of labour by not considering the direct relationship between the worker (labour) and production. It is true that labour produces wonderful things for the rich – but for the worker it produces privation. It produces palaces – but for the worker, hovels. It produces beauty – but for the worker, deformity. It replaces labour by machines, but it throws one section of the workers back to a barbarous type of labour, and it turns the other section into a machine. It produces intelligence – but for the worker, stupidity, cretinism.

The direct relationship of labour to its products is the relationship of the worker to the objects of his production. The relationship of the man of means to the objects of production and to production itself is only a *consequence* of this first relationship – and confirms it. When we ask, then, what is the essential relationship of labour we are asking about the relationship of the *worker* to production.

Till now we have been considering the estrangement, the alienation of the worker only in one of its aspects, i.e., the worker's *relationship to the products of his labour*. But the estrangement is manifested not only in the result but in the *act of production*, within the *producing activity* itself. How could the worker come to face the product of his activity as a stranger, were it not that in the very act of production he was estranging himself from himself? The product is after all but the summary of the activity, of production. If then the product of labour is alienation, production itself must be active alienation, the alienation of activity, the activity of alienation. In the estrangement of the object of labour is merely summarised the estrangement, the alienation, in the activity of labour itself.

What, then, constitutes the alienation of labour?

First, the fact that labour is *external* to the worker, i.e., it does not belong to his intrinsic nature; that in his work, therefore, he does not affirm himself but denies himself, does not feel content but unhappy, does not develop freely his physical and mental energy but mortifies his body and ruins his mind. The worker therefore only feels himself outside his work, and in his work feels outside himself. He feels at home when he is not working, and when he is working he does not feel at home. His labour is therefore not voluntary, but coerced; it is *forced labour*. It is therefore not the satisfaction of a need; it is merely a *means* to satisfy needs external to it. Its alien character emerges clearly in the fact that as soon as no physical or other compulsion exists, labour is shunned like the plague. External labour, labour in which man alienates himself, is a labour of self-sacrifice, of mortification. Lastly, the external character of labour for the worker appears in the fact that it is not his own, but someone else's, that it does not belong to him, that in it he belongs, not to himself, but to another. Just as in religion the spontaneous activity of the human imagination, of the human brain and the human heart, operates on the individual independently of him – that is, operates as an alien, divine or diabolical activity – so is the worker's activity not his spontaneous activity. It belongs to another; it is the loss of his self.

As a result, man (the worker) only feels himself freely active in his animal functions – eating, drinking, procreating, or at most in his dwelling and in dressing-up, etc.; and in his human functions he no longer feels himself to be anything but an animal. What is animal becomes human and what is human becomes animal.

Certainly eating, drinking, procreating, etc., are also genuinely human functions. But taken abstractly, separated from the sphere of all other human activity and turned into sole and ultimate ends, they are animal functions.

We have considered the act of estranging practical human activity, labour, in two of its aspects. (1) The relation of the worker to the *product of labour* as an alien object exercising power over him. This relation is at the same time the relation to the sensuous external world, to the objects of nature, as an alien world inimically opposed to him. (2) The relation of labour to the *act of production* within the *labour* process. This relation is the relation of the worker to his own activity as an alien activity not belonging to him; it is activity as suffering, strength as weakness, begetting as emasculating, the worker's *own* physical and mental energy, his personal life – for what is life but activity? – as an activity which is turned against him, independent of him and not belonging to him. Here we have *self-estrangement*, as previously we had the estrangement of the *thing*.

We have still a third aspect of *estranged labour* to deduce from the two already considered.

Man is a species-being, not only because in practice and in theory he adopts the species (his own as well as those of other things) as his object, but – and this is only another way of expressing it – also because he treats himself as the actual, living species; because he treats himself as a *universal* and therefore a free being.

The life of the species, both in man and in animals, consists physically in the fact that man (like the animal) lives on inorganic nature; and the more universal man (or the animal) is, the more universal is the sphere of inorganic nature on which he lives. Just as plants, animals, stones, air, light, etc., constitute theoretically a part of human consciousness, partly as objects of natural science, partly as objects of art – his spiritual inorganic nature, spiritual nourishment which he must first prepare to make palatable and digestable – so also in the realm of practice they constitute a part of human life and human activity. Physically man lives only on these products of nature, whether they appear in the form of food, heating, clothes, a dwelling, etc. The universality of man appears in practice precisely in the universality which makes all nature his *inorganic* body – both inasmuch as nature is (1) his direct means of life, and (2) the material, the object, and the instrument of his life activity. Nature is man's *inorganic body* – nature, that is, insofar as it is not itself human body. Man *lives* on nature – means that nature is his *body*, with which he must remain in continuous interchange if he is not to die. That man's physical and spiritual life is linked to nature means simply that nature is linked to itself, for man is a part of nature.

In estranging from man (1) nature, and (2) himself, his own active functions, his life activity, estranged labour estranges the *species* from man. It changes for him the *life of the species* into a means of individual life. First it estranges the life of the species and individual life, and secondly it makes individual life in its abstract form the purpose of the life of the species, likewise in its abstract and estranged form.

For labour, *life activity*, *productive life* itself, appears to man in the first place merely as a *means* of satisfying a need – the need to maintain physical existence. Yet the productive life is the life of the species. It is life-engendering life. The whole character of a species – its species-character – is contained in the character of its life activity; and free, conscious activity is man's species-character. Life itself appears only as a *means to life*.

The animal is immediately one with its life activity. It does not distinguish itself from it. It is *its life activity*. Man makes his life activity itself the object of his will and of his consciousness. He has conscious life activity. It is not a determination with which he directly merges. Conscious life activity distinguishes man immediately from animal life activity. It is just because of this that he is a species-being. Or it is only because he is a species-being that he is a conscious being, i.e., that his own life is an object for him. Only because of that is his activity free activity. Estranged labour reverses this relationship, so that it is just because man is a conscious being that he makes his life activity, his *essential being*, a mere means to his *existence*.

In creating a *world of objects* by his practical activity, in his *work upon* inorganic nature, man proves himself a conscious species-being, i.e., as a being that treats the species as its own essential being, or that treats itself as a species-being. Admittedly animals also produce. They build themselves nests, dwellings, like the bees, beavers, ants, etc. But an animal only produces what it immediately needs for itself or its young. It produces one-sidedly, whilst man produces universally. It produces only under the dominion of immediate physical need, while man produces even when he is free from physical need and only truly produces in freedom therefrom. An animal produces only itself, whilst man reproduces the whole of nature. An animal's product belongs immediately to its physical body, whilst man freely confronts his product. An animal forms objects only in accordance with the standard and the need of the species to which it belongs, whilst man knows how to produce in accordance with the standard of every species, and knows how to apply everywhere the inherent standard to the object. Man therefore also forms objects in accordance with the laws of beauty.

It is just in his work upon the objective world, therefore, that man really proves himself to be a *species-being*. This production is his active species-life. Through this production, nature appears as *his* work and his reality. The object of labour is, therefore, the *objectification of man's species-life*: for he duplicates himself not only, as in consciousness, intellectually, but also actively, in reality, and therefore he sees himself in a world that he has created. In tearing away from man the object of his production, therefore, estranged labour tears from him his *species-life*, his real objectivity as a member of the species, and transforms his advantage over animals into the disadvantage that his inorganic body, nature, is taken away from him.

Similarly, in degrading spontaneous, free activity to a means, estranged labour makes man's species-life a means to his physical existence.

The consciousness which man has of his species is thus transformed by estrangement in such a way that species[-life] becomes for him a means.

Estranged labour turns thus:

(3) *Man's species-being*, both nature and his spiritual species-property, into a being *alien* to him, into a *means* for his *individual existence*. It estranges from man his own body, as well as external nature and his spiritual aspect, his *human* aspect.

(4) An immediate consequence of the fact that man is estranged from the product of his labour, from his life-activity, from his species-being is the *estrangement of man* from *man*. When man confronts himself, he confronts the *other* man. What applies to a man's relation to his work, to the product of his labour and to himself, also holds of a man's relation to the other man, and to the other man's labour and object of labour.

The estrangement of man, and in fact every relationship in which man [stands] to himself, is realised and expressed only in the relationship in which a man stands to other men.

Hence within the relationship of estranged labour each man views the other in accordance with the standard and the relationship in which he finds himself as a worker.

We took our departure from a fact of political economy – the estrangement of the worker and his product. We have formulated this fact in conceptual terms as *estranged, alienated* labour. We have analysed this concept – hence analysing merely a fact of political economy.

Let us now see, further, how the concept of estranged, alienated labour must express and present itself in real life.

If the product of labour is alien to me, if it confronts me as an alien power, to whom, then, does it belong?

To a being *other* than myself.

Who is this being?

The *gods*? To be sure, in the earliest times the principal production (for example, the building of temples, etc., in Egypt, India and Mexico) appears to be in the service of the gods, and the product belongs to the gods. However, the gods on their own were never the lords of labour. No more was *nature*. And what a contradiction it would be if, the more man subjugated nature by his labour and the more the miracles of the gods were rendered superfluous by the miracles of industry, the more man were to renounce the joy of production and the enjoyment of the product to please these powers.

The *alien* being, to whom labour and the product of labour belongs, in whose service labour is done and for whose benefit the product of labour is provided, can only be *man* himself.

If the product of labour does not belong to the worker, if it confronts him as an alien power, then this can only be because it belongs to some *other man than the worker*. If the worker's activity is a torment to him, to another it must give *satisfaction* and pleasure. Not the gods, not nature, but only man himself can be this alien power over man.

We must bear in mind the previous proposition that man's relation to himself only becomes for him *objective* and *actual* through his relation to the other man. Thus, if the product of his labour, his labour objectified, is for him an *alien*, *hostile*, powerful object independent of him, then his position towards it is such that someone else is master of this object, someone who is alien, hostile, powerful, and independent of him. If he treats his own activity as an unfree activity, then he treats it as an activity performed in the service, under the dominion, the coercion, and the yoke of another man.

Every self-estrangement of man, from himself and from nature, appears in the relation in which he places himself and nature to men other than and differentiated from himself. For this reason religious self-estrangement necessarily appears in the relationship of the layman to the priest, or again to a mediator, etc., since we are here dealing with the intellectual world. In the real practical world self-estrangement can only become manifest through the real practical relationship to other men. The medium through which estrangement takes place is itself *practical*. Thus through estranged labour man not only creates his relationship to the object and to the act of production as to powers {MS here has *Menschen* – men – not *Machte*, powers} that are alien and hostile to him; he also creates the relationship in which other men stand to his production and to his product, and the relationship in which he stands to these other men. Just as he creates his own production as the loss of his reality, as his punishment; his own product as a loss, as a product not belonging to him; so he creates the dominion of the person who does not produce over production and over the product. Just as he estranges his own activity from himself, so he confers upon the stranger an activity which is not his own.

We have until now considered this relationship only from the standpoint of the worker and later we shall be considering it also from the standpoint of the non-worker.

Through *estranged, alienated labour*, then, the worker produces the relationship to this labour of a man alien to labour and standing outside it. The relationship of the worker to labour creates the relation to it of the capitalist (or whatever one chooses to call the master of labour). *Private property* is thus the product, the result, the necessary consequence, of *alienated labour*, of the external relation of the worker to nature and to himself.

Private property thus results by analysis from the concept of *alienated labour*, i.e., of *alienated man*, of estranged labour, of estranged life, of estranged man. True, it is as a result of the *movement of private property* that we have obtained the concept of *alienated labour* (*of alienated life*) in political economy. But analysis of this concept shows that though private property appears to be the reason, the cause of alienated labour, it is rather its consequence, just as the gods are *originally* not the cause but the effect of man's intellectual confusion. Later this relationship becomes reciprocal.

Only at the culmination of the development of private property does this, its secret, appear again, namely, that on the one hand it is the *product* of alienated labour, and that on the other it is the *means* by which labour alienates itself, the *realisation of this alienation*.

This exposition immediately sheds light on various hitherto unresolved conflicts:

(1) Political economy starts from labour as the real soul of production; yet to labour it gives nothing, and to private property everything. Confronting this contradiction, Proudhon has decided in favour of labour against private property. We understand, however, that this apparent contradiction is the contradiction of *estranged labour* with itself, and that political economy has merely formulated the laws of estranged labour.

We also understand, therefore, that *wages* and *private property* are identical. Indeed, where the product, as the object of labour, pays for labour itself, there the wage is but a necessary consequence of labour's estrangement. Likewise, in the wage of labour, labour does not appear as an end in itself but as the servant of the wage. We shall develop this point later, and meanwhile will only draw some conclusions.

An enforced *increase in wages* (disregarding all other difficulties, including the fact that it would only be by force, too, that such an increase, being an anomaly, could be maintained) would therefore be nothing but better *payment for the slave*, and would not win either for the worker or for labour their human status and dignity.

Indeed, even the *equality of wages*, as demanded by Proudhon, only transforms the relationship of the present-day worker to his labour into the relationship of all men to labour. Society is then conceived as an abstract capitalist.

Wages are a direct consequence of estranged labour, and estranged labour is the direct cause of private property. The downfall of the one must involve the downfall of the other.

(2) From the relationship of estranged labour to private property it follows further that the emancipation of society from private property, etc., from servitude, is expressed in the *political* form of the *emancipation of the workers*; not that *their* emancipation alone is at stake, but because the emancipation of the workers contains universal human emancipation – and it contains this, because the whole of human servitude is involved in the relation of the worker to production, and all relations of servitude are but modifications and consequences of this relation.

Just as we have derived the concept of *private property* from the concept of *estranged, alienated labour* by *analysis*, so we can develop every *category* of political economy with the help of these two factors; and we shall find again in each category, e.g., trade, competition, capital, money, only a *particular* and *developed expression* of these first elements.

Before considering this phenomenon, however, let us try to solve two other problems.

(1) To define the general *nature of private property*, as it has arisen as a result of estranged labour, in its relation to *truly human* and *social property*.

(2) We have accepted the *estrangement of labour*, its *alienation*, as a fact, and we have analysed this fact. How, we now ask, does *man* come to *alienate*, to estrange, his *labour*? How is this estrangement rooted in the nature of human development? We have already gone a long way to the solution of this problem by *transforming* the question of the *origin of private property* into the question of the relation of *alienated labour* to the course of humanity's development. For when one speaks of *private property*, one thinks of dealing with something external to man. When one speaks of labour, one is directly dealing with man himself. This new formulation of the question already contains its solution.

As to (1): *The general nature of private property and its relation to truly human property.*

Alienated labour has resolved itself for us into two components which depend on one another, or which are but different expressions of one and the same relationship. *Appropriation* appears as *estrangement*, as *alienation*; and *alienation* appears as *appropriation*, *estrangement* as truly *becoming a citizen*.

We have considered the one side – *alienated* labour in relation to the worker himself, i.e., the *relation of alienated labour to itself*. The product, the necessary outcome of this relationship, as we have seen, is the *property relation of the non-worker to the worker and to labour*. *Private property*, as the material, summary expression of alienated labour, embraces both relations – the *relation of the worker to labour and to the product of his labour and to the non-worker*, and the relation of the *non-worker to the worker and to the product of his labour*.

Having seen that in relation to the worker who *appropriates* nature by means of his labour, this appropriation appears as estrangement, his own spontaneous activity as activity for another and as activity of another, vitality as a sacrifice of life, production of the object as loss of the object to an alien power, to an *alien* person – we shall now consider the relation to the worker, to labour and its object of this person who is *alien* to labour and the worker.

First it has to be noted that everything which appears in the worker as an *activity of alienation, of estrangement*, appears in the non-worker as a *state of alienation, of estrangement*.

Secondly, that the worker's *real, practical attitude* in production and to the product (as a state of mind) appears in the non-worker confronting him as a *theoretical* attitude.

Thirdly, the non-worker does everything against the worker which the worker does against himself; but he does not do against himself what he does against the worker.

Let us look more closely at these three relations. {The MS breaks off here, unfinished}
[Economic and philosophic manuscripts of 1844; 1844c: 270–82][119]

9.2 I examine the system of bourgeois economy in the following order: *capital, landed property, wage-labour; the State, foreign trade, world market.*[120] The economic conditions of existence of the three great classes into which modern bourgeois society is divided are analysed under the first three headings; the interconnection of the other three headings is self-evident. The first part of the first book, dealing with Capital, comprises the following chapters: 1. The commodity; 2. Money or simple circulation; 3. Capital in general. The present part consists of the first two chapters. The entire material lies before me in the form of monographs, which were written not for publication but for self-clarification at widely separated periods; their remoulding into an integrated whole according to the plan I have indicated will depend upon circumstances.

A general introduction {that of 1857}, which I had drafted, is omitted, since on further consideration it seems to me confusing to anticipate results which have still to be substantiated, and the reader who really wishes to follow me will have to decide to advance from the particular to the general. A few brief remarks regarding the course of my study of political economy may, however, be appropriate here.

Although I studied jurisprudence, I pursued it as a subject subordinated to philosophy and history. In the year 1842–43, as editor of the *Rheinische Zeitung*, I first found myself in the embarrassing position of having to discuss what is known as material interests. The deliberations of the Rhenish Landtag on forest thefts and the division of landed property; the official polemic started by Herr von Schapper, then Oberpräsident of the Rhine Province, against the *Rheinische Zeitung* about the condition of the Moselle peasantry, and finally the debates on free trade and protective tariffs caused me in the first instance to turn my attention to economic questions.[121] On the other hand, at that time when good intentions 'to push forward' often took the place of factual knowledge, an echo of French socialism and communism, slightly tinged by philosophy, was noticeable in the *Rheinische Zeitung*. I objected to this dilettantism, but at the same time frankly omitted in a controversy with the *Allgemeine Augsburger Zeitung*[122] that my previous studies did not allow me to express any opinion on the French theories. When the publishers of the *Rheinische Zeitung* conceived the illusion that by a more compliant policy on the part of the paper it might be possible to secure the abrogation of the death sentence passed upon it, I eagerly grasped the opportunity to withdraw from the public stage to my study.

The first work which I undertook to dispel the doubts assailing me was a critical re-examination of the Hegelian philosophy of law {1843b}; the introduction to this work being published in the *Deutsch-Französische Jahrbücher* issued in Paris in 1844.[123] My inquiry led me to the conclusion that neither legal relations nor political forms could be comprehended whether by themselves or on the basis of a so-called general development of the human mind, but that on the contrary they originate in the material conditions of life, the sum total of which Hegel, following the example of English and French thinkers of the eighteenth century, embraces within the term 'civil society'; that the anatomy of this civil society, however, has to be sought in political economy. The study of this, which I began in Paris, I continued in Brussels, where I moved owing to an expulsion order issued by M. Guizot. The general conclusion at which I arrived and which, once reached, became the guiding principle of my studies can be summarised as follows. In the social production of their existence, men inevitably enter into definite relations, which are independent of their will, namely relations of production appropriate to a given stage in the development of their material forces of production. The totality of these relations of production constitutes the economic structure of society, the real foundation, on which arises a legal and political superstructure and to which correspond definite forms of social consciousness. The mode of production of material life conditions the general process of social, political and intellectual life. It is not the consciousness of men that determines their existence, but their social existence that determines their consciousness. At a certain stage of development, the material productive forces of society come into conflict with the existing relations of production or – this merely expresses the same thing in legal terms – with the property relations within the framework of which they have operated hitherto. From forms of development of the productive forces these relations turn into their fetters. Then begins an era of social revolution. The changes in the economic foundation lead sooner or later to the transformation of the whole immense superstructure. In studying such transformations it is always necessary to distinguish between the material transformation of the economic conditions of production, which can be determined with the precision of natural science, and the legal, political, religious, artistic or philosophic – in short, ideological forms in which men become conscious of this conflict and fight it out. Just as one does not judge an individual by what he thinks about himself, so one cannot judge such a period of transformation by its consciousness, but, on the contrary, this consciousness must be explained from the contradictions of material life, from the conflict existing between the social forces of production and the relations of production. No social order is ever destroyed before all the productive forces for which it is sufficient have been developed, and new superior relations of production never replace older ones before the material conditions for their existence have matured within the framework of the old society. Mankind thus inevitably sets itself only such tasks as it is able to solve, since closer examination will always show that the problem itself arises only when the material conditions for its solution are already present or at least in the course of formation. In broad outline, the Asiatic, ancient, feudal and modern bourgeois modes of production may be designated as epochs marking progress in the economic development of society. The bourgeois mode of production is the last antagonistic form of the social process of production – antagonistic not in the sense of individual antagonism but of an antagonism that emanates from the individuals' social conditions of existence – but the productive forces developing within bourgeois society create also the material conditions for a solution of this antagonism. The prehistory of human society accordingly closes with this social formation.

Frederick Engels, with whom I maintained a constant exchange of ideas by correspondence since the publication of his brilliant essay on the critique of economic categories (printed in the *Deutsch-Französische Jahrbücher*), arrived by another road (compare his *Lage der arbeitenden Klasse in England*)[124] at the same result as I, and when in the spring of 1845 he too came to live in Brussels, we decided to set forth together our conception as opposed to the ideological one of German philosophy, in fact to settle accounts with our former philosophical conscience. The intention was carried out in the form of a critique of post-Hegelian philosophy {1846a}. The manuscript, two large octavo volumes, had long ago reached the publishers in

Westphalia when we were informed that owing to changed circumstances it could not be printed. We abandoned the manuscript to the gnawing criticism of the mice all the more willingly since we had achieved our main purpose – self-clarification. Of the scattered works in which at that time we presented one or another aspect of our views to the public, I shall mention only the *Manifesto of the Communist Party*, jointly written by Engels and myself, and a *Discours sur le libre échange*,[125] which I myself published. The salient points of our conception were first outlined in an academic, although polemical, form in my *Misère de la philosophie* {1847a}, this book which was aimed at Proudhon appearing in 1847. The publication of an essay on *Wage-Labour*,[126] written in German in which I combined the lectures I had held on this subject at the German Workers' Association in Brussels, was interrupted by the February Revolution and my forcible removal from Belgium in consequence.

The publication of the *Neue Rheinische Zeitung* in 1848 and 1849 and subsequent events cut short my economic studies, which I could only resume in London in 1850. The enormous amount of material relating to the history of political economy assembled in the British Museum, the fact that London is a convenient vantage point for the observation of bourgeois society, and finally the new stage of development which this society seemed to have entered with the discovery of gold in California and Australia, induced me to start again from the very beginning and to work carefully through the new material. These studies led partly of their own accord to apparently quite remote subjects on which I had to spend a certain amount of time. But it was in particular the imperative necessity of earning my living which reduced the time at my disposal. My collaboration, continued now for eight years, with the *New York Tribune*, the leading Anglo-American newspaper, necessitated an excessive fragmentation of my studies, for I wrote only exceptionally newspaper correspondence in the strict sense. Since a considerable part of my contributions consisted of articles dealing with important economic events in Britain and on the Continent, I was compelled to become conversant with practical details which, strictly speaking, lie outside the sphere of political economy.

This sketch of the course of my studies in the domain of political economy is intended merely to show that my views – no matter how they may be judged and how little they conform to the interested prejudices of the ruling classes – are the outcome of conscientious research carried on over many years. At the entrance to science, as at the entrance to hell, the demand must be made:

Qui si convien lasciare ogni sospetto
Ogni vilta convien che qui sia morta

[Preface to the *Critique of political economy*, 1859; 1859a: 19–23.
The final quote, from Dante's *Divina Commedia*, translates as:
'Here must all distrust be left; all cowardice must here be dead'.]
In *Capital* 1, Marx added a footnote bearing on this Preface:

9.3 I seize this opportunity of shortly answering an objection taken
by a German paper in America, to my work 'Zur Kritik der Pol.
Oekonomie, 1859'. In the estimation of that paper, my view that each
special mode of production and the social relations corresponding to
it, in short, that the economic structure of society, is the real basis on
which the juridical and political superstructure is raised, and to which
definite social forms of thought correspond; that the mode of production
determines the character of the social, political, and intellectual life
generally, all this is very true for our own times, in which material
interests preponderate, but not for the middle ages, in which
Catholicism, nor for Athens and Rome, where politics, reigned supreme.
In the first place it strikes one as an odd thing for anyone to suppose
that these well-worn phrases about the middle ages and the ancient
world are unknown to anyone else. This much, however, is clear, that
the middle ages could not live on Catholicism, nor the ancient world
on politics. On the contrary it is the mode in which they gained a
livelihood that explains why here politics, and there Catholicism, played
the chief part. For the rest, it requires but a slight acquaintance with
the history of the Roman republic, for example, to be aware that its
secret history is the history of its landed property. On the other hand,
Don Quixote long ago paid the penalty for wrongly imagining that
knight errantry was compatible with all economic forms of society.
[*Capital* 1, 1867; 1867a: 81n]

9.4 Philosophy, as long as a drop of blood shall pulse in its
world-subduing and absolutely free heart, will never grow tired of
answering its adversaries with the cry of Epicurus:

Not the man who denies the gods worshipped by the multitude, but
he who affirms of the gods what the multitude believes about them,
is truly impious.

Philosophy makes no secret of it. The confession of Prometheus:

In simple words, I hate the pack of gods,

is its own confession, its own aphorism against all heavenly and earthly gods who do not acknowledge human self-consciousness as the highest divinity. It will have none other beside.

But to those poor March hares who rejoice over the apparently worsened civil position of philosophy, it responds again, as Prometheus replied to the servant of the gods, Hermes:

Be sure of this, I would not change my state
Of evil fortune for your servitude.
Better to be the servant of this rock
Than to be faithful boy to Father Zeus.

Prometheus is the most eminent saint and martyr in the philosophical calendar.
[Foreword to doctoral dissertation, 1841; 1841: 30–31][127]

Notes

Publication details of all works cited in these notes are given in the bibliography. Methods of citation and the organization of the bibliography are explained more fully on pp. 220–1.

1. I refer to MEGA 2. On this and MEGA 1, see bibliography.
2. The major larger works of Marx finalized for press were: 1844e; 1847a; 1848b; 1850a; 1852a; 1859b; 1860; 1867a; 1871d.
3. First German edition 1867; Russian edition, with minor revisions and additions, 1872; 2nd German edition, wholly restructured (seven parts and twenty-five chapters, each subdivided into sections, instead of the original six large chapters and appendix; Part 1 substantially rewritten), 1871–3; further changes in French edition of 1872–5 (some additions, new division into eight parts and thirty-three chapters). Marx said in the Preface to the French edition that it possesses 'a scientific value independent of the original' and 'should be consulted even by readers familiar with German'; I give an example of one major amendment in my comment on 4.3 (p. 34). This still holds; not all Marx's changes were incorporated into later German editions, the basis of English translations.

The 3rd and 4th German editions were edited by Engels in accord with directions found in Marx's MSS: see Engels 1885 and 1894b for details. Materials from the first German edition of *Capital* (original Chapter 1 and appendix on 'The form of value') are available in *Value*.

4.Quoted in McLellan 1973: 284. Major journalistic contributions (as distinct from essays) were to: *Rheinische Zeitung*, 1842–3; *Neue Rheinische Zeitung*, 1848–9; *New York Daily Tribune*, 1852–62; *Neue Oder Zeitung*, 1855; *People's Paper* and *Free Press*, 1856; *Das Volk*, 1859; *Die Presse*, 1861–3. All are now in CW. Anthologies based wholly or largely on Marx's journalism include: *The American journalism of Marx and Engels*, *Articles on Britain*, *Marx on China*, *The civil war in the United States*, *Marx on colonialism and modernization*, *The first Indian war of independence*, *Articles from the Neue Rheinische Zeitung*, and *Revolution in Spain*. Newspaper articles are also included in many other collections listed in the bibliography. Articles written by Engels have often been ascribed to Marx, notably those in *Revolution and counter-revolution in Germany* (London 1896, ed. Eleanor Marx-Aveling; many subsequent edns). Mention should also be made here of Marx's contributions to the *New American Cyclopedia*, 1857–8. See CW 18, and *Articles in the New American Cyclopedia*.

5.An excellent anthology of Marx's early writings, giving all the major 1843–4 texts in full, is CEW; Colletti's Introduction is a masterpiece of Marx commentary. See also *Writings of the young Marx*; this draws on a wider range of materials than CEW, but gives generally shorter extracts. CW 1, and 3–4 contain most of Marx's pre-*German Ideology* writings, though omission of his Paris notes on political economy (except those on Mill, 1844b) is to be regretted; on these see Rubel, 1957; 1959. CW 2 is devoted to the young Engels: it is a revealing collection, showing both Engels's superior acquaintance with industrial conditions and political economy at the time, and a significantly different philosophical itinerary to Marx's. On the Marx/Engels relationship, see note 40. The dates of first full publication, and English translation, of Marx's major (posthumously published) early writings are as follows: Doctoral dissertation, 1927/67; Critique of Hegel's *Rechtsphilosophie*, 1927/70; 1844 MSS, 1932/59; *German Ideology*, 1932/64 (part 1, 1924/26; part 3 translation 1938).

Most of Marx's *Rheinische Zeitung* articles appeared in full in English for the first time only in CW 1 (1975); on these see McGovern; McLellan 1970. On the status of Marx's early writings in his intellectual legacy, compare Althusser 1977, Avineri 1968, and Colletti's Introduction to CEW. McLellan 1969 and 1970 are balanced, scholarly treatments of the young Marx; see also Draper 1977, vol. 1, part 1, which has the rare merit of recognizing the impact of Marx's own experience as editor of the *Rheinische Zeitung* on the development of his ideas, a topic too often treated as a mere philosophical odyssey. Other works that deal with the young Marx include Arthur; Colletti 1973; Hyppolite; Jones 1977; Korsch; Lichtheim; Maguire 1972; Meszaros; Ollman 1976; Rosen; Sayer 1985; Schmidt; Sherover-Marcuse; Teeple; Walliman.

6. See Marx 1859a, reproduced as passage 9.2, p.190; Engels 1886: 2–3. Before abandoning the MS, Marx and Engels did make considerable efforts to get it published. It is extensively used here. See further notes 44, 106.

7. The phrase is McLellan's (his selections from 1858a: 9); on this basis he argues that the *Grundrisse*, because it contains material not developed in *Capital*, is 'the most fundamental work Marx ever wrote'. The same, however, could be argued with regard to other drafts of the 'economics', including the enormous one of 1861–3; see note 10. The evolution of Marx's plans for his 'economics' is discussed, *inter alia*, in McLellan, 1973; foreword to Nicolaus edition of 1858a; Rosdolsky; Rubel 1981; Sayer 1983a, Chapter 4; and (in most detail) Oakley 1983. See also Engels 1885; 1894b; the editorial prefaces to 1863a–c; Mandel 1971; and *Letters on Capital*.

8. Nicolaus 1968. The first publication of the full manuscript of 1857–8, since known as the *Grundrisse*, was actually in Moscow in 2 vols in 1939/41; but only three or four copies reached the West – not surprisingly, considering the date! The 1953 edition (Berlin, Dietz) was a reprint of this. The 'Chapter on money' (about one-seventh of the whole MS) was first published slightly earlier, in AME, 1935. The 1857 'General Introduction' to this text and the fragment 'Bastiat and Carey' had been published in 1903–4 in *Neue Zeit* by Kautsky, and the former translated into English in 1904. Apart from very small extracts in anthologies (rare), the only other English translations from this huge work before 1973 were the section on 'precapitalist economic formations' (1964), and extracts by

McLellan (in 1971); see bibliography under 1858a. On the *Grundrisse* see Nicolaus 1968; Oakley 1983; Rosdolsky; and editorial material in the Nicolaus edition and McLellan selections.

9. See Engels 1885; 1894b for details. The extent of Engels's editing will not be known before the full MSS are published in MEGA 2. See also Oakley 1983.

10. The part of Marx's 1861–3 MS known as *Theories of Surplus Value* was to form the basis for what would have been *Capital* 4. It is a critical exposition of the history of political economy; as such, it is a major source for reconstructing Marx's own methodology (see Chapter 4 (this book) and Sayer 1983a, especially Chapter 5). Kautsky first published an edition of this, with Marx's material much rearranged, and numerous cuts, in 1905–10; selections from this edition were first published in English in 1951 (London, eds G. Bonner and E. Burns). The first full edition was published in three parts in 1956–66, and translated into English 1963–72. It should be noted that *Theories* forms only slightly over one-half of Marx's 1861–3 MS, entitled by him *Zur Kritik der Politischen Oekonomie*. The rest of the MS drafts what was to become vol. 1 of *Capital* (with the exception of the present Part 1, treated in the 1859 *Critique*), as well as covering many topics later dealt with in vols 2 and 3. See Oakley 1983. The full MS is now in MEGA 2.

11. The title is Marx's own. According to a plan of January 1863 (1863a: 414) this was intended to follow the chapter on Wakefield with which *Capital* 1, as he eventually published it, closes. The MS is extremely useful for the light it sheds on (1) fetishism of capital (see 5.23–5.25) and (2) the relation of social and technical change in the early development of capitalism (see 6.4; 6.22–6.24). 'Results' was first published in AME in 1933; the first English translation was in 1976.

12. The two drafts of *The civil war*, written in English, were first published in AME in 1934. The drafts gained wider currency with their inclusion in the Peking edition of *The Civil War* (FLP 1966), *Writings on the Paris Commune* (1971), and *Marx and Engels on the Paris Commune* (1971). I give a substantial extract (7.30). See Sayer 1985, and Corrigan and Sayer 1987, for fuller commentary on these texts, and their relationship to the view of the state in Marx's early writings. As well as the drafts, Marx left a long preparatory notebook

(1871a) for *The Civil War*. The drafts of Marx's reply to Zasulich (see further note 20) were first published in AME in 1924. A bowdlerized English translation was included in *The Russian Menace to Europe* (1952); the first draft was included in *Selected Works*, vol. 3, Moscow 1970. Hobsbawm (ed.) *Precapitalist Economic Formations* (see Marx, 1858a) also includes extracts. The first full English translation of all four of the drafts was in Shanin (1983), which also contains fulsome commentary on their context. I give a long extract from these drafts (8.2).

13. On the history of Marxism, see note 36. On the 'Marxism of the Second International', Colletti 1972; also Anderson; on Bolshevism, Corrigan *et al.*

14. See 7.25–7.28.

15. See Shanin; also Dunayevskaya; Krader 1973; 1975; 1977.

16. The words are Marx's; see 3.24.

17. Along with Marx's journalism, this is the category of his work *least* represented in the present anthology. A useful introduction is the three-volume PW. DFI and *The Hague Congress of the First International* are also extremely valuable, giving documents, drafts, records of speeches, and minutes; see also 1872a; 1873a. Marx's earlier period of political activity around the Communist League is well reflected in the materials in *Cologne Communist Trial* (including 1850b,c; 1852b,c). Of post-IWMA 'political' statements, mainly in connection with the socialist movement in Germany, 1875b and 1879b are especially famous. See also note 38. On Marx's relations with the Russian revolutionary movement in his later years, see Shanin. Ollman 1978 attempts a detailed 'retrieval' of Marx's vision of socialism and communism. A good biography (see note 32) is a crucial guide through this maze; here editorial commentary in Moscow editions is more than usually tendentious. Works on Marx's politics include Collins and Abramski; Cummings; Draper 1977–8; Gilbert; Hunt; McGovern; Maguire 1978; Thomas; and among biographies, Nicolaievski; Raddatz.

18. 1852b; 1860.

19. On the drafts, see note 12. Some of the English trade unionists on the GC of the IWMA had grave doubts on its politics; the furniture-maker Lucraft said it 'defended ruffians who had done deeds that he abhorred', and both he and the shoemaker Odger resigned from the GC in protest at Marx's text being

issued under its name. Both were founder-members of the
IWMA and Odger was at one time its President; Odger was
also a founder of the London Trades Council and its Secretary
from 1862–72. See minutes of GC meetings of 20 and 27 June
1871, in DFI: 4.

20.Marx wrote four preparatory drafts, but the last is only a few
lines long. Marx considered the Black Repartition group
around Plekhanov, Axelrod, and Zasulich to be 'mere
doctrinaires', and the People's Will (whom they opposed) to be
'sterling people through and through' (Letter to Jenny Longuet,
April 11; 1881d: written little more than a month after the
drafts of the reply to Zasulich. The same letter relates Marx's
first, unflattering impressions of Karl Kautsky). Marx had
enormous regard for the major theorist of Russian 'populism',
Nicolai Chernyshevsky, and sought to help him publish in the
West and even translated some of his *Unaddressed letters*
himself. Posterity 'forgot' this: the Zasulich correspondence
was buried until 1924 (and then published with a warning note
by Riazanov as to Marx's 'failing powers': this is in Shanin).
Plekhanov was meantime canonized as 'the father of Russian
Marxism', and 'populism' consigned to oblivion. The
unorthodoxy of Marx's drafts lies in his endorsing of the
'populist' view that the Russian peasant commune could be a
'direct starting-point' for socialism, and the revision of the
'standard' Marxist conception of the peasantry as a historically
obsolete and invariably reactionary class (see, for instance,
Marx's own oft-quoted remarks in *The Eighteenth Brumaire* on
French peasants [1852a: 187–8]), which this implied. See 4.3
and 8.2, plus 1882b; and Shanin.

21.See Prinz. I think the point can be overstated, but needs to be
borne in mind given attempts to read the Preface as holy writ.
The real problem with this text – given in full as 9.2 – as with
all generalizing, summary statements in Marx, lies with the
meaning of its key terms: productive forces, relations of
production, economic structure, superstructure, correspond,
determine, condition, etc. Marx was notoriously (and if Ollman
1976, Chapter 1 is right, necessarily, in view of his method)
lax in his use of terms, so texts like the Preface can easily be
interpreted far too rigidly. The only way sensibly to understand
what Marx meant by a productive force or production relation
is to examine the *variety* of his usages of such terms *across*
his work. Cohen 1978 takes the Preface, interpreted along

'traditional' lines, as a definitive summary of Marx's 'theory of history': it is by far the best defence of this conception. My own work (Sayer 1987) is a critique of Cohen. See also Engels 1890a,b,c; 1893; 1894a; Carver 1982; more generally, works cited in note 39.

22.1881a; see also 1879a. This material is impossible to anthologize. The notes on Mill (1844b), Bakunin (1874) and Wagner (1880b) are all worth reading, only the last excerpted here (3.7, 4.13, 7.21). On Marx's notes more generally, see Draper *Cyclopedia*; all Krader and Rubel entries; Oakley 1983; Sayer 1983b; Struick.

23.1882a. 1880a, first published in Russian in 1947, is roughly contemporary with this. The origins of capitalism is a major issue in modern Marxist historiography: see Hilton; Aston and Philpin.

24.Rubel and Manale, p. 243.

25.1882c; see Struick, and material cited in note 22.

26.Not all of Marx's letters of course survive, and some were destroyed by his children, notably any that would hurt Engels. The Marx–Engels correspondence was first published in Stuttgart in 1913, edited by Bebel and Bernstein. This edition was heavily bowdlerised, especially to protect Lassalle and Liebknecht, by then patron saints of German Social Democracy. The first unexpurgated edition of the correspondence was published in MEGA 1, in 4 volumes, 1929–31; full editions (of material known at the time) of the Marx–Engels correspondence plus letters to third persons were later published in both Russian and German (MEW) *Collected Works*. The Marx correspondence is – at long last – being published in full in English, in CW (CW 1, and 38 onwards). It is an amusing exercise to compare the successive editions of the *Selected Correspondence* emanating from Moscow. Selection here usually means sanitization, and the criteria of selection are clearly more political than scholarly. A superb collection, very much more revealing of Marx the man, is Padover's *Letters of Karl Marx*. Other anthologies of Marx's correspondence are listed in the bibliography, section 1C; and letters are also included in many of the anthologies listed in section 1D. See also *The Daughters of Karl Marx: family correspondence 1866–98*, Harmondsworth, 1984, and the correspondence of Friedrich Engels with Paul and Laura Lafargue, London, 3 vols., 1959–63.

27.1846b; excerpts 2.7 and 3.25.

28.1868c; excerpt 5.4.

29.Extracts from some of these are are given in 4.12, 4.20, 4.22, and especially 4.15. See also *Letters on Capital*.

30.1877; also 4.3.

31.1836–7. Some are interesting, like these lines of 1837 on Hegel:

Kant and Fichte soar to heavens blue
Seeking for some distant land
I but seek to grasp profound and true
That which – in the street I find.

[CW 1: 567–8].

32.The 'Confessions' are given as 1.1. On Marx's literary tastes, see Prawer. This is, perhaps, the place to make clear that a good biography is an indispensible aid to reading Marx; see bibliography, section 3B. Soviet biographies (e.g. Fedoseyev) are earnest, hagiographic, and stunningly boring, but they sometimes contain information, not found elsewhere, based on material in the CPSU archives. The first volume of Yvonne Kapp's *Eleanor Marx* is far and away the best portrait I have come across of Marx's family life, the better for displacing Karl himself, for once, from the centre of attention. See also family correspondence cited in note 26. Also of interest is *Reminiscences of Marx and Engels*, a set of memoirs of people who knew them. Draper's *Marx–Engels Chronicle* is the most exhaustive and reliable chronology.

33.For a sample of Marx's views on colonialism, see 8.3–8.5, but compare 6.30–6.32, where he anticipates 'dependency theory'; on the peasantry, compare the famous remarks in *The Eighteenth Brumaire*, where he likens peasants to 'sacks of potatoes' (1852a: 187–8), with his assessment of Russian peasants in 8.2. Marx's support for both Irish and Polish self-determination (in part because this would weaken Britain and Russia) is well-known; but as editor of the *Neue Rheinische Zeitung* he published Engels's notorious anti-Slavic article (1849) which argues, *inter alia*, that 'apart from the Poles, the Russian, and at most the Turkish Slavs, no Slav people has a future'; 'the Czechs have never had a history of their own [...] and this historically absolutely non-existent "nation" puts forward claims to independence?' (1849: 367). Other NRZ pieces, by Engels and other correspondents, push a similar line. There is no indication that Marx dissented from these views, which Engels presented as those of the paper. On all these issues, as elsewhere, Marx's legacy is far from uniform. Discussions include Cummings; Krader 1975; Melotti; Paul; Shanin; Turner.

34.1872b. Barrett discusses Marx's views on the family and wage labour in detail, arguing that Marx 'cannot be "let off the hook" by saying that gender inequality had yet to be discovered at the time he lived and wrote [...] To exonerate Marx by an appeal to a supposedly "pre-feminist" culture is both to underestimate the currency of feminist ideas in the nineteenth century and to underestimate the usual level of perception of Marx' (199–200).

35.DFI 3: 147 (August 17, 1869; see also Minutes of August 10).

36.The history of Marxism (and the opposition to it) is beyond this volume, but has had enormous impact on how Marx has been interpreted. He has of course been variously twisted by both sides. See *inter alia* Anderson; Colletti 1972; Corrigan *et al.*; Kolakowski; McLellan 1979.

37.Compare the 'progressive' optimism of 6.29 with the darker extracts immediately following it; and consider the declaration that opens the Manifesto ('the history of all hitherto existing society is the history of class struggles') in the light of the passages given in Chapter 8, particularly those bearing on the supposed millennial social stability of Asiatic society.

38.The 'correction', a quote from *The Civil War* (the draft version is given at the end of 7.30) was made in the Preface to the 2nd German edition (1872c).

39.The diversity of modern interpretations of Marx can be seen *inter alia* from the following: Althusser and Balibar; Avineri; Bottomore 1981; Carver 1982; Cohen 1978; Elster 1985; McMurtry; Ollman 1976; Rader; Sayer 1987; Shaw. I cite here only major works on Marx's *overall* social theory.

40.I refer of course to Friedrich Engels. There is now considerable controversy on both the differences between Marx and Engels, and the degree to which, in popularizing Marx's ideas in *Anti-Dühring* (which Marx, incidentally, both read and wrote a chapter for) and other of his later writings, Engels actually bastardized them. But there can be little doubt that the impact of Engels on the *young* Marx was enormous. On the Marx–Engels relationship see Carver 1983; Colletti 1972; Coulter; Hodges; Jones 1973, 1977; Krader 1973, 1977.

41.On Marx's politics see note 17. On his economics, a good brief anthology is *Marx on Economics*. Accessible introductions to

Marx's economic theory include Sweezy (still in my view the best); Brewer; Mandel 1970; Roth and Eldred. Meek is an old, but still outstanding, study of the background; see also Walker. Mandel 1971 is an excellent account of the development of Marx's economic theory. More advanced discussions of Marxist economics include de Brunhoff; Elson; Fine; Harris and Fine; Howard and King; Pilling; Rosdolsky; Rubin; Sayer 1983a; Steedman 1977, 1981; Wolff.

42.In many ways the inspiration for this anthology is Bottomore and Rubel's superb *Karl Marx on Sociology and Social Philosophy*. For its time, it was pathbreaking. But it is now dated, both in terms of the texts drawn upon, and its references to editions of Marx's writings (now, so out of date as to be very misleading) and secondary discussions. Bottomore and Rubel have shown, however, that a 'bits and pieces' collection *can* be worthwhile.

43.This is the earliest of Marx's letters, and the only one from his student years, to have survived. Several letters to Marx from his father are extant (in CW 1).

44.*The German Ideology* is discussed on p. xvi and in notes 5 and 6. Its major target is the Young Hegelians. Vol. 1, Part 1, intended to deal with Feuerbach, actually says little about him and is unfinished. This is by far the best-known section of the text, and amounts to the fullest outline anywhere in Marx's writings of the general 'premises' of his conception. Vol. 1, Part 2 is a short critique of Bruno Bauer, whom Marx had attacked at greater length previously in *The Holy Family* (1844e). Vol. 1, Part 3, the longest section of the book, is an extended but turgid critique of Max Stirner, author of *The Ego and his Own*, and a precursor of anarchism. Vol. 2 is a critique of the Utopian socialism current in Germany at the time, which Marx and Engels christen 'True Socialism'. Karl Grün and Rudolph Matthäi (referred to in some extracts on p. 17) were amongst those attacked. Marx viewed Ludwig Feuerbach as the most progressive of the Young Hegelians, and had praised his 'real humanism' in both the 1844 Manuscripts and *The Holy Family*; his disagreements with Feuerbach's materialism can be gleaned from 2.5 and 2.6. See note 46. On Marx and the Young Hegelians, see McLellan 1969; 1970; Rosen; and material cited in note 5.

45.This 'trick' is elaborated, at greater length, in a famous section of *The Holy Family* entitled 'The mystery of speculative construction' (1844e: 57–61). See also the recurrent criticisms of Hegel's method in 1843b, and the section of the 1844 MSS entitled 'Critique of Hegelian dialectic'.

46. This text is celebrated. Written in the spring of 1845, it was first published in an edited version by Engels in 1888 as an appendix to his 1886. The title is Engels's. He said of Marx's MS that 'these are notes hurriedly scribbled down for later elaboration, absolutely not intended for publication, but invaluable as the first document in which the brilliant germ of the new world outlook is deposited'. There is no more succinct formulation of Marx's materialism.

47. The letter to Annenkov anticipates much of the argument of *The Poverty of Philosophy* (1847a), a polemic against Proudhon which Marx later referred to as the first 'academic, though polemical' outline of 'the salient points of our conception' to find its way into print (see 9.2). Proudhon was a noted French socialist thinker; his response to Marx's *Poverty* was to label Marx 'the tape-worm of socialism' (McLellan 1973: 166). Marx's 1865b, written shortly after Proudhon's death, is an interesting retrospective note on their differences. Annenkov published extracts from Marx's letter in his reminiscences in 1880, and these were translated into German in *Neue Zeit* in 1883. The French original was published in full in 1912.

48. The *Deutsch-Französische Jahrbücher* was edited by Marx and Ruge; only one number appeared, in Paris in 1844. It led to warrants being issued in Prussia for the arrest of Marx, Ruge, Heine and other contributors, and the beginning of a lifetime of political exile for Marx. The journal was discontinued largely because of differences between the editors. Marx contributed two major articles, referred to in this passage, which are both landmarks in his development (1843c,d). I give two extracts from 1843c (7.12 and 7.13), and one from 1843d (7.24). The latter is also famous for its hailing of the proletariat, for the first time in Marx's writings, as the agent of human emancipation (1843d: 186–7). Marx's two D-FJ articles were first translated into English in 1926 (*Selected essays*, London, Parsons). The D-FJ also published Engels's 'Outlines of a critique of political economy'; on the impact of this on Marx, see 9.2, and note 40.

49. On the 1844 MSS see note 5. Not all of the text has survived. The best-known parts of the work are the sections on

'Estranged labour' (given in full in 9.1), 'Private property and communism' (1844c: 293–305; extracts 3.1 and 3.2 are from this), and 'Critique of the Hegelian dialectic and philosophy as a whole' (ibid: 326–348). Closely linked with these MSS are Marx's Paris reading notes on political economy; see note 5.

50.First published in 1958; first English translation in 1971.

51.The notes on Adolph Wagner's *Lehrbuch der politischen Oekonomie* are one of Marx's 'late' texts; they represent his 'last word' in the critique of political economy. They were first published in AME 1930, and first translated into English in 1971. They are valuable mainly for the retrospective commentary they give on the method of *Capital* (see 4.13). Also of note are passages on law (7.21) and language (Carver: 190–191); as with his criticisms of 'Man' (cf. 2.4–2.6), what Marx has to say on language in these notes strikingly recalls *The German Ideology* of thirty-five years before. Carver provides a useful commentary.

52.On the publication history of the 1857 General Introduction see note 8. Marx decided to replace it with the 1859 Preface (9.2) when he came to publish the *Critique of Political Economy*, for reasons he explains there. The 1857 text is one of Marx's fullest discussions of method, and further extracts from it are given in Chapter 4. 'Robinsonades' is a satirical reference to Defoe's *Robinson Crusoe*. On the concept of *bürgerliche Gesellschaft* see my comment on 3.16 (p. 25). Sir James Steuart was the author of *An Inquiry into the Principles of Political Economy*, London, 1767. Marx discusses his work in 1863a: 41–3.

53.Marx prepared *Wage Labour and Capital* as a lecture series for the German Workers' Society in Brussels in December 1847. It was first published as a series of leading articles in the *Neue Rheinische Zeitung* in April 1849; a surviving MS of the 1847 lectures is virtually identical to the 1849 published text. It was separately republished several times in the 1880s. The 1891 edition, edited by Engels, revised the text in accord with Marx's later theory of surplus value. CW 9 gives the original text, with Engels's amendments in footnotes.

54.This passage occurs in a polemic against Nassau Senior's and others' attempts to criticize Adam Smith's distinction of productive and unproductive labour, and Marx defends the distinction. For Marx, a particular form of labour (like, say, that of a state functionary or a soldier) may be necessary under a given social regime without being productive in the economic sense, i.e. in a capitalist society, productive of surplus value. See 1863a: Chapter 4 and Addenda. This does not alter the point he is making here *vis-à-vis* production in general.

55.This passage is a good example of one which, when quoted out of context, can mislead. The context, which immediately precedes it, is given in 8.7. This makes it clear that for Marx, in societies in which the direct producer effectively possesses the means of production, surplus can be 'pumped' only by 'other than economic pressure' and 'conditions of personal dependence are requisite'. The feudal lords' 'ownership', in other words, is constituted on the basis of 'forcible domination of one section of society over another' (8.6). To define 'property' for Marx is to delineate the set of social relations of which it is the 'legal expression', which vary historically; see 4.7.

56.This famous passage occurs at the beginning of the *18th Brumaire*, a study of Napoleon III's *coup d'état* of December 1852. The 18th Brumaire of the title is an ironical reference to Napoleon Bonaparte's coup of 9 November, 1799 (the 18th Brumaire in the republican calendar), which overthrew the Directory. *The 18th Brumaire* is perhaps Marx's most incisive analysis of current events, and an excellent antidote to temptations to apply his 'theory' mechanistically. For this reason Engels several times commended it as an exemplar of Marx's method (Engels 1890b,c; 1894a). *The 18th Brumaire* was first published in 1852, in the USA, as the first issue of the 'non-periodic journal' *Die Revolution*; few copies reached Europe. It was republished, with revisions, in 1869. The first full English translation was 1897, though long extracts had appeared in the Chartist *People's Paper* in 1852.

57.The handmill/steam-mill sentence is another one frequently quoted out of context, to portray Marx as a technological determinist. A perusal of Chapter 6 should set the record straight.

58.Sayer 1983a; 1987. Other works dealing specifically, or centrally, with Marx's method include: Althusser; Althusser and Balibar; Bologh; CEW intro.; Della Volpe; Kain; Mepham and Ruben; Mandel introduction to Penguin edition of Marx 1867a; Nicolaus introduction to his edition of 1858a; Ollman 1976; Zeleny.

59.Marx changed his mind on the proper order of analysis in

Capital following this text, and arguably developed a clear
distinction of historical and transhistorical categories that
resolved some of its uncertainties and ambiguities. See Sayer
1983a: Chapter 4, and Afterword. On Marx's changing plans
for *Capital*, see note 7. Later comments on method which have
to be put beside the 1857 text include 1873b; 1880b; and –
less accessibly – the many comments in *Capital* and *Theories
of Surplus Value* on the errors of other economists. See also
Letters on Capital. For Marx's earlier writings on method, see
notes 45, 60, and 67.

60. 1843b is an excellent source on Marx's method, but does not
lend itself to comprehensible excerpting in this regard. See also
the material cited in note 45. Colletti in CEW brilliantly relates
the methodology in the 1843 Critique to that of Marx's later
works; a point often lost in the largely sterile debate around
Althusser's dismissal of the early writings (see note 5). I
include this brief extract merely to give a 'feel' of such
methodological continuity (which does not preclude
development) in Marx: compare, for example, 4.13, 4.21–4.22.

61. The traditional dating of this is November 1887; Wada argues
it hails from late 1888. Marx did not in fact send the letter;
Engels supposes this was because it might jeopardize the
survival of the journal (see Wada, in Shanin: 60). It was found
amongst Marx's papers after his death. Engels sent a copy to
Vera Zasulich in 1884, who published it in Russian in 1884 or
1886 (sources differ on this). The first English translation was
in *The Russian Menace to Europe* (1952). It was first included
in the 1965 edition of the *Selected Correspondence*. Herzen
and Chernyshevsky were major Russian populist theorists; on
Marx's views on the latter see note 20. The section of *Capital*
to which Marx refers is excerpted as 6.2 and 6.3; Marx's drafts
of the letter to Zasulich, in which he expands his views on
Russian 'exceptionalism', as 8.2.

62. I take it Marx means that Darwin explains 'rationally' (via the
mechanism of natural selection) what *appears* to be a
teleological process (the adaptation of species to their
environments). The point is important because evolutionist
readings of Marx have often been more Lamarckian than
Darwinian.

63. On the General Introduction, see notes 52 and 59. I believe
that Marx is posing a *problem* of the dual reference – both
transhistorical and historical – of the 'abstractions' of political

economy in this passage (and 4.8), which he does *not* fully resolve in this text. The eventual resolution, which also explains why Marx does *not* begin *Capital* with a section on production in general as mooted in the 1857 work, but begins with a concrete social form, the commodity (4.13), lies in a clear *distinction* of historical and transhistorical, and this in turn becomes a linchpin of Marx's 'critique of the economic categories'. The 'material side, which the most disparate epochs of production may have in common [...] lies beyond political economy' (4.11). Marx's object is *not* production in general, but its specific social forms, which can only be apprehended in determinate historical categories. This is emphasized in many of the passages in this chapter. Economists' identification of the socially specific with the materially universal aspects of productive phenomena is in turn basic to what Marx calls their 'Fetishism'. See passages 5.6–5.9 and 5.21–5.26. On these issues, see Sayer 1983a.

64. These are the opening lines of a fragment, entitled 'On value', which occurs at the very end of the *Grundrisse*. For the first time, Marx definitively arrives at the commodity as the proper starting-point (a problem which had plagued him through the *Grundrisse*) of his critique. Compare the opening sections of both 1859b and 1867a (given as 5.2).

65. This letter is roughly contemporary with the last notebook of the *Grundrisse*.

66. Marx explains the useful/abstract labour distinction in Chapter 1 of *Capital* 1. (See 5.2 and 5.7.) It is an example of the transhistorical/historical distinction discussed in note 63. Useful labour is any labour which produces a use-value, or article which satisfies human wants, irrespective of the mode of production. Abstract labour is a specific social form found only in generalized commodity production. This resolves the ambivalence in the simple abstraction 'labour' discussed in 4.8. See further 1863b: 164; Sayer 1983a, Chapter 2; Rubin.

67. This passage, along with 3.26, 4.25, and 6.32, comes from the important first section of Chapter 2 of *Poverty of Philosophy* (1847a), which comprises 'seven observations' on the method of political economy. The whole is well worth reading alongside the other methodological comments of Marx's cited in notes 45, 59, and 60.

68. This is the opening paragraph of *Capital* 3.

69. Marx accuses Adam Smith of having two theories of value, an

'esoteric' one which (for Marx, correctly) sees value as being determined by the labour requisite for the *production* of a good, and an 'exoteric' one which equates value with the labour it will *command*, i.e. the number of hours that would have to be worked in order to purchase it. This latter is for Smith determined by the summation of revenues: in his own words 'wages, profit and rent, are the three original sources of all revenue, as well as of all exchangeable value'. Smith restricted his 'esoteric' theory to pre-capitalist conditions, in which the labour that a commodity contained and commanded were identical. It was the discrepancy between the two under capitalism which led him to formulate his 'exoteric' theory. Marx explained this discrepancy by the fact that although commodities exchanged on the basis of the labour they contained, not all such labour was *paid* (see 5.15 and 5.16). Profit, rent and wages were thus *divisions* of value, not its sources: see 4.23, 5.26, and for fuller discussion, 1863a: Chapter 3; Sayer 1983a: 122–6, and Meek. *Capital* 3 in fact does end with a chapter entitled 'Classes' (1865a: 885–6), identifying wage-labourers, capitalists and land-owners as the 'three big classes of modern society based on the capitalist mode of production', but noting also that 'middle and intermediate strata [...] obliterate lines of demarcation everywhere'. Unfortunately the MS is unfinished, and runs to only 40 lines or so. On Marx on class, see also note 89.

70. This is a brief extract from a long discussion of classical political economy and what Marx dubbed its 'vulgar' successor. He explains these terms in 1867a: 80n2; 1873b. The criticisms of the 'analytic' method of political economy made in this passage are elaborated in detail in *Theories of surplus value* (1863a,b,c), but this text does not readily lend itself to easy excerpting. But see, *inter alia*, 1863a: 81–2, 87–90; 1863b: 106, 164–9, 174, 190–1, 437. Sayer 1983a: 113–35 provides detailed commentary on Marx's critique of classical economy's procedures of abstraction.

71. The best book I have read on Marx's *Capital* is Isaak Rubin's *Essays on Marx's Theory of Value*, where he argues this case in detail; see also Colletti 1972. Rubin was an active participant in the Russian revolutionary movement from 1905. He became a research associate at the Marx–Engels Institute in 1926. In 1930 he was arrested. An official source explained that 'the followers of Rubin and the Menshevising Idealists [...]

treated Marx's revolutionary method in the spirit of Hegelianism'. Rubin was imprisoned, 'confessed' to belonging to a non-existent oppositional organization, was tried, exiled, and 'disappeared'. Others of the same generation of theorists, like Pashukanis, Volosinov, and Chayanov have also only latterly been 'discovered' in the West. If Rubin is right about the intimacy of the link between Marx's theory of value and his analysis of fetishism – I myself think his case incontrovertible – recent Marxist attempts to state Marx's supposed 'theory of history' on the basis of such disclaimers as '*The theses of the labour theory of value are not presupposed or entailed by any contentions advanced in this book*' (Cohen 1978: 353; see also Cutler *et al.*; Elster 1985) are simply absurd. The labour theory might be wrong, but it is a cornerstone of Marx's thought. Marx of course analyses far more than the commodity, money and capital in *Capital*; so this chapter only deals with what his 1862b calls the 'quintessence' of his 'economics'.

72. Chapter 1 of *Capital* 1 was extensively revised by Marx through successive editions, and it is sometimes worth comparing the different treatments of the material. See note 3.

73. For Marx, proportionality between different branches of production on the basis of the law of value is actually ensured through the play of supply and demand. When supply exceeds demand, price falls below value, and capital is withdrawn from a sector; when demand exceeds supply, prices rise above value, and capital is attracted. The underlying tendency is always toward equilibrium – i.e., the point at which price and value (or more strictly, given the transformation of prices into values under capitalism, market price and price of production; see note 77) coincide. Contrary to a widespread misconception, then, Marx did *not* ignore supply and demand in his theory; he merely argued that the relative prices of different commodities *at* equilibrium could not be explained on its basis, since there the two cancel out. It was the axis *around* which market-prices revolve, which was in need of explanation. This was the problem of 'natural price' in classical political economy. See 1865a: Chapter 10.

74. Thomas Hodgskin was one of a group of early socialist economists who anticipated Marx in using Ricardo's theory of value to develop a critique of the capitalist system. See 1863c: Chapter 21.

75. Marx distinguishes the circulation of commodities (C – M – C)

and of capital (M – C – M). In the first case, commodities are sold for money to buy other commodities; thus money merely facilitates the exchanges. In the second, the objective is to realise a *profit* on the money advanced; purchase and sale of commodities is simply a vehicle for capital expansion. Money advanced as *capital* is thus a sum of value advanced with a view to realizing a *surplus value*. It is the source of this surplus value Marx is concerned with here. The form of capital which he considers is money advanced to purchase *means of production* and *labour power*. The commodities his capitalist buys are these latter; what he sells is the product of their utilization in a material production process.

76. In 'Value, Price and Profit' (1865c). This is the text of lectures given to the GC of the IWMA on 20 and 27 June, 1865. Along with 'Wage Labour and Capital' (see note 53), this is one of the most 'popular' and accessible introductions to Marx's economic theory. It was first published in 1898 in London by Eleanor Marx and Edward Aveling; the title is theirs. This work is also known under the title 'Wages, price and profit'.

77. This 'trinity formula', as Marx dubs it, is a theory both of the composition of value and the sources of revenues. It follows Adam Smith's 'exoteric' theory of value as comprising the sum of revenues, discussed in note 69. For Marx, labour is the sole source of value; the value of a commodity is thus made up of c (constant capital) + v (variable capital) + s (surplus value). C is the sum expended on means of production; since the labour-time necessary to produce these is part of the *total* labour-time necessary to produce the final product, this value is transferred to the product. No revenues can arise from this source. V is the capital advanced as wages, the labourer's revenue; the labourer reproduces this in the necessary labour-time. S is surplus-value. Circulation adds no value or surplus-value. S must therefore be the *sole* source of revenue for the capitalist and rentier classes. Marx sees profit, interest, and rent as being *post festum* divisions of the surplus-value created in the process of production. The landlord's monopoly of land, a means of production, allows the interception of some surplus value that would otherwise go to functioning capital; interest is a further interception, which stems from the fact that capital as capital may be sold as a commodity, whose 'price' is the going rate of interest. The profit on an individual capital, we might note, is *not* identical to the surplus value it extracts,

even before these deductions. If it were, then, other things being equal, capitals with a lower organic composition (c/v) would reap higher profits than those with a higher (since the rate of surplus value is s/(c + v)). In practice, Marx argues, capitals will migrate in search of higher profits, and imbalances in supply and demand will yield systematic deviations of price from value, and an average rate of profit. Thus the connection between surplus labour and profit is obscured: profit *appears* to be a function simply of the size of the capital advanced, and therefore a reward to capital as a factor of production. Land similarly appears to be the source of rent. All these economic forms are treated at length in *Capital* 3. Marx's discussions of the trinity formula, in 1865a: Chapter 48, and in 1863c: addenda, are amongst his best analyses of ideology and fetishism. I review these in Sayer 1983a.

78. The following is an edited summary of the long discussion of 'the so-called primitive accumulation' in Part 8 of *Capital* 1. Marx takes England as his exemplar, as throughout *Capital* 1, for reasons he explains in the Preface to the first German edition. He was later to deny the generalisability of this account and modify the relevant passage in the Preface accordingly: see 4.3. Part 8 of *Capital* 1 is perhaps the best example to be found in his work of 'historical investigation'; it is far more accessible than much of Marx's writing. It is worth noting that Marx intended to use Russian history comparably for the sections on ground-rent in *Capital* 3, and according to Engels this was one factor that prevented him completing vols 2 and 3 for the press (Engels 1894b: 7). This might be borne in mind when reading selections on Russia in this anthology, especially 8.2.

79. Marx refers to the Elizabethan Poor Law, enshrined in statutes of 1597 and 1601. This established a compulsory parish poor rate, levied by overseers under the supervision of JPs, and set up houses of correction for 'sturdy beggars'. Marx discusses vagrancy legislation in England in 1867a: Chapter 28.

80. Feudal tenures were abolished during the interregnum, but the parliament of 1660 confirmed this. Larger landlords effectively gained rights of private property. Copyhold tenure was excluded from the 1660 law, so many peasants did *not* gain comparable security of tenure.

81. The 1662 Act of Settlement severely restricted mobility of the poor; it authorized justices to send back to their last place of

domicile any newcomer to a parish likely to become a charge on the rates.

82. Of 1688–9; often described as neither glorious, nor a revolution.

83. In *Grundrisse* Marx writes similarly that: '*governments*, e.g. of Henry VII, VIII, etc. appear as conditions of the historic dissolution process and as makers for the conditions of existence of capital' (Nicolaus: 507).

84. The statute followed the black death, and ensuing shortage of labour. It gave JPs wide powers to force labourers to work at legal wages, and severely restricted labour mobility. The labour statutes of 1349/51 were part of a Europe-wide 'feudal reaction' to the crisis.

85. Marx distinguishes 'manufacture' and 'machine industry' as successive stages in the development of a properly capitalist mode of production. See 6.16. The characteristics of each, and the transition from one to the other, are discussed in detail in later passages in this chapter.

86. Marx's remarks in this passage on the role of usurers' and merchants' capital in the development of capitalism are expanded in 1865a: Chapters 20 and 36.

87. See note 77.

88. Marx distinguishes between *absolute* and *relative* surplus value. The former originates from extending the length of the working day beyond necessary labour time (the time taken to reproduce the value of the wage); the latter from diminishing necessary labour time as a *proportion* of the working day. This is an indirect consequence of capitalist competition: increases in productivity which initially give an individual capital a market advantage become generalized throughout a sector, with a resulting fall in the value of its products, since the labour time *socially* necessary for their production has now decreased. In so far as these products enter either directly (as means of subsistence) or indirectly (as means of their production) into the labourer's consumption, the value of labour power, which is determined by the labour time necessary to produce the labourer's means of subsistence, falls, and with it, necessary labour time. It is therefore quite possible, incidentally, that a rising *rate* of exploitation (s/v) may coincide with a stationary, or even a rising, real *standard* of living: an important point given that Marx is often misread as predicting the inexorable *absolute* immiseration of the

working class; he did not hold this view by the time he wrote *Capital*. See 1867a: Parts 3 – 5.

89. This passage is of note, since Marx has sometimes been accused of failing to anticipate the 'managerial revolution' and growing separation of ownership and control of capital. He went so far as to see in the modern joint stock company 'a necessary transitional phase towards the reconversion of capital into the property of producers [...] the abolition of the capitalist mode of production within the capitalist mode of production itself' (1865a: 438–9). Relatedly, he criticized Ricardo for forgetting to emphasize 'the constantly growing number of the middle classes, those who stand between the workman on the one hand and the capitalist and landlord on the other. The middle classes maintain themselves to an ever increasing extent directly out of revenue, they are a burden weighing heavily on the working base and increase the social security and power of the upper ten thousand' (1863b: 573). His empirical studies, notably 1850a and 1852a, do *not* operate with the crude 'two-class model' of society so often attributed to him by the authors of sociology textbooks, but distinguish a large variety of classes and class fractions.

90. Compare the early 3.2, and more generally, 1844b.

91. Thompson argues this in his *Poverty of Theory*.

92. See 4.19. Marx's distinction between the 'essential relations' of society and their 'phenomenal forms' – which may be deceptive – is a central theme in his work. Sayer 1987a, Chapter 4, (contentiously) interprets Marx's base/superstructure metaphor in these terms, and documents this *vis-à-vis* his analysis of the state, a central concern of this chapter. On Marx's account of ideology (to which this distinction is central) see Larrain; Lukács; McMurtry; Mepham; Parekh; Sayer 1983a; Seliger; Thompson.

93. In his 1862b, Marx says that the question of 'the relations of the different state forms to the different economic structures of society' is the one part of his projected opus that could *not* be easily developed by others on the basis of *Capital*.

94. On these drafts, see notes 12 and 19.

95. This 'domination of ideas' theme is anticipated in *The German Ideology*: 1846a: 406.

96. This is one of many instances in Marx where the supposed 'base' of social life (production/property relations) is

constituted by 'superstructural' factors; see Sayer 1987,
Chapter 4.

97. Maine is best known to sociology for his contrast of status and
contract, formulated in *Ancient Law* (1861). Marx excerpted
Maine's *Lectures on the Early History of Institutions* in
1880–1; see Krader's introduction to 1881a.

98. Marx's linking, here and in the next few passages, of state
formation and individualization strikingly anticipates Durkheim
1957; a much neglected work.

99. Marx's critique is organized in the form of
paragraph-by-paragraph commentary on part of Hegel's book. I
have reproduced only Marx's comments here; I hope, not
incomprehensibly. For commentary see Colletti, intro. to CEW,
and note 5.

100. Marx's characterization of bureaucracy here is strikingly
anticipated in his 1843a. Marx himself cites this as a crucial
formative moment in his intellectual development (see 9.2).

101. Marx refers to the Declaration of the Rights of Man and the
Citizen which prefaces the French constitution of 1791.

102. On this article, see note 48.

103. This (like 7.3) suggests that class is, for Marx, in one sense at
least an *historical* category (like 'labour' in 4.8). We can apply
the abstraction 'class' to describe any set of social relations
predicated on surplus extraction; but the bourgeoisie is the first
group to rule *as* a class, in the sense that its social power
derives from its property ownership alone. This implies, *inter
alia*, the existence of the civil society/state division (where, for
example, bourgeois individuals may *not* themselves control
political apparatuses) Marx discusses in these passages. The
contrast is with rule organized through personal domin- ation,
as epitomized in the medieval system of estates, where
'economic' and 'political' power – the very division being an
anachronism – coincide. Godelier (1984) is one of the very
few commentators to pick up on this; see also Sayer 1985.

104. Pashukanis (who had no knowledge of the *Grundrisse*) was
attempting to link legal forms to the conditions of commodity
production and exchange, on the basis of *Capital*, in Russia in
the 1920s – his *Law and Marxism: a General Theory*, a
pioneering work in this field, was not published in English
until 1978. On Marx and law see *Marx and Engels on Law*;
Buchanan; M. Cohen; Corrigan and Sayer 1981; Phillips.

105. Christian Wolff was a disciple of Leibniz, known for his common-sense adaptation of Leibniz's ideas.

106. Marx discusses utilitarianism more fully in *The German Ideology* (1846a: 408–14). See also 1844e: 124–34.

107. This long passage comes from the drafts of *The Civil War in France*; see note 12. Marx is talking of the development of the French state. The main events referred to in the text are the 'first French revolution' of 1789; the (first) Empire of Napoleon Bonaparte, established in 1804 (though Napoleon had been 'First Consul' since his coup of November 1799); the Restoration of the Bourbons in 1815; the July Monarchy of Louis Philippe from 1830; the revolution of 1848, which established the Second Republic; the Second Empire of Napoleon III, from 1852 (after his coup of 2 December, 1851) to 1870; and the Paris Commune. The Commune of 1871 lasted 72 days, before it was bloodily suppressed by the provisional government under Thiers.

108. Charles Dickens's satirical description of bureaucracy in *Little Dorrit*.

109. This so-called 'development thesis' is a cornerstone of G. A. Cohen's influential account of Marx; see Cohen 1978. It has a long pedigree in Marxist thought; Dobb, for example, replies to Sweezy's critique of his pioneering *Studies in the Development of Capitalism* (1946) by accusing Sweezy of making feudalism (which Sweezy regards as economically static) 'an exception to the general Marxist law of development that economic society is moved by its own internal contradictions' (in Hilton 1978: 59).

110. Had I space, I would also have included substantial excerpts from the three historical chapters in *Capital* 3; 1865a: Chapters 20, 36, 47. See also the anthology *Pre-capitalist Socio-economic Formations*, 1974; Gandy; Godelier; Hilton 1978; the Hobsbawm edn of 1858a; all Krader references; Melotti; Rigby; Sawer; Turner.

111. This is a substantial part of the self-contained section of the *Grundrisse* entitled 'Forms which preceded capitalist production'. It was published in English before the *Grundrisse* as a whole; see note 8.

112. For discussion of this text, see p. xvii and notes 12 and 20. It should be carefully compared with section 8.1, written fifteen years earlier and before Marx's copious reading of the 1870s and early 1880s on precapitalist societies. Two differences are

very apparent: Marx's emphasis here on the 'vitality' of the primitive commune; and his perception of its eventual disintegration as conditional upon historical context, not inevitable.

113. Marx refers to the emancipation of the serfs by Tsarist decree in 1861.

114. The *artel* was a team working jointly, usually under an elected leader and sharing its net proceeds.

115. 'Federation of North Russian republics' refers to the city states of Russia, the most prominent of which was Nijni Novgorod. *Volost* was a territorial subdivision of specifically peasant administration, closely controlled by state officialdom.

116. Richard Jones, *An Essay on the Distribution of Wealth*, London, 1831, Part 1.

117. The Physiocrats were an 18th-century French school of political economy, whose most famous representative is Quesnay. See 1863a: Chapter 2.

118. This is one of several long parenthetical notes in the text, and it is not altogether clear what personal service is different *from*. I would say wage-labour, discussed by Marx before the parentheses. In any event, it is for what it says about feudal society that I include this passage here.

119. On the 1844 MSS, and the debates they have inspired, see notes 5 and 49.

120. On this text (1859a), see p. xviii and note 21.

121. Relevant articles are in CW 1. See also note 100.

122. See CW 1: 215–21.

123. See note 48.

124. Engels 1843; 1845; see notes 40 and 48.

125. 1848a.

126. 1847b. See note 53.

127. Marx wrote his doctoral dissertation, 'Difference between the Democritean and Epicurean philosophy of nature', between 1840 and March 1841. Both this, and the notebooks for it (1839), are in CW 1, the latter appearing in English for the first time. Parts of the MS (which survives only in a copy, but one annotated in Marx's own hand) are missing. It was published, with some omissions, in Stuttgart in 1902; the first complete publication was in MEGA 1, 1927. The first full English translation was in N. Livergood, *Activity in Marx's Philosophy*, Hague, 1967; the Foreword was previously translated in *On religion* (1957).

Select bibliography

This bibliography is not simply a listing of texts cited in this book, but a guide to English sources for Marx's writings, and modern secondary literature on Marx. Whilst not exhaustive, it aims to be reasonably comprehensive. It is organized under the following headings:

Part 1 MARX: COLLECTIONS
A. Collected works; B. Selected works; C. Correspondence; D. Anthologies on specific topics.

By collections is meant compilations of Marx's writings, large or small, as distinct from editions of individual works like *Capital* or *The German Ideology*. These collections are often the source volumes for the individual texts listed in Part 2. Collections in 1A, 1B, and 1C are listed in rough order of comprehensiveness; in 1D, alphabetically by title.
Items listed in Part 1 are cited in my text and notes by title, or, in some cases, by abbreviations (explained on p. x).

Part 2 MARX: INDIVIDUAL TEXTS

These are individual writings by Marx – anything from a letter to a book – drawn on, or referred to, in this anthology. In some cases they exist as independent publications (e.g. *Capital*), in others they can only be found in one of the collections listed in Part 1, so cross-referencing is necessary to find full details.

These texts are listed chronologically, by year of composition. In the text and notes, these are cited by date-code: e.g. 1867a is *Capital*, vol. 1.

Part 3 OTHER WORKS:

A. Reference works on Marx; B. Biographies and reminiscences of Marx; C. Writings by Engels; D. Commentary on Marx.

This contains all works cited in my text or notes not by Marx, plus some literature on Marx not otherwise mentioned in this book. Chronologies, dictionaries, and bibliographies are given in 3A; biographies and reminiscences in 3B; commentaries (works of interpretation, rather than pure information) in 3D. I list Engels's writings separately in 3C.

Listing here is alphabetical by author's surname, and chronological within an author's output. In the text and notes all works in Part 3 are cited by author's name plus, where necessary, date.

1. MARX: COLLECTIONS

This listing is not exhaustive. Except in section A, only English language collections are given. Smaller collections are in general omitted from section B. Many of the works listed contain texts by both Marx and Engels.

A. Collected works

Historische-Kritische Gesamtausgabe, Werke-Briefe-Schriften, Frankfurt and Moscow, 1927–36, 12 vols (uncompleted). [MEGA 1]

Gesamtausgabe, Berlin, 1975 onwards. (This will be a complete edition, publishing everything surviving of Marx and Engels in the original languages of composition, including MSS, drafts, notes, excerpts, marginalia, etc. It will amount to over 100 vols.) [MEGA 2]

Werke, Berlin 1956–68. (39 vols plus 2 suppl. vols.) [MEW]

Collected Works, Moscow/London/New York, 1975 onwards. (To comprise 50 vols. *Not* a complete works.) [CW]

Archiv K. Marksa i F. Engelsa, Moscow, 1924 onwards. (Not a collected works as such, but the first, and in some cases only, place in which many of Marx's posthumous texts were published.) [AME]

B. Selected works

Selected Works, 3 vols, Moscow, 1969–70.
Selected Works, 1 vol., Moscow, 1968.
The Portable Karl Marx, ed. E. Kamenka, Harmondsworth, 1983.
The Marx-Engels Reader, ed. R. Tucker, New York, 1972.
Essential writings, ed. R. Bender, New York, 1972.
Selected writings, ed. D. McLellan, Oxford, 1977.
Karl Marx: a Reader, ed. J. Elster, Cambridge, 1986.
Selected Writings in Sociology and Social Philosophy, eds. T. Bottomore and M. Rubel, Harmondsworth, 1963.
Thought of Karl Marx, ed. D. McLellan, 2nd edn, London 1980.

C. Correspondence

Selected Correspondence, ed. D. Torr, Moscow, 1934. [SC 1934]
Selected Correspondence, Moscow, 1956, 1965, 1975. (Editions differ slightly from each other and radically from SC 1934; the 1975 edn. is used here unless otherwise indicated.) [SC]
Letters of Karl Marx, ed. S. Padover, Englewood Cliffs, 1979.
Selected Letters, ed. F. Raddatz, Boston 1981.
[43 letters by Marx.] Instituto Giangiacomo Feltrinelli *Annali*, 1, 1958.
Letters to Americans, New York, 1963.
Letters on Capital, London, 1983.
On the Eastern Question, ed. E. Aveling, London, 1969.
Letters to Kugelmann, London, n.d. [1934?].

D. Anthologies on specific topics

American Journalism of Marx and Engels, New York, 1966.
Anarchism and Anarcho-syndicalism, Moscow, 1972.
Articles from the Neue Rheinische Zeitung, Moscow, 1972.
Articles in the New American Cyclopaedia, ed. H. Draper, Berkeley, 1969.
Articles on Britain, Moscow, 1971.
Civil War in the United States, New York, 1969.
Documents of the 1st International, 5 vols, Moscow, 1962 onwards. [DFI]
Early Texts, ed. D. McLellan, Oxford, 1971.
Early Writings, ed. L. Colletti, Harmondsworth, 1975. [CEW]
First Indian War of Independence, Moscow, 1975.
Ireland and the Irish Question, Moscow, 1978. [*Ireland*]

Karl Marx: Interviews and Recollections, ed. D. McLellan, New Jersey, 1981.

Late Marx and the Russian Road, ed. T. Shanin, London, 1983. [Shanin]

Love Poems of Karl Marx, eds. R. Lettau and L. Ferlinghetti, San Francisco, 1977.

Marx and Engels on Law, eds. M. Cain and A. Hunt, London, 1979.

Marx, Engels and Australia, ed. H. Mayer, Sydney, 1964.

Marx on China 1853–60, London, 1968.

Marx on Colonialism and Modernization, ed. S. Avineri, New York, 1969.

Marx on Economics, ed. R. Freeman, Harmondsworth, 1962.

On Britain, Moscow, 1962.

On Colonialism, Moscow, 1968.

On Communist Society, Moscow, 1978.

On Literature and Art, Moscow, 1978.

On Literature and Art, eds. L. Baxandall and S. Morawski, St. Louis, 1973.

On Means of Communications, ed. Y. de la Haye, New York, 1980.

On Religion, Moscow, 1957.

On the Paris Commune, Moscow, 1971.

On the United States, Moscow, 1979.

[Political Writings.] 3 vols: *Revolutions of 1848*; *Surveys from Exile*; *1st International and After*, ed. D. Fernbach, Harmondsworth, 1973–4. [PW 1–3]

Precapitalist Socioeconomic Formations, Moscow, 1974.

Revolution in Spain, 1854–6, London, 1939.

Russian Menace to Europe, eds. P. Blackstock and B. Hoselitz, London, 1955.

Texts on Method, ed. T. Carver, Oxford, 1974. [Carver]

The Cologne Communist Trial, ed. R. Livingstone, London, 1971.

The Hague Congress of the 1st International, 2 vols, Moscow, 1976, 1978.

The 'Karl Marx Library', ed. S. Padover, has issued the following anthologies: *On America and the Civil War*; *On Education, Women, and Children*; *On Freedom of the Press and Censorship*; *On History and People*; *On Religion*; *On Revolution*; *On the 1st International*, New York, 1971–7.

Value: Studies by Karl Marx, ed. A. Dragstedt, London, 1976. [Value]

Writings of the Young Marx, eds. L. Easton and K. Guddat, New York, 1967.

Writings on the Paris Commune, ed. H. Draper, New York, 1971.

2. MARX: INDIVIDUAL TEXTS

I list here only works excerpted in this anthology or mentioned in the notes. English versions are given except where none exists, or, in the case of 1875a, where Marx himself altered his work in translation. In all cases the *first* source given is the one I have used. For bibliographies of Marx, see section 3A. The numbers in round brackets after entries cross-refer to discussions in notes.

1836–7 [Poems and Literary Experiments], CW 1. (31)

1837 Letter to his Father, 10–11 Nov, CW 1. (43)

1839 Notebooks on Epicurean Philosophy, CW 1. (127)

1841 Difference between the Democritean and Epicurean Philosophy of Nature [doctoral dissertation], CW 1. Alt. tr: see note 127. (127)

1842 Leading article in no. 179 of the *Kölnische Zeitung*, CW 1.

1843a Justification of the correspondent from the Mosel, CW 1. (5, 100)

1843b Critique of Hegel's *Rechtsphilosophie*, CW 3. Alt. tr: J. O'Malley (ed), Cambridge, 1970; CEW. (5, 45, 60, 99)

1843c On the Jewish Question, CW 3. Alt tr: CEW. (48)

1843d Contribution to the Critique of Hegel's Philosophy of Law: Introduction, CW 3. Alt. tr: CEW. (48)

1844a Critical notes on the article 'The King of Prussia and Social Reform', CW 3. Alt. tr: CEW.

1844b Comments on James Mill. CW 3. Alt. tr: CEW. (5,22)

1844c Economic and Philosophic Manuscripts of 1844 [Paris Manuscripts], CW 3. Alt. tr: CEW. (5, 45, 49)

1844d Letter to L. Feuerbach, 11 August, CW 3. (50)

1844e The Holy Family, with F. Engels, CW 4. (44, 45, 106)

1845a Draft of an article on Friedrich List, CW 4.

1845b Theses on Feuerbach, CW 5. Alt. tr: CEW. (46)

1846a The German Ideology [1845–6], with F. Engels, CW 5. (5, 6, 44, 103, 106)

1846b Letter to P. Annenkov, 28 Dec, CW 38. (47)

1847a The Poverty of Philosophy, CW 6. (47, 57, 67)

1847b Wage Labour and Capital, CW 9. (53, 76)

1848a Speech on the question of free trade, CW 6. (125)

1848b Manifesto of the Communist Party, with F. Engels, CW 6. (Many separate editions: *The Communist Manifesto*, ed. A. J. P.

Taylor, Harmondsworth, 1967, gives all prefaces, and is as good as any. *Birth of the Communist Manifesto*, ed. D. J. Struick, New York, 1971, is the most scholarly edn, giving early drafts by Engels and other supplementary material.) (37, 38, and the in-text comment on 7.30)

1850a Class Struggles in France, 1848–50. CW 10. Alt. tr: PW 1. (89)

1850b Address to the central authority of the Communist League, March, with F. Engels, CW 10. (17)

1850c Address to the central authority of the Communist League, June, with F. Engels, CW 10. (17)

1852a 18th Brumaire of Louis Bonaparte, CW 11. Alt. tr: PW 2. (20, 33, 56, 89)

1852b Great Men of the Exile, with F. Engels, CW 11. (17)

1852c Revelations concerning the communist trial in Cologne, CW 11. (17)

1853a British Rule in India [NYDT article], CW 12. (4, 33)

1853b Future Results of the British Rule in India [NYDT article], CW 12. (4, 33)

1857 General Introduction [to the *Grundrisse*], CW 28. Alt. tr: Nicolaus and McLellan edns. of 1858a; Carver. (8, 52, 59, 63)

1858a. *Grundrisse* [1857–8], CW 28, 29 [all citations here from 28]. Alt. tr: Nicolaus, *Grundrisse*, Harmondsworth 1973; and of extracts in *Marx's Grundrisse*, ed. D. McLellan, London 1971, and *Precapitalist Economic Formations*, ed. E. Hobsbawm, London, 1964. (7, 8, 64, 83, 104, 110, 111, 112)

1858b Letter to F. Engels, 1 Feb, CW 40.

1858c Letter to F. Lassalle, 22 Feb, CW 40.

1858d Letter to F. Engels, 2 April, CW 40. (65)

1859a Preface to 1859b, with the latter. (21)

1859b *A Contribution to the Critique of Political Economy*, London, 1971. (10, 64)

1860s [date uncertain] 'Confessions', in D. Riazanov (ed.) *Karl Marx: man, thinker, revolutionist*, London, 1927, p. 269. (32)

1860 Herr Vogt, CW 17.

1861a Letter to F. Lassalle, 16 Jan, CW 41.

1861b The Crisis in England [*Die Presse* article], CW 19.

1862a Letter to Engels, 30 July, in S. Padover (ed.) *Letters of Karl Marx*.

1862b Letter to L. Kugelmann, 28 Dec, CW 41.

1863a,b,c *Theories of Surplus Value* [1861–3], 3 vols, Moscow, 1963, 1968, 1971. (7, 10, 54, 59, 69, 77, 89, 117)

1864 Inaugural address of the IWMA, CW 20.

1865a *Capital*, vol. 3 [1863–5], ed. F. Engels, Moscow, 1971. Alt. tr: Harmondsworth, 1981. (7, 9, 10, 55, 68, 73, 77, 78, 86, 89, 110)

1865b Letter to J. Schweitzer, 24 Jan, SC. (47)

1865c Value, Price and Profit, CW 20. (76)

1866 Results of the Immediate Process of Production [between 1863 and 1866]. With Penguin (Harmondsworth) edn. of 1867a. Alt. tr: *Value*. (7, 11)

1867a *Capital*, vol. 1. London, Lawrence & Wishart, tr. E. Aveling and S. Moore, 1967. Alt. tr: Chicago, Kerr, 1906; London, Dent, 1930; Harmondsworth, Penguin, 1976. (3, 10, 51, 59, 66, 71, 72, 75, 78, 88)

1867b Letter to F. Engels, 24 Aug, SC.

1867c Outline of a Report on the Irish Question, *Ireland*.

1868a Letter to F. Engels, 8 Jan, SC.

1868b Letter to F. Engels, 30 April, SC.

1868c Letter to L. Kugelmann, 11 July, SC.

1871a *Notebook on the Paris Commune*, ed. H. Draper, Berkeley, 1971. (12)

1871b First draft of 1871d, CW 22. (12, 107)

1871c Second draft of 1871d, CW 22. (12, 38, 107, and in-text comment on 7.30)

1871d The Civil War in France, CW 22. (12, 19, 107)

1872a Fictitious splits in the International, with F. Engels, DFI 5. Alt. tr: PW 3. (17)

1872b American split [in the IWMA], DFI 5. (34)

1872c Preface to 2nd German edn of the Communist Manifesto, in Taylor and Struick edns of 1848b. (38)

1873a Political Indifferentism, PW 3. (17)

1873b Afterword to 2nd German edn of *Capital*. With 1867a. (59, and in-text comment on 4.21)

1874 Notes on Bakunin's *Statism and anarchy*. Full text, *Etudes de Marxologie*, 2, 1959; Marx's comments, PW 3. (22)

1875a *Le Capital* (French edn of 1867a; first published in installments 1873–5), Paris, Flammarion, 1969. (3, and in-text comment on 4.3)

1875b Critique of the Gotha programme, PW 3. (17)

1877 [Or possibly 1878] Letter to editors of *Otechestvenniye Zapiski*, in Shanin. Alt. tr: SC, all edns; *On colonialism and modernization*. (20, 61)

1878 *Capital*, vol. 2 [1865–78], ed. F. Engels, Moscow, 1967. Alt.
  tr: Harmondsworth, 1978. (9)
1879a Notes on Kovalevsky, in Krader 1975. (22)
1879b Circular letter to Bebel, Liebknecht, Bracke *et al.*, with F.
  Engels, PW 3. (17)
1880a *Notes on Indian History* [?1879–80], Moscow, 1986. (23)
1880b Notes on Adolph Wagner [1879–80], Carver. Alt. tr:
  Theoretical practice, 5, 1972; *Value*. (22, 51, 59)
1881a *Ethnological notebooks* [1880–1], Assen, 1972. (22, 97)
1881b Drafts of 1881c, Feb/March, in Shanin. (12, 20, 33, 61, 78,
  112)
1881c Letter to Vera Zasulich, 8 March. With 1881b.
1881d Letter to Jenny Longuet, 11 April, SC 1934. (20)
1882a Chronological notes, in AME, vols 5–8, Moscow. (23)
1882b Preface to Russian edn of the Communist Manifesto, with F.
  Engels. With Taylor and Struick edns of 1848b. (20)
1882c *Mathematical manuscripts* [1878–82], London, 1983. (25)

3. OTHER WORKS

A. Reference works on Marx

Beckerman, G. *Marx and Engels: a Conceptual Concordance*,
  Oxford, 1983. (Guide to concepts)
Bottomore, T. (ed.) *Dictionary of Marxist Thought*, Cambridge,
  Mass., 1983.
Draper, H. *Marx–Engels Cyclopedia*, vol. 1 *Marx–Engels Chronicle*
  [day-by-day chronology]; vol. 2 *Marx–Engels Register* (complete
  bibliography of Marx's and Engels's individual writings); vol. 3
  Marx–Engels Glossary (dictionary of all proper names mentioned
  in vols 1 and 2), New York, 1984 onwards. (The best general
  work of reference, and an incomparable research tool.)
Eubanks, C. L. *Karl Marx and Friedrich Engels: an Analytical
  Bibliography*, New York, 2nd edn, 1984. (Lists books, articles,
  doctoral theses on Marx and Engels to 1984.)
Oakley, A. *The Making of Marx's Critical Theory: a
  Bibliographical Analysis*, London, 1983. (Chronological guide to
  notebooks, plans, drafts, texts of Marx's 'economics'.)
Rubel, M. *Marx: Life and Works*, London, 1980. (Chronology.)
Sayer, D. Karl Marx 1867–83; a Biographical Note [1983b] in
  Shanin. (Chronology.)

B. Biographies and reminiscences of Marx

Berlin, I. *Karl Marx: his Life and Environment*, Oxford, 1939. (Short, readable introduction.)

Blumenberg, W. *Karl Marx*, London, 1971. (Probably the best short modern biography.)

Fedoseyev, P. *et al. Karl Marx: a Biography*, Moscow, 1973.

Kapp, Y. *Eleanor Marx*. London, 2 vols, 1979. (Vol. 1 is on 'Family life: 1855-1883'.)

McLellan, D. *Karl Marx: his Life and Thought*, London, 1973. (The major modern biography; clear outline of Marx's ideas as well as his life.)

Mehring, F. *Karl Marx*, London, 1936. (The classic biography, now dated.)

Nicolaevski, B. and Maenchen-Helfen, O. *Karl Marx: Man and Fighter*, London, 1973.

Padover, S. *Karl Marx: an Intimate Biography*, New York, 1978.

Raddatz, F. *Karl Marx: a Political Biography*, Boston, 1978.

Reminiscences of Marx and Engels, Moscow, n.d. Abridged as *Marx and Engels through the Eyes of their Contemporaries*, Moscow, 1972.

Rowbotham, S. (ed.) *Daughters of Karl Marx*, Harmondsworth, 1984. (Family correspondence.)

Rubel, M. and Manale, M. *Marx without Myth*, Oxford, 1975.

C. Engels

I list only works referred to in this anthology.

1843 Outlines of a critique of political economy, CW 3.

1845 *Condition of the Working Class in England in 1844*, CW 4.

1849 Democratic pan-Slavism, CW 8.

1878 *Anti-Dühring*, New York, 1972.

1885 Preface to *Capital* 2, with Marx, 1878.

1886 *Ludwig Feuerbach*, Peking, 1976.

1890a Letter to C. Schmidt, 5 Aug, 1890, SC.

1890b Letter to J. Bloch, 21–22 Sept, 1890, SC.

1890c Letter to C. Schmidt, 27 Oct, 1890, SC.

1893 Letter to F. Mehring, 14 July, 1893, SC.

1894a Letter to W. Borgius (erroneously published before as to Starkenburg), 25 Jan, 1894, SC.

1894b Preface to *Capital* 3, with Marx, 1865a.

Correspondence with Paul and Laura Lafargue, 3 vols, London, 1959–63.

D. Commentary on Marx

This is a select listing. With a few exceptions, and unavoidable overlaps, works listed here treat of *Marx* rather than Marx*ism*; this means some important areas of current debate in the social sciences (e.g. Marxism and feminism) are omitted. This list also excludes articles, except where specifically cited in the notes, or where they are mainly informative rather than interpretative, and most books written before 1970, except obvious 'classics'.

Althusser, L. *For Marx*, London, 1977.

Althusser, L. and Balibar, E. *Reading Capital*, London, 1975.

Anderson, P. *Considerations on Western Marxism*, London, 1977.

Arthur, C. *Dialectics of Labour: Marx and his Relation to Hegel*, Oxford, 1986.

Aston, T. and Philpin, C. *The Brenner Debate*, Cambridge, 1985.

Avineri, S. *Social and Political Thought of Karl Marx*, Cambridge, 1968. (See also under 1D.)

Barrett, M. 'Marxism–feminism and the work of Karl Marx', in B. Matthews (ed.) *Marx: a hundred years on*, London, 1983.

Bologh, R. *Dialectical Phenomenology: Marx's Method*, London, 1979.

Bottomore, T. *Marxist Sociology*, London, 1975.

Bottomore, T. (ed.) *Modern Interpretations of Marx*, Oxford, 1981. (See also under 1B, 3A.)

Brewer, A. *Guide to Marx's Capital*, Cambridge, 1984.

Buchanan, A. *Marx and Justice*, London, 1982.

Carver, T. *Marx's Social Theory*, Oxford, 1982.

Carver, T. *Marx and Engels: the Intellectual Relationship*, Brighton, 1983. (See also under 1D.)

Clarke, S. *Marx, marginalism and modern sociology*, London, 1983.

Cleaver, H. *Reading Capital Politically*, Austin, 1979.

Cohen, G. A. *Karl Marx's Theory of History: a Defence*, Oxford, 1978.

Cohen, M. *et al.* (eds) *Marx, Justice, and History*, Princeton, 1980.

Colletti, L. (ed.) 'Bernstein and the Marxism of the Second International', in *From Rousseau to Lenin*, London, 1972.

Colletti, L. *Marxism and Hegel*, London, 1973. (See also under 1D.)

Collins, H. and Abramski, C. *Karl Marx and the British Labour Movement*, London, 1985.

Corrigan, P. and Sayer, D. 'How the law rules: variations on some themes in Karl Marx', in B. Fryer (ed.) *Law, State and Society*, London, 1981.

Corrigan, P. and Sayer, D. 'Revolution against the state: context and significance of Marx's later writings', in *Dialectical Anthropology*, *12* (1), 1987.

Corrigan, P., Ramsay, H., and Sayer, D. *Socialist Construction and Marxist Theory*, London/New York, 1978.

Coulter, J. 'Marx and the Engels paradox', *Socialist Register*, 1971.

Cummings, I. *Marx, Engels, and National Movements*, New York, 1980.

Cutler, A., Hindness, B., Hirst, P., and Hussain, A. *Marx's Capital and Capitalism Today*, 2 vols, London, 1978.

de Brunhoff, S. *Marx on Money*, New York, 1976.

Della Volpe, G. *Rousseau and Marx*, New Jersey, 1979.

Dobb, M. *Studies in the Development of Capitalism*, London, 1946.

Draper, H. *Karl Marx's Theory of Revolution*, 2 vols, New York, 1977–8. (See also under 1D, 2, 1871a, 3A.)

Dunayevskaya, R. *Rosa Luxemburg, Women's Liberation, and Marx's Philosophy of Revolution*, New Jersey, 1981.

Durkheim, E. *Professional Ethics and Civic Morals*, London, 1957.

Elson, D. (ed.) *Value: the Representation of Labour in Capitalism*, New Jersey, 1979.

Elster, J. *Making Sense of Marx*, Cambridge, 1985.

Elster, J. *An introduction to Karl Marx*, Cambridge, 1986. (See also under 1B.)

Evans, M. *Karl Marx*, Bloomington, 1975.

Fine, B. *Marx's Capital*, New Jersey, 1975.

Gandy, D. R. *Marx and History*, Austin, 1979.

Geras, N. *Marx and Human Nature*, London, 1983.

Gilbert, A. *Marx's Politics: Communists and Citizens*, London, 1981.

Godelier, M. *L'Idéel et le Matériel*, Paris, 1984.

Gould, C. *Marx's Social Ontology*, Cambridge, Mass., 1978.

Harris, L. and Fine, B. *Rereading Capital*, New York, 1979.

Heller, A. *The Theory of Need in Marx*, London, 1976.

Henry, M. *Marx: a Philosophy of Human Reality*, Bloomington, 1983.

Hilton, R. (ed.) *Transition from Feudalism to Capitalism*, London, 1978.

Hodges, D. 'Engels's contribution to Marxism', *Socialist Register*, 1965.

Howard, M. and King, J. *Political Economy of Marx*, 2nd edn, London, 1985.

Hunt, R. *Political Ideas of Marx and Engels*, London, 1984.

Hyppolite, J. *Studies on Marx and Hegel*, London, 1969.

Jones, G. S. 'Engels and the end of classical German philosophy',

New Left Review 79, 1973.

Jones, G. S. Engels and the genesis of Marxism, *New Left Review 106*, 1977.

Kain, P. *Marx's Method, Epistemology, and Humanism*, Sovietica, 1986.

Kolakowski, L. *Main Currents of Marxism*, 3 vols, Oxford, 1978.

Korsch, K. *Marxism and Philosophy*, London, 1971.

Krader, L. 'Works of Marx and Engels in ethnology compared', *International Review of Social History 18* (2), 1973.

Krader, L. *The Asiatic Mode of Production*, Assen, 1975.

Krader, L. 'Still more on Marx, Engels, and Morgan', *Current Anthropology 18*, 1977. (See also under 2, 1879a, 1881a.)

Larrain, J. *Marxism and Ideology*, London, 1983.

Lefebvre, H. *Sociology of Karl Marx*, London, 1968.

Lichtheim, G. *From Marx to Hegel*, London, 1971.

Lippi, M. *Value and Naturalism in Marx*, New York, 1980.

Lukács, G. *History and Class Consciousness*, London, 1970.

McBride, W. *Philosophy of Marx*, London, 1977.

McCarthy, T. *Marx and the Proletariat*, Westport, 1978.

McGovern, A. 'Karl Marx's first political writings: the *Rheinische Zeitung* 1842–3', in F. Adelmann (ed.) *Demythologising Marxism*, Hague, 1969.

McLellan, D. *The Young Hegelians and Karl Marx*, London, 1969.

McLellan, D. *Marx before Marxism*, London, 1970.

McLellan, D. *Marxism after Marx*, London, 1979. (See also under 1B, 1D, 2, 1858a, and 3B.)

McLellan, D. (ed.) *Marx: the First 100 Years*, London, 1983.

McMurtry, J. *The Structure of Marx's World View*, Princeton, 1978.

McQuarie, D. (ed.) *Marx: Sociology, Social Change, Capitalism*, London, 1978.

Maguire, J. *Marx's Paris Writings*, Dublin, 1972.

Maguire, J. *Marx's Theory of Politics*, Cambridge, 1978.

Mandel, E. *Introduction to Marxist Economic Theory*, New York, 1970.

Mandel, E. *Formation of Marx's Economic Thought*, London, 1971.

Matthews, B. (ed.) *Marx: a Hundred Years On*, London, 1983.

Meek, R. *Studies in the Labour Theory of Value*, 2nd edn, London, 1973.

Melotti, U. *Marx and the 3rd World*, London, 1977.

Mepham, J. 'Theory of ideology in *Capital*', in Mepham and Ruben (eds) *Issues in Marxist Philosophy*, vol. 3, 1979.

Mepham, J. and Ruben, D. *Issues in Marxist Philosophy*, 3 vols, Brighton, 1979.

Meszaros, I. *Marx's Theory of Alienation*, London, 1970.

Nicolaus, M. 'The unknown Marx', *New Left Review 48*, 1968. (See also under 2, 1858a.)

Oakley, A. *Marx's Critique of Political Economy: Intellectual Sources and Evolution*, 2 vols, London, 1984–5. (See also under 3A.)

Ollman, B. *Alienation: Marx's Critique of Man in Capitalist Society*, 2nd edn, Cambridge, 1976.

Ollman, B. 'Marx's vision of communism', *Critique*, 1978.

Parekh, B. *Marx's Theory of Ideology*, London, 1982.

Pashukanis, E. *Law and Marxism*, London, 1978.

Paul, D. 'In the interest of civilisation: Marxist views of race and culture in the 19th century', *Journal of the History of Ideas 42*, 1981.

Perez-Diaz, V. *State, Bureaucracy and Civil Society: a Critical Discussion of the Political Theory of Karl Marx*, London, 1978.

Phillips, P. *Marx and Engels on Law and Laws*, Oxford, 1980.

Pilling, G. *Marx's Capital: Philosophy and Political Economy*, London, 1980.

Prawer, S. *Marx and World Literature*, Oxford, 1976.

Prinz, A. 'Background and ulterior motive to Marx's Preface of 1859', *Journal of the History of Ideas 30*, 1969.

Rader, M. *Marx's Interpretation of History*, Stanford, 1978.

Rattansi, A. *Marx and the Division of Labour*, London, 1983.

Riazanov, D. *Karl Marx: Man, Thinker, Revolutionist*, London, 1927.

Rigby, S. *Marxism and History*, Manchester, 1987.

Rosdolsky, R. *Making of Marx's Capital*, London, 1968.

Rosen, Z. *Bruno Bauer and Karl Marx*, Hague, 1977.

Roth, M. and Eldred, M. *Guide to Marx's Capital*, London, 1978.

Rubel, M. 'Les cahiers de lecture de Karl Marx. I. 1840–53', *International Review of Social History 2*, 1957.

Rubel, M. 'Les premières lectures économiques de Karl Marx', *Etudes de Marxologie 2*, 1959.

Rubel, M. 'Les cahiers d'étude de Karl Marx. II. 1853–6', *International Review of Social History 5*, 1960.

Rubel, M. *Rubel on Marx: 5 essays*, Cambridge, 1981. (See also under 1B, 3A, 3B.)

Ruben, D. *Marxism and Materialism*, New Jersey, 1977.

Rubin, I. *Essays on Marx's Theory of Value*, Detroit, 1972.

Sawer, M. *Marxism and the Question of the Asiatic Mode of Production*, Hague, 1978.

Sayer, D. *Marx's Method: Ideology, Science and Critique in*

Capital, 2nd edn, Brighton, 1983 [1983a].

Sayer, D. 'Critique of politics and political economy; capitalism, communism and state in Marx's writings of the mid-1840s', *Sociological Review 33* (2), 1985.

Sayer, D. *The Violence of Abstraction*, Oxford, 1987. (See also under 3A, and 3C, Corrigan.)

Schmidt, A. *Concept of Nature in Marx*, London, 1971.

Seliger, M. *Marxist Conception of Ideology*, Cambridge, 1979.

Shanin, T. (See under 1D.)

Shaw, W. *Marx's Theory of History*, London, 1978.

Sherover-Marcuse, E. *Emancipation and Consciousness: Dogmatic and Dialectical Perspectives in the Early Marx*, Oxford, 1986.

Singer, P. *Marx*, London, 1980.

Steedman, I. *Marx after Sraffa*, London, 1977.

Steedman, I. *et al. The Value Controversy*, London, 1981.

Struick, D. 'Marx and mathematics', *Science and Society 12*, 1948.

Suchting, W. *Marx: an Introduction*, New York, 1983.

Sweezy, P. *Theory of Capitalist Development*, New York, 1942.

Teeple, G. *Marx's Critique of Politics 1842–7*, Toronto, 1984.

Thomas, P. *Karl Marx and the Anarchists*, London, 1980.

Thompson, E. P. *Poverty of Theory*, London, 1978.

Tucker, D. F. *Marxism and Individualism*, New York, 1980.

Turner, B. *Marx and the End of Orientalism*, London, 1978.

Walker, A. *Marx: his Theory and its Context*, London, 1978.

Walliman, I. *Estrangement: Marx's Conception of Human Nature and the Division of Labour*, Westport, 1981.

Wolff, R. P. *Understanding Marx: a Reconstruction and Critique of Capital*, Oxford, 1985.

Worsley, P. *Marx and Marxism*, London, 1982.

Zeleny, J. *The Logic of Marx*, London, 1980.

Index

Proper names, subjects and major concepts are indexed. In the case of the latter, Marx often used synonyms, so there are many cross-references. The index is strictly alphabetical; thus for instance 'natural law' comes before 'nature'. There are no sub-headings, except for the entry 'Marx, Karl': Marx's individual writings are indexed here, alphabetically by title. The text and introduction are indexed much more fully than the notes. The chronology and bibliography are not indexed; nor are the purely bibliographic citations in the notes, whether of Marx or others.